AUGUSTINE'S TRAVELS

AUGUSTINE'S TRAVELS

A World-Class Leader
Looks at Life, Business, and
What It Takes to Succeed at Both

Norman R. Augustine
Chairman
Lockheed Martin Corporation

AMACOM
American Management Association

New York • Atlanta • Boston • Chicago • Kansas City • San Francisco • Washington, D.C.
Brussels • Mexico City • Tokyo • Toronto

Library of Congress Cataloging-in-Publication Data

Augustine, Norman R.
    Augustine's travels : a world-class leader looks at life,
business, and what it takes to succeed at both / Norman R.
Augustine.
        p.   cm.
    Includes bibliographical references and index.
    ISBN 0-8144-0397-2 (hardcover)
    1. Management.   2. Leadership.   3. Chief executive officers.
4. Success in business.   I. Title.
HD91.A8194   1997
658—dc21   97-28985
                                                       CIP

Printing number

10 9 8 7 6 5 4 3 2 1

To my family:
Meg, son **Greg,** daughter **René,**
and son-in-law **Mark**

Contents

Acknowledgments

As with so much else in my life, the writing of this book reflects the generous assistance of many dedicated and talented individuals. It draws in part upon a number of my speeches and writings from the past, which Zack Russ helped me draft, and for which Laura Cooper did most of the typing. Jean Ross contributed to the gathering of material and, perhaps even more importantly, did such a skillful job of managing my time that I had occasional evenings and weekends free to think and to write.

My special thanks go to John Greenya, one of the most able writers I've ever met. (His own books include *Blood Relations* and *The Real David Stockman*, as well as collaborations with F. Lee Bailey, former U.S. Attorney General William French Smith, and Pierre Salinger, among others.) John worked with me every step of the way to turn the nearly random set of ideas I wanted to convey into a coherent and (we hope) interesting whole. I also want to thank John—and Susan Pearce, Lockheed Martin's head of corporate communications—for convincing me that this book had commercial, not just in-house, possibilities. Along those same lines, I wish to thank John's literary agent, Frank Weimann, of The Literary Group International, for placing the book, and the most able and cooperative Adrienne Hickey of AMACOM Books, our editor, for acquiring it, and for making John and me hew the line, both literally and figuratively, under what turned out to be a very tight deadline. Barbara Horowitz, also of AMACOM, and freelancer Beverly Miller, made the copy-editing process almost enjoyable.

I am deeply grateful to each of these individuals.

Preface

"You Don't Have to Be a Rocket Scientist—But If You're a CEO, It Helps!"

It just so happens that I *am* a rocket scientist—or, to be more precise, an aeronautical engineer who has worked on and around some of America's most exciting space projects—but my real job has been chairman and chief executive officer of Lockheed Martin, the largest aerospace company in the world (that is, until Boeing and McDonnell Douglas finish their merger; then we'll be second . . . for a while). With nearly 200,000 employees, annual revenues of $30 billion, a backlog of $50 billion, and business in forty-seven countries, we are number 22 on the Fortune 500 list, which means we have a *lot* of responsibilities and a lot of challenges (one of which, in our industry, involves trying to defy gravity, a pretty heavy task, given that it's the law).

While some of my fellow CEOs say I'm lucky and tell me they envy me, others say they consider themselves lucky *not* to be me. Why do they say that? Because I've got this little problem with . . . timing.

Here are a few examples. The very first rocket I was assigned to work on blew up after a "flight" of 250 milliseconds. Yes, *milliseconds!* My next rocket project was canceled one week before its first flight—which at least saved us the "explosion phase." Early on in my business career, I agreed to join the

1

board of directors of a small company at the very moment it was bought by a big company. So long, board membership.

Later, I left Douglas Aircraft shortly before it was acquired by McDonnell Aircraft. I did so because I wanted to accept a position at the Pentagon, where Secretary of Defense Robert McNamara was forming two groups of young managers, one of which would become the highly lauded Whiz Kids. I was in the other group.

Just as I arrived at the Pentagon, the Vietnam war exploded into full force. A few years after that, I went to work for the giant LTV Corporation the very same week that its founder, the entrepreneurial Jimmy Ling, with whom I'd looked forward to working, was relieved of control.

Still on a roll, I left the private sector to become a presidential appointee in the U.S. government just in time to catch the resignation of President Richard Nixon. Not long after that, my Pentagon boss, the Secretary of Defense, was fired. Taking the hint, I left government and joined Martin Marietta Aerospace, and after a couple of years I assumed the presidency of its largest and most profitable division, Astronautics, at the exact moment the Bendix Corporation launched its widely publicized (and ultimately unsuccessful) takeover attempt on our "corporate body." Shortly after that—apparently figuring I must be due for something positive—the board of directors made me CEO of what was by then largely a defense company, just in time for the Berlin Wall to tumble down, along with the defense business. Businesspeople talk a lot about "just-in-time-manufacturing"; I seemed to have discovered the "just-in-time-career."

I wish that were the end of my Oops Chronicle, but there were others (some of which involved space; and that's real—not cyber—space). And at none of my embarrassing moments did I notice any of my fellow CEOs casting envious looks.

As a result of these events, I believe I have had more opportunities to learn from my mistakes than the vast majority of men and women in business today. (Of course, I didn't *want* all those opportunities, but they came my way nonetheless. Some people are just lucky, I guess.) I like to think that I've learned from these "mistakes in timing," and also that what I have learned is worth passing on, especially in the **Don'ts** category. At least that's what the folks told me who suggested I write this book.

Some years ago, despite the fact that I had no intention of doing so, I wrote another book. While alone and out of town on business, I had an attack of appendicitis so sudden and severe—once again, my great sense of timing—that a *cab driver* had to find me a surgeon. I was laid up for a while, and my teenage daughter, wisely recognizing that if I did not have a project I would quickly drive everyone around me nuts, suggested I write a book. As a result, I lost an appendix but gained a book. Some of my friends say it was a bad trade.

The organizing principle behind this cautionary tale was the idea of learning from mistakes others made in business. (Once when I'd asked a fellow executive if he'd learned from *his* mistakes, he said, "Yes, I could repeat all of them exactly." That was *not* the idea behind *my* book.) The content was based on anecdotes and vignettes—"stories"—I'd been using for years in speeches and articles on management. Since I didn't think anybody outside my immediate family would read it—and, as it turned out, not all of my family did; apparently even familial loyalty has its limits, although my wife, Meg, in the words of Samuel Goldwyn, did claim she had "read part of it all the way through"—I dispensed with false modesty and gave it the rather grandiose title of *Augustine's Laws*. (A sarcastic friend suggested that *Augustine's Flaws* would be a more descriptive title; I ignored him.)

The book contained fifty-two of them. Here are a few samples: "Augustine's Law number 1—The best way to make a silk purse from a sow's ear is to start with a silk sow. The same is true of money"; "number 4—If you can afford to advertise, you don't need to"; "number 9—Acronyms and abbreviations should be used to the maximum extent possible to make trivial ideas profound . . . Q.E.D."; "number 21—It's easy to get a loan unless you need it"; "number 28—It is better to be the reorganizer than the reorganizee"; and "number 31—By the time the people asking the questions are ready for the answers, the people doing the work have lost track of the questions."

All of the laws are dedicated to the proposition that if one had a better understanding of history, one could generate a happy ending—sort of like running a movie backward. Kierke-gaard put it this way: "A life must be understood backwards, but it must be lived forwards."

The book first saw the light of day in 1983. The publisher was the American Institute of Aeronautics and Astronautics, be-cause my target audience was people like myself—managers of large aerospace engineering projects. To the Institute's delight, and my utter amazement, the book quickly sold out the first printing of 10,000 copies, almost all of them by mail order. Ap-parently we had tapped some sort of vein.

In 1986, after another edition had come out, I was ap-proached by an editor at a commercial publishing house, Viking Penguin, who said it was time to bring out a new and expanded version, one to be read by "regular people" (his term, not mine). Only slightly offended, I agreed, and Viking Penguin published a handsome edition—with a statesmanlike photo of me on the cover looking off into the distance like a proper lawgiver—that sold well. In fact, to this day it continues to have, as they say in show biz, "legs." When I learned that the book was being re-printed in Germany, Italy, and perhaps even other countries, I thought that would be my final surprise.

However, it soon became a paperback, and then sales really took off. (Only recently, I was in Japan visiting Mr. Toyoda of Toyota—yes, for some reason he spells it differently—and he showed me a copy of my book in *Japanese,* which I had never seen before!) A few years ago, *Augustine's Laws* was in the proc-ess of being reprinted in the Soviet Union when it disappeared—the Soviet Union, not the book. That timing thing again.

Not long ago, my daughter the troublemaker asked me if I were going to write a second volume. I told her I regretted that I had but one appendix to give for my country's libraries, an answer that either satisfied her or confused her sufficiently that she didn't ask again. (By then she'd grown up and become a lawyer. I am now a lot more careful about what I say to her, especially about my laws concerning lawyers. However, and for the record, I have to say that she is fairly understanding—and *very* patient. For example, when she was little, she wanted a doll-house, exactly the kind of project that I, as an avid woodworker, get caught up in, and, if I do say so myself, it turned out superbly. Her enthusiasm, I'm compelled to admit, was somewhat tempered by the fact that I completed it the year she graduated from law school.)

After the book was finished (and my insides were back inside) I resumed my regular life as a CEO, if there is such a thing, and continued to write the occasional article on management. I gave even more speeches, to even more varied groups, essentially all at the request of key customers or very close friends. And then one day a funny thing happened on the way to yet another forum. I realized I *wanted* to write another book. (Actually, I *had* written another book, but it was a super-serious tome on national security policy done with Ken Adelman, former arms negotiator and U.S. deputy to the UN. Today collectors vie for *un*signed copies!)

But what kind of book, I asked myself, should I now write? I wasn't ready to do *Laws II,* and I certainly didn't want to do a memoir (I don't even want my own radio talk show). Nor did I really want to do another treatise on national defense. Who, me? The guy who took over a major defense contractor just as the Evil Empire imploded and the U.S. defense budget exploded, the latter undergoing the greatest collapse in half a century?

So I did a "product review," a look back at the specific topics that this specific manager had been talking and writing about over the past decade. As I scrolled back through the speech titles, it soon became clear that certain subjects came up more frequently than others. Of course, issues relating to defense and aerospace were high on the list, as were topics of interest to business and engineering groups, in particular management and leadership. But educational, economic, and social and environmental issues were not far behind.

In *Augustine's Laws,* my approach had been to examine mistakes made in business in hopes of learning from them. In this book I've broadened the focus, because by now I've had time to make mistakes in a whole *variety* of fields. So, in order to illustrate the many and varied issues a manager must deal with on a daily basis, in everyday life as well as in business, I have included outside-the-workplace themes and topics because these issues ultimately have an enormous impact on all of us, from the veteran CEO to the brand-new entry-level employee. The days when corporate executives dealt only with Wall Street, factories, and balance sheets are long gone.

Solving problems is a big part of my job, right after avoiding problems, and it's a major factor in all of our lives. Fortunately, I enjoy solving problems (which is a good thing because that's one of the main things Lockheed Martin pays me to do), and I frequently try to think about how I *enjoy* solving them. I do this because then when they show up—and they always do—they don't frustrate me as much. It's sort of a case of mind over (what's the) matter.

Accordingly, I want this book to help readers deal with issues, make decisions, and solve problems. As in *Augustine's Laws,* I've used lots of stories to illustrate my points. I've learned over the years that this is a much more effective way of conveying ideas than deep philosophical musing. In this book, I've tried to duplicate the tone of *Augustine's Laws,* which was to treat serious issues in a relatively lighthearted manner. I also raise the issue of the changing nature of the CEO position. As we poise on the brink of the twenty-first century, many of our institutions have undergone dramatic changes, and the job of CEO is no exception.

Today, external issues—contact with the media, politicians, regulators, foreign competitors, major investors—have taken on importance matching that of more traditional internal issues. And even internally you don't get much done anymore by giving orders. When I was a young employee and the boss said, "Jump," we asked, "How high?" Today's young members of the workforce are more likely to ask, "Why?" That's progress.

I had the same general objective in mind in writing this book as I had with my first. In the preface to *Laws,* I wrote, "The author hopes through this treatise on organizational misbehavior to contribute toward improving upon that process, which has, in spite of its many pratfalls, demonstrated truly enormous inherent strength and accomplishment, largely because of the dedication and native ability of the individuals who make it work."

In that book, "process" referred exclusively to business, but in this one I have tried to embrace many more aspects of life faced by businesspeople in America as we hurtle toward the year 2000 and the beginning of the third millennium. I think it's good to keep in mind that, in business as in life, we don't know how long it's going to last. Or, as my hero Yogi Berra sagaciously observed, "It ain't over 'til it's over."

This is a serious book about serious issues, but I have tried my best to see that it isn't overly serious (for fear of making readers seriously bored). To that end, I've unabashedly employed humor whenever and wherever it seemed appropriate, and in places where I felt fairly certain readers would not find humor distracting.

While I'm at it, I should mention another point that I hope readers will not find distracting, and that is the frequency of references to Lockheed Martin. Unfortunately (or fortunately, as the case may be—certainly fortunate for me) much of my business life *has been and is* Lockheed Martin; thus, many of my points are illustrated by reference to the corporation for which I work. I hope readers will not mind the number of times I mention LM, but the problem is a bit like that of a man who has been married to the same woman for many years: When he talks about wives, he had better be careful not to generalize too much (like the time I introduced my one and only wife of thirty-five years to an audience as "my first wife." Not funny.) So I apologize in advance for the number of times I will mention our corporation. Nonetheless, Lockheed Martin *is* surprisingly representative of American business in general—especially those that have recently undergone tectonic change—and, being a part of its management has put me in touch with a large number of others who manage the companies that, collectively, comprise much of what we think of when we say American Business or Corporate America.

In his new book, *Business as a Calling: Work and the Examined Life*, Michael Novak writes, "Business has a vested interest in virtue." He says this view is both good *and* good business. That's the same idea I was trying to get across fifteen years ago in *Augustine's Laws* when I wrote, "Integrity is the *sine qua non* of all human endeavors, including business. It has even been said that if rascals knew the value of honesty they would be honest simply because of their rascality."

It seems to me that while it may be true, as Calvin Coolidge is reported to have said, that the chief business of America is business, that does not mean that the *business of business* has to be limited to materialistic ends. That our daily lives as individuals who work for a living can be a growing experience instead of a necessary evil is a subtheme of this book. As I once told a newspaper reporter, if you don't have a boss you admire, then you should "go out and get one—otherwise your career will be in grave danger." All that ties in with my personal definition of "success": being happy in life and leaving the world a little bit better than you found it.

One last point. It's based on my own experience of almost forty years as an employee who has been fortunate enough to have been given increasingly greater amounts of responsibility. To borrow the words of General Custer, who knew a good bit about the subject, "The privilege of leadership is not to have a bigger tent." Thus, I'd like to give younger readers a bit of un-asked-for advice: Don't plan your careers *too* carefully or in too much detail. (Later, I'll explain why not.)

But whatever the case, I'm fairly confident that any advice I offer will be better than that given to Michael Jordan by one of his grade school teachers, who said, "Study math, Michael. That's where the big money is."

In the following pages I attempt to make my point that the time to come to terms with the issues raised in this book is right now. Not later, now. Because anyone who wants to be a business—and a personal—success in the twenty-first century had better take full advantage of what little is left of the twentieth.

N.R.A.

SECTION ONE

Values

AROUND THE WORLD IN EIGHT DAYS, I

On a particularly miserable day in the particularly miserable winter of 1995, in the midst of the last weeks of the corporate pregnancy that would produce a fine new offspring named Lockheed Martin, I received a letter inviting me on a trip around the world: all expenses paid, no duties or obligations, total R&R, and a ton of learning, both corporate and personal.

No, it was not from Ed McMahon, and, no, I didn't have to buy or donate anything other than one week of my life. It was a legitimate invitation from Reg Brack, the chairman of Time, Inc., inviting me to join a group of American CEOs and some more normal people (including a university professor and a diva-turned-opera-company-executive) on a week's jaunt around the globe.

Scheduled for October, the trip would take us to some of the most troubled—and therefore most interesting—spots on earth, places that would be in the headlines in the coming years and would profoundly affect the future of business, particularly the aerospace business.

The last paragraph of the invitation letter stated that Time did not want us to be mere tourists; the magazine wanted us to be "honorary journalists." Clearly that was meant to be an added inducement, but, my quirky sense of humor never being far from the surface, it caused me to recall a Neil Simon line: "Would you want an honorary mechanic to work on your brand-new Mercedes?"

Actually, the trip sounded like a great opportunity. The group was to visit such past, present, and future global hot spots as Havana, Beirut, and Hanoi, as well as such "garden spots" as Pyongyang, North Korea, and Bangalore, India. Nonetheless, many of the stops on the itinerary were places I'd always wanted to visit. I'm an avid and inveterate traveler. In recent years I have visited more than sixty countries and every continent.

Within a year or so of this invitation, I'd journeyed from China to the Persian Gulf and from Estonia to the South Pole, but I had despaired of ever seeing several of the places on Time's list because of my almost four decades of involvement in national security affairs. (The problem was that I had been told so many defense secrets over the years that the U.S. government wouldn't let me *in* those countries—and I was afraid that those countries might, in turn, not let me back *out!*) The idea of seeing from ground level places that I'd come to know only from the view of a satellite camera was pretty exciting.

But, sure enough, there was my old bugaboo: timing. Because Lockheed and Martin Marietta were still in the throes of the U.S. government's antitrust review of our plans to become Lockheed Martin, I suspected that mid-October could prove to be a very bad time for me to be out of the office for a week. Nonetheless, I thought long and hard about accepting, but in the end my conscience got out of hand, and I wrote Reg and, with great reluctance, declined the invitation.

The following month I happened to run into a CEO-friend who had been on a previous "Time Newstour." I'd thought they were annual events, but he said, "Oh, no. I think the one coming up is the first in ten years!"

"So how was it?" I asked him, of his Newstour.

"The experience of a lifetime. And you, Norm, by turning it down, have made the *mistake* of a lifetime!"

A couple of weeks later, however, at a reception in New York City, I happened, by chance, to meet someone who worked in the executive offices of Time, Inc. I blurted out that I felt terrible about blowing my big chance, and, lo and behold, a week later I got a second letter from Reg Brack. It began, ". . . a little bird told me," and was a reinvitation . . . for the slow to learn. I accepted by phone, fax, FedEx, UPS, e-mail, the U.S. Postal Service—and messenger.

For the next three months, a homework package arrived in the mail almost every week with a carefully selected book and a set of fact sheets relating to one of the stops planned for the trip. Unfortunately, the visit to North Korea was eventually canceled at the last minute. As things turned out, the visit to Lebanon was also canceled (just days before our departure, the jury in the New York City trial of the Muslim fundamentalists accused of bombing the World Trade Center had returned a guilty verdict).

A stop in Moscow was added to replace the Lebanon visit. And we were told that we'd have a bit more time in various other cities along the way, which turned out to be welcome since the schedule we were given somehow had neglected one minor thing—to allot any time for sleep.

At 7:30 P.M., on Thursday, October 5, at the Willard Hotel in downtown Washington, I met my fellow travelers for the first time as a group. Our troupe of honorary journalists totaled thirty-two in all, and we were joined by about fifteen of Time's senior executives and perhaps ten of what some of our group began referring to as "legitimate" correspondents. (Somehow, I didn't like what that seemed to imply about the rest of us). Just being with this group for a week would have been an education in itself had we simply remained in the hotel and shot the bull for the entire period.

Among the people I'd already met were: Don Beall, chairman and CEO of Rockwell; Reg Brack of Time; Bill Esrey, chairman and CEO of Sprint; Carla Hills, former U.S. trade representative; and John Smale, chairman of General Motors. Some of the others on the trip whom I already knew were chief executives from such organizations as General Mills, FMC, the Gap, and Zenith.

The next day, following a heavy breakfast, we were given instructions on how to act like journalists: "The only dumb question is the one you don't ask." "Ask hard questions, but ask them diplomatically." We were told that anyone could be a journalist—"It was not a genetic affliction." The "Sacred Trust of Journalism" was discussed at some length, after which Time's editor indicated to us that we would be focusing on the "New World Re-order," to wit: "Can capitalism exist without individual freedom?"

After the breakfast briefing, we boarded a bus in front of the hotel and were driven the short distance to the Old Executive Office Building adjacent to the White House. There we were briefed, on their special areas of expertise, by top officials of the State Department, the Department of Defense, the CIA, and the White House.

And then we were off, by bus, for Dulles Airport where our aircraft was waiting at the Signature Terminal, a terminal through which I'd passed several times a week for the last eighteen years. When we got to Dulles, I saw that the aircraft most of us would be on for the trip was a Lockheed L-1011. It had better work, I thought to myself, or I'd be hearing a lot about it. Or, then, maybe I *wouldn't!* A smaller Gulfstream aircraft accompanied us as a trailblazer.

The Time staff and aircraft crew finally got all the CEOs loaded onto the airplane, an undertaking that reminded me of trying to herd chickens from horseback. CEOs do not herd well. The L-1011 aircraft, which was designed to hold some 400 passengers, had been outfitted in an all-first-class configuration for our trip, but even at that, it was less than half full. Champagne and a huge bowl of shrimp were awaiting us at a large horseshoe bar, which had been built into the middle of the aircraft. Clearly, this was not going to be a hardship tour.

I soon discovered that the flight attendants could make piña coladas, but that shouldn't have surprised me, as we were on our way to Cuba.

Within a few minutes, we were flying down the Potomac River, over the city of Washington southward toward Havana, happily sipping piña coladas. And there I was, on the road again.

⊕   ⊕   ⊕   ⊕   ⊕

Two and one-quarter hours after leaving Washington, we landed at Cuba's José Martí Airport, a bedraggled-looking site just outside Havana. As we taxied toward the terminal, our L-1011 was the only moving aircraft in sight. It was a bit disconcerting, though not surprising, to see that most of the planes parked on the ramp were of Russian origin.

We boarded our air-conditioned Mercedes (read: capitalist) buses and, complete with police escort, headed toward Havana. There were very few cars along the way, but large numbers of people were riding bicycles, and we noticed a few goats munching on the roadside grass.

We spent an hour riding around Havana gawking out of the windows of the bus. Over the years, I've found that I can get a pretty good feeling for a country by doing exactly that. Unfortunately, the overall impression of Cuba was depressing. Large numbers of people were standing around the streets simply staring off into space—not laughing, not talking to one another, not going anywhere or doing anything—just staring.

It looked as if no paint had been used in Havana since the revolution in 1959, and there were no signs of new construction anywhere. It was said that in one part of the city, several buildings collapse each week. In fact, everything appeared to be in disrepair. Here we were, only 90 miles from Florida, but in terms of lifestyle, it could have been 90 light-years.

After the bus tour of Havana, we returned to the hotel and quickly dressed for the 7:30 P.M. dinner, to be hosted by Fidel Castro himself. We'd been told that before dinner, he would make a "few remarks" and answer a few questions, which turned out to be the understatement of the year.

Dinner was served in the country's principal government building, which, as far as we could tell, was the only well-kept building in all of Cuba. It was a rather impressive, white-marble affair, mindful of the "standard impressive building" from the Russian architectural catalog. However, Castro quickly dispelled that notion, explaining with some embarrassment that the building had been built many years earlier by his predecessor, dictator Fulgencio Batista. Therefore, he, Castro, was not responsible for its opulence! (As we left the building, someone noticed the date on the cornerstone; it was years after Batista was "toast.")

With great care and formality, each one of us was introduced to President Castro. He was very cordial to everyone and showed no reaction at all when I told him I was from Lockheed Martin, a firm that most of the communist world must have viewed as a bitter enemy, inasmuch as we'd built much of the equipment that underpinned America's military might. When he made his remarks to the group, he did so standing in one place, without a podium, for the entire time. In fact, he stood continuously for well over five hours. Later, we learned through the media that this was the first time in Cuba that Castro had ever worn a suit rather than his standard military fatigues.

Castro was really quite gracious—and a true performer. He seemed to be enjoying himself thoroughly and from time to time spoke in a very animated fashion. Although his remarks were somewhat rambling (a typical answer, including his translation into English, lasted at least fifteen minutes), he managed to hold the audience spellbound. And this was a tough audience.

With regard to President Clinton's announcement that very morning that certain restrictions with Cuba would be eased, Castro said he couldn't comment on it because he hadn't seen the actual document, and then proceeded to comment on it for thirty minutes. He asserted that "we intend to preserve the conquests of communism even during this 'special period,' " yet another euphemistic reference to the financial difficulties the country had faced since the Russians' abrupt withdrawal in 1993.

One of the faults of the communist system, he said, was that it made life too easy for people, that they didn't have to worry about retirement, medical care, education, or even food. (He should have added, "for the first ten days of the month," since that is the extent of the ration afforded each Cuban.)

At this point, Beverly Sills, who was sitting near me, winced at a chauvinistic reference, a speaking practice we would notice throughout the trip. Political Correctness had not yet reached the communist-heritage world. On the other hand, Castro's most vehement response of the entire evening was triggered by a questioner's suggestion that Cuba was ignoring women and minorities. He also decried the situation that has evolved in Cuba whereby a person who opens a restaurant can make "three times as much in a day as a teacher can make in a month." (This was one of the few things Castro said with which I agreed.)

By this point, it was quite late, and Castro, in the middle of a long and rambling answer to a question, suddenly suggested, "Please feel free to go to sleep, take a nap." He then went on . . . and on! But in fact, even though many of us had had very little sleep the previous night, no one was having any problem staying awake. Castro was simply fascinating.

When Reg Brack, Time's chairman, finally made the suggestion—at 11:45 P.M.!—that we eat dinner, a brave gesture that made Reg the instant folk hero of our trip, everyone adjourned to another hall, where we were greeted with a magnificent buffet.

The fare included lobster, shrimp, suckling pig, rich ice cream—the works. Castro, in his engaging style, offered what may have been the final communist grace: "Please enjoy your meal, and eat all you want. We're already broke."

We grazed at the buffet table until the wee hours of the morning, finally returning to the hotel at 1:30 A.M. Nonetheless, Castro still kept working the room, visiting with every person.

When it was my turn, I asked where he, for so long an admirer of the Soviet system, thought they had gone wrong. He answered that Gorbachev had tried to do things too fast, that this was like "trying to rebuild a ship in the middle of an ocean."

Screwing up my courage, I decided to tell Castro a joke, which is always dangerous when the joke has to be translated. It was a story I'd often used in speeches (but this time I gave it a Russian context). It told of a Cuban deep-sea diver who received an urgent message over his intercom from the Russian ship floating above him: "Come up at once. We're sinking." To my great relief, Castro thought this was hilarious.

It was almost 2:00 A.M. when our day finally ended. We'd only traveled about 100 miles off U.S. shores, but we had made quite a start nonetheless.

1

Ethics

Nine times out of ten, doing the right thing turns out also to be the smart thing.

Looking back on the Newstour, it's hard to pick out a "best" experience. But if I were forced to do so, I'd have to say that as fascinating as it was to meet and listen to someone like Fidel Castro or any of the other national leaders we encountered, the daily, ongoing interaction among the American business leaders was for me the most fascinating aspect of the tour.

Wherever we flew, there was always an interesting conversation going on somewhere in the huge aircraft. I joined as many of these confabs as I could, because I'd quickly learned that no matter what the topic, the discussion would be instructive or entertaining, and usually both.

One person would barely finish a story when someone else would pick up the theme and relate his or her anecdote about it. The discussions had a lot of the flavor of, "Yeah, we had that problem too, and let me tell you how we handled it." So there was a great deal of learning to be had of the sort you don't pick up in business school. After a while, it hit me that what we had was an airborne seminar in which these American business leaders were talking, directly as well as indirectly, about their personal values. And when I say personal, I don't mean to limit that

to just their business values, but also to whatever, in their opinion, it takes to be a success and a contributor in every aspect of
life.

⊕   ⊕   ⊕   ⊕   ⊕

My assumption, from the very beginning of this book, is that
many readers will read it in part because they want to know
how American business leaders, circa 1997, as typified by the
people on the Time Newstour (which includes me), made it to
their respective positions. What worked for them? What didn't
work? What game plan (if any) did they follow?

My strong belief, which was only strengthened by the time
I've spent with such people, is that people succeed in business,
as well as in life, because of their values. Now I'm not talking
about how high your salary is compared to the person in the
office next to you. Warren Buffett once told me he knew people
on Wall Street who'd been happy making $1.5 million a year—
until they discovered the person next to them was making $1.6
million, at which point they became despondent. Similarly, I'm
not talking about how many people you have in your division
compared to Brenda's or Fred's, or how close your parking place
is to the main entrance. No, I'm talking about what you believe
in, what makes you tick. It's been my experience, and I would
guess you already agree with me, that at the core of most successful businessmen and businesswomen in today's America is
a personal value system based on a strong sense of ethics.

Ethics: "Knowing the Difference Between What You Have a Right to Do and What Is the Right Thing to Do"

Here are two stories, both true, that have to do with the business
of ethics *and* the ethics of business.

The first is about a survey done a few years ago by Donald
McCabe, who teaches business ethics at Rutgers. According to
his poll of 15,000 juniors and seniors at thirty-one different col-

leges and universities, more than 87 percent of the business majors responding said they had cheated at least once in college. That caused Professor McCabe to speculate that "business courses attract students looking to make a quick buck and willing to cut corners to do it." (Do you believe that? I do not. Yes, it may be true of a few of them, but then it's also true of a lot of other fields.) Before you nonbusiness majors get too smug, here are some more survey results. Students in engineering, my own profession, ranked second with 74 percent, followed by science majors with 67 percent, and those in the humanities with 63 percent. Rather sobering stats, wouldn't you say?

Here's the second story.

In 1959, the legendary hitter Ted Williams was forty years old and closing out his career with the Boston Red Sox. At $125,000 per year, he was the highest salaried player in all of professional sports. That season, Williams was suffering from a pinched nerve in his neck. "The thing was so bad," he later explained, "that I could hardly turn my head to look at the pitcher."

For the first time in his career, Williams batted under .300, hitting just .254, with only ten home runs. The following winter, the Red Sox sent him the same contract he had during his disappointing season. When he got the proposal, Williams sent it back with a note saying that he would not sign it until they gave him the full pay *cut* allowed.

"I was always treated fairly by the Red Sox when it came to contracts," Williams said. "Now they were offering me a contract I didn't deserve. And I only wanted what I deserved."

What happened? Williams cut his own salary by 25 percent. (By the way, that year he had a great season.)

Everybody's Doing It—or So It Seems

It's not easy to talk about ethics without feeling awkward. There seem to be very few absolute standards as to what constitutes ethical behavior, which is what makes the subject so difficult. Most everyone would agree that cheating is wrong—but how many of us would carry our ethics to the extent that Ted Williams did? Suffice it to say that ethics is a highly personal matter, and I'm certainly not going to put my own beliefs up as some kind of standard. But there *are* ethical guideposts that I've noted are fundamental to American business—as well as to anyone's life.

Things weren't always so complicated. There was a time when ethics *seemed* simple to explain. For example, a young girl who'd been assigned a term paper on ethics went home and asked her father to explain the meaning of ethics. The father, who owned a dry cleaning establishment, replied that he had settled an ethical question that very day. He told her he had found a $100 bill in the pocket of a customer's coat. "Now," he explained, "ethics is: Do I tell my partner?"

A news clip tells of a bookstore in Boston that phoned its Washington, D.C., branch in search of a book called *Some Honest Men*. When the Bostonian asked, "Do you have *Some Honest Men* in Washington?" the surprised clerk paused for a moment and replied, "Perhaps two or three."

By now almost everyone is familiar with the plot of John Grisham's best-seller *The Firm*, in which fresh-out-of-law-school attorneys are recruited by a fictional Memphis law firm for what certainly sounds like a dream job—$80,000 to start, plus such perks as a new BMW and frequent trips to the Caymans! The only drawback for the rookie lawyers is that in exchange, they lose their souls. Gradually and inextricably, sometimes almost imperceptibly, they are trapped into crossing the ethical line— and once over it, they discover, it is incredibly hard to return to the other side insofar as the law is concerned, and impossible to do insofar as their personal reputation is concerned.

While the book and its movie counterpart both have a happy ending, it presents a lonely hero (where's Diogenes when we really need him?) set against a landscape of unethical, truly evil people. So what's the message?

These (fictional) people are, like those caught up in the Watergate and Iran-contra scandals, people with no record of wrongdoing who would seldom set out with the deliberate intent to break the law. They are drawn into it slowly and gradually, almost as a boa constrictor consumes its prey.

In the past, I labored under the impression that the boa constrictor drops out of a tree on its victims and quickly crushes them in the powerful folds of its body. A quick look in the encyclopedia reveals that, instead, "the snake places two or three coils of its body around the chest of its prey. Then each time the victim exhales its breath, the boa simply takes up the slack. After three or four breaths there is no more slack. The prey quickly suffocates and is then swallowed by the boa."

This deadly phenomenon of a victim's becoming the unwitting accomplice of its own destruction is not confined to the world of reptiles. Modern life is nothing if not a constant effort to stay one step ahead of the stealthy approach of the boa constrictor.

Where else do we see evidence of an ethical breakdown? How about:

Politics: From Watergate to Whitewater, with stops along the way marked "Keating Five," "Monkey Business," and "Campaign Spending," you may take your pick.

Athletics: Pete Rose, Rosie Ruiz (who used the subway to better her time in the Boston Marathon), steroid-taking Olympians, and all too many heavyweight boxers.

Academia: (Otherwise) distinguished professors who falsify their research to win new grants and chase fleeting prestige.

Religious broadcasters: I'm sure you have your own favorites, but mine are Jimmy Swaggart and Tammy Faye Bakker.

Hotel management: The clear winner is Leona "Only-Little-People-Pay-Taxes" Helmsley.

Religion (yes, apparently nothing is sacred): As reported in a recent newspaper story, a Church of England priest suggested that it is no sin to shoplift—when the victim is a big supermarket. The "good" reverend drew a distinction between stealing from individuals or small stores—which he said *is* wrong—and stealing from giant retailing corporations.

Wall Street: Ivan Boesky, who, in a speech at the UCLA Business School, said, "Greed is a good thing." (Sentenced to three years in a federal prison, he had plenty of time to rethink that statement.) In the movie *Wall Street,* the main character, Gordon

Gekko, was still in phase one, saying, "Greed is good! Greed is all right! Greed works!" Back in real life, so to speak, arbitrageur Marylou Bates assured us, "Greed is all right. Greed is healthy. You can be greedy and still feel good about yourself."

Self-improvement(?) books and games: Looking Out for Number One, Winning Through Intimidation, and *Cheating 101: The Benefits and Fundamentals of Earning the Easy 'A'.* And who can forget the sports trading card genius who brought out a set of cards featuring famous serial killers?

1-800/ETHICAL

I can't really say if ethical lapses—perhaps "collapses" is the better word—are worse now than they were in the past. I do know, however, that at the company I serve, Lockheed Martin, we have an Ethics Hot Line—1-800/ETHICAL—and we keep careful track of the calls. You can call with a complaint that someone is doing something wrong, or you can call for advice. If you want to be anonymous, you just leave a code number (which you make up), and when you call back one of the ethics advisers will give you a report on how they're dealing with your issue (which can range from "I should have been promoted," to "I'm being sexually harassed," to whatever). When we initiated the program, the line managers didn't like it at all, because they don't like something going around them, but it has worked out very well.

Our ethics advisers don't come to me with case reports; they're expected to deal with each caller professionally, themselves. Interestingly, over time it has gotten to the point where fewer and fewer of the calls are anonymous, which suggests that people are building some trust. When the number of calls goes down, our board of directors asks if we have lost interest in ethics; when it goes up, the board invariably asks if we are less ethical! (But then it is exactly to ask such questions that we *have* boards.)

Some years ago, while testifying before a congressional committee, GE's CEO Jack Welch cogently laid out the case for ethical behavior from a corporation's standpoint: "We have no police force, no jails. We must rely on the integrity of our people as our first defense."

"But I Know It When I See It!"

What does "ethics" mean? I like the definition of Potter Stewart, the highly regarded former U.S. Supreme Court justice: "Ethics is knowing the difference between what you have a right to do and what is the right thing to do."

Some people believe that if it's legal, it's ethical. Well, it's clear Justice Stewart doesn't believe that. I know I don't, and I bet you don't either. It's legal to burn the flag, but I believe it's the wrong thing to do. At one time racial discrimination was legal, but it was always wrong. And in business, hostile take-overs are legal—but I *definitely* think they are the wrong thing to do. The great French writer François La Rochefoucauld defined ethics as "doing without witnesses what one would be capable of doing with the world looking on."

Here's a homespun definition: "Ethics is being unafraid to give your pet parrot to the town gossip."

Let me offer a personal checklist that I've used for years:

1. Is it legal?
2. If someone else did "this" to you, would you think it was fair?
3. Would you like it if what you were doing were to appear on the front page of your hometown newspaper?
4. Would you be proud if your mother were to see you doing this?

If you can say yes to all four of these questions, then whatever it is you are doing, or are about to do, is probably ethical.

I think Robert Fulghum nailed it in his book *All I Really Need to Know . . . I Learned in Kindergarten.* Fulghum wasted no words in laying out his rules for ethical living:

Play fair.
Share.

Don't hit people.
Don't take things that aren't yours.
Put things back where you found them.
Clean up your own mess.
Say you're sorry when you hurt someone.

Hard to beat, wouldn't you say?

Institutionalizing Ethics

Sometimes the ethical choices faced by large corporations are relatively easy to make—but that doesn't mean they are easy to take. Such was the case some time ago when Lockheed Martin was in competition for a major contract, and the day before we were to submit our proposal, we received in the mail a copy of our competitor's price sheet. Presumably it came from a disgruntled employee of our competitor. Once we realized what we had, we promptly handed the package to our attorneys, who in turn told the government *and* the competitor what had happened. We did not change our bid price.

As things turned out, we lost the contract—and some of our employees lost their jobs due to the resultant lack of work. By any measure, we—and especially the laid-off employees—paid a heavy price for acting ethically, but I am convinced beyond any question of a doubt that we did the right thing and that in the long run it does pay off to do so. That is, incidentally, one of the problems with business and with life: Good decisions do not necessarily guarantee good outcomes.

Lockheed Martin has been asked to participate in any number of projects not only because we have the technical talent (some *62,000* scientists and engineers), but because we are known as an ethical company, and we are trusted. As we all know, the truly difficult ethical choices in life involve day-to-day decisions where the cost is very real and the "payoff" or advantage seems remote at best. Nonetheless, the ethical course is always the right course to take.

When Lockheed Martin was born, both Dan Tellep (Lockheed's CEO, the same post I held at Martin Marietta) and I—as its parents, so to speak—knew that given the nature of the businesses we were in, the new corporation would have to be especially aware of possible ethical conflicts. Each and every one of us would have to commit ourselves, individually and collectively, to the highest ethical standards.

Whenever Dan talks about our corporate family responsibility, he stresses the point that "ethical conduct" is the very first of the "overarching principles" that was adopted for our new corporation. I strongly endorse Dan's comments and add my own admonition about professional behavior on the job. While it's true that ethics is a very personal matter, it's also true that what we do on the job eventually, if not immediately, has an impact on every other person among the nearly 200,000 strong who make up Lockheed Martin. All of us can be hurt and endangered by the lapses of any one of us, just as we can take pride in each other's accomplishments. So, while ethics is in fact a personal matter, ethical behavior at work is the concern of every one of us.

The concern for ethical behavior on the job stems in part from the unfortunate reputation that business in general has today. Big business is an institution that is viewed by the public as not particularly concerned about ethics, and, unfortunately, there is at least some justification for this view. Just a few years ago, insider trading was considered a symbol of the way unscrupulous traders took advantage of, by "cashing in" on, unsuspecting investors. And recently I read an article suggesting that maintaining high ethical standards is simply untenable in the world of business, especially now that we all must compete in a global marketplace where ethical standards vary widely from place to place. Once again, I didn't agree with that.

The Golden Rule—or, He Who Has the Gold Rules?

When I was an undergraduate at Princeton, it was interesting to watch the evolution of students' attitudes toward the university's honor code, which was a *very* central part of the educational scheme of things.

Freshmen, during an exam, were afraid even to lift their eyes for fear it would appear that they were cheating. By the sophomore year, there was such great pride in the honor system that no one would have dreamed of violating it. By the upper-class years, it was just a normal aspect of everyday student life, like eating and sleeping, and the idea of cheating simply didn't occur to the overwhelming majority of students. In fact, in four years, I never saw a single person cheat. (I wish I could say that about my large public high school! I even had one classmate who answered true-false questions by flipping a coin! Not cheating, but . . .)

I'm told that at the University of Virginia, when a violation of the ethics code does happen, there's a small announcement (surrounded by a black border) simply stating that a student, unnamed, has left the university.

Similarly, the athletes' entrance to the stadium at Olympia, where the original Olympic Games were held, is lined with statues. But these are not representations of those athletes who achieved great and courageous victories, but of those who cheated. When I first saw those statues some years ago, it gave me a hollow feeling in the pit of my stomach that I can still recall. Twenty-seven centuries later, those stone statues still shout out their message of contempt.

It All Depends on How You Look at It (Oh, Really?)

Ethics is not simple, as I am sure you have already found out—as an employee, a manager, a boss. Not only do you have to know the right thing to do, but you have to have the moral fortitude to do it. And that's not always easy. People who are ethical, of course, believe in honoring their word, obeying the law, acting honestly, respecting other people's property, exhibiting loyalty, giving a day's work for a day's pay.

But even these values can be misplaced. Optimism is not unethical. In fact, in most cases, it's even admirable. But in business, misrepresentation under the guise of optimism is a crime.

Information is valuable, but it's ethical only as long as you have a right to have it. Profit is valued, as long as you've earned it. Loyalty is appreciated, as long as it isn't misplaced. (The Iraqis following Saddam Hussein could have been said to have been loyal.)

Professional football teams work hard all season long to get into the playoffs and to get the home field advantage. But a letter to a Washington, D.C., newspaper once asked if, as happened a couple of years ago, it is ethical for the coach to urge the fans to make so much noise cheering that the other team can't hear its quarterback call the signals. And what about those basketball fans, seated directly behind the basket, who wave towels and balloons and whoop and holler in hopes of causing a missed free throw? Do those fans—50,000 strong in the case of the football stadium—think what they are doing is unethical? Do you? (Don't ask about me. I'm too much of a Washington Redskins fan to be objective; I'm going to punt on this one.)

In mid-April 1997, toward the end of the regular season in the National Basketball Association, something happened at the end of a game that was so unusual that the *Washington Post* asked its readers for their opinion. While losing to the Washington Bullets 113–110, the Philadelphia 76ers called three last-minute timeouts in order to give Allen Iverson three more chances to extend his record of consecutive 40-point games by a rookie. The Bullets chose not to guard Iverson, and in the final seconds he hit a three-pointer to up his record to five games in a row. The *Post* asked its readers this question: "Did the 76ers create a tainted record by their actions? And did the Bullets act irresponsibly by their inaction?" Should the record books show an asterisk?

Seeing as my son-in-law once played for the Bullets, I'd have to excuse myself on this one too, but it sounds very much like an ethics question to me. In any event, several days later, the newspaper printed the results of its query. For whatever it's worth, the respondents were about evenly split between those who were disgusted by the situation and those who said it was "no big deal."

Unfortunately, people sometimes adjust their ethical values to meet the pressures of the moment (like the 76ers and the Bul-

lets?). Take Charlie Brown, Mr. Schultz's brilliant cartoon creation. Charlie was practicing with his bow and arrow one day.
As soon as he'd hit the fence, he would run over to it with a
piece of chalk and draw a target around the arrow. When Lucy
saw this, she reacted with predictable hysteria. "Charlie
Brown," she screamed, "you're supposed to draw the target first
and *then* shoot at it!"

"I know that, Lucy," said an unrepentant Charlie Brown.
"But if you do it my way, you never miss."

Ethics has to do with hitting the target the hard way. You
have to have a set of ethical values to aim at. You can't make up
the ethics as you go along. That's the most common pitfall of all:
rationalizing one's ethics to meet the circumstances. That's when
the boa gets its first grip.

Despite all the evidence of illegal or unethical behavior,
however, and at the risk of being labeled naive, I must say I still
believe that most people do try to do the right thing. If so, one
might ask, if most people are basically ethical, then why do so
many end up doing something *un*ethical? The answer is that
being ethical almost always entails a short-term cost that not
everyone is willing to pay.

It All Depends on How *They* Look at It
(Oh, Really?)

Further complicating the ethical dilemma is that what may be
deemed ethical at one time in history, or in one part of the world,
may not be considered so in another. In some societies, taking
advantage of a business counterpart is not considered unethical
and may even be considered admirable, at least to the extent that
cleverness is admired. In other societies, the clarity of a "no"
answer to a business proposition may be lost in the desire to
maintain a polite decorum.

In some highly developed countries, the payment of bribes
in an effort to win business abroad and thereby create jobs at
home is fully legal, the argument being that the ends justify the
means. Even more unfathomable, in some of these countries

such bribes are tax deductible. (When the U.S. government has objected to such practices, it has on occasion produced the remarkable result that the foreign government permits bribes to be tax deductible only *with prior approval!*)

Whatever the disparities of standards, bribes have no place in business and are a cancer on the operation of the free enterprise system.

Woe Is Thee, and Woe Is Me . . . But Not My Wife

The elevation of probity over personal gain is more prevalent than you might think. Golfers like to joke about the player who cheated so badly that when he once had a hole in one, he wrote down "zero" on his scorecard. But a more typical approach to ethical behavior on the links was exhibited during a major golf tournament.

The great professional golfer Tom Kite warned his playing partner, Grant Waite, that Waite was about to commit a rules infraction that would cost him two strokes. Waite corrected his behavior, avoided the two-stroke penalty, and went on to win the tournament, eking out a one-stroke victory—over Tom Kite. Not only did Kite lose the first-place trophy, but as a result of coming in second, he also lost $94,000 in prize money.

I can give a similar example of the "cost of ethics" from my own life. About ten years ago, while traveling in Europe, my wife and I had dinner one weekend with a very wealthy friend and business associate who owned, among other things, a company that happened to be one of our company's suppliers. At the end of dinner, as a thoughtful gesture, he presented two small packages as gifts to my wife and me, and said that he had picked them up off the assembly line as he left the plant. When we returned to our hotel, we saw that the boxes contained wristwatches manufactured by his firm.

The following Monday morning, as I was preparing to leave for my office, I asked my wife for her watch. In answer to her not-unreasonable question, "Why?" I explained that since it came from a supplier, company rules required that I turn both gifts in to our company, which would in turn give them to charity. But my wife liked her watch. Incredulous, she said it was a gift to *her*, not to the company; that *she* didn't work for the company; and furthermore that our friend would be genuinely and justifiably offended if he knew that the company, suspecting some ulterior motive, had taken away from her what was intended purely as a very thoughtful gift.

Therefore, she said, I could do whatever I wanted with *my* watch, but she was keeping *hers!*

What to do? After a prolonged discussion, our corporation's legal counsel suggested I write a check to the company for the value of her watch. That amount would in turn be given by the company to charity. Together, the counsel and I looked up the cost of a similar-appearing watch in a catalog we'd managed to dig up: $120, which I paid.

A few weeks later, our legal counsel stopped by my office to say that he had bad news. (General counsels never have *good* news; like auditors, the only good news is that there is no bad news.) It turned out that he had seen exactly the same watch in a jewelry store—and I owed another $1,500!

I had the worst of both worlds. I was out over $1,600 for a watch I had bought my wife, and my wife was mad at *me* for trying to take it away from her. And my wife is one of the most ethical people I know!

Well, no one ever said being ethical is easy!

⊕   ⊕   ⊕   ⊕   ⊕

A century ago, Richard Sears—founder of Sears Roebuck and Company—started the modern mail order industry, exposing a continent of people to new products that improved their lives in a huge number of ways. While supplying a burgeoning nation with these products, he also built a business that gave employment to thousands of people.

In the early days, Mr. Sears occasionally strayed from a strictly ethical path, as he later confessed. On occasion, in his zeal to sell merchandise, he would get carried away with catalog descriptions, and the praise he heaped on his own products would transcend the actual truth. This, in turn, led to returned merchandise and reduced profits. But Sears learned his lesson.

In later years, he was fond of saying, "Honesty is the best policy. I know because I've tried it both ways." Sears found that no matter what the short-term cost, honesty pays, because a customer who gets a fair deal from a merchant tends to return to that merchant in the future for other products.

Honesty *Is* the Best Policy (Honest!)

Let me relate a somewhat similar example of a challenging ethical decision I encountered on the job. Back when I was managing our company's Astronautics operation, our space launch vehicle contract with the Air Force included a special incentive clause rewarding the company with several million dollars for every time one of our rockets successfully launched a spacecraft.

One day a representative in our insurance department wrote to me that he had just learned we could insure our launches for a very low premium cost. (This certainly was more useful information than most of what comes in the many letters that CEOs of high-tech companies regularly get from would-be geniuses; in one memorable case I received a letter telling of the low-cost goldfish-powered [really!] spaceship the writer had invented to travel to the sun. When we responded—we *always* respond; that's important—that his spaceship would be incinerated long before it got close to the sun, our pen pal's quick solution was: "Go at night.") What our insurance department discovered was that the Air Force would give us our incentive award if we succeeded, and the insurance company would give us almost the same amount of money if we failed. This sounded like the proverbial self-eating watermelon.

Truthfully, I am absolutely certain that no one involved in any of our launches ever did anything one bit better because there was a bonus to the company for success. Nor do I believe that anyone would do less than their level best if the launch were insured against failure.

Nonetheless, we faced an ethical question. It would clearly undermine the idea of the incentive intended by our customer if we went out and bought insurance to hedge against failure. At the same time, our lawyers were quick to point out that we also had a responsibility to our shareholders to conduct our business in a prudent fashion. Was it not sound business practice to purchase insurance that would in effect guarantee most of the reward to the shareholders?

How would you have decided?

Frankly, I struggled a bit with that one. Finally, I decided that the first step in our ethical solution was, as it often is, full disclosure. I called the Air Force general who was in charge of the project and explained our opportunity and my dilemma. Noting that I was seeking advice, not guidance, I told him that if the Air Force were indifferent to what we elected to do, then we intended to buy the insurance. If, on the other hand, the Air Force felt the insurance undermined their intent, we would weigh that factor in our decision.

After having thought about the matter for a few days, the general called me back to say that anything that would appear to weaken the incentive for a successful launch did in fact undermine the government's intent. So I decided against purchasing the insurance against future failures. Certainly one could argue that this was not the proper resolution of the matter, but to me it seemed *equitable*. And it passed my four rules-of-thumb tests.

As already noted, there's no virtue in consistency if you're consistently wrong. What may be appropriate to do in one situation may not be in another. The world of ethics is, unfortunately, not often without an array of choices. And it's a world of gray, not black and white. In this spectrum of choices, honest people can honestly disagree on what is honest.

In this continuum of choices, I have found large numbers of people who consider themselves to be quite ethical, yet disagree over the point at which the boundary of propriety was actually transgressed . . . where the boa was lying in wait.

An Ill Wind

A real-world high stakes ethical dilemma in a business setting concerned the Citicorp Center building in New York City, a 716-

foot tall skyscraper that had been built with an innovative bracing system that allowed the building to rest on four massive columns. The building met all New York City building codes, including those relating to wind forces.

But after the building was completed, the engineer in charge of the structural design conducted more sophisticated analyses to assess the building's ability to withstand unusual wind forces. To his great alarm, the calculations revealed that the building might be subject to failure in "quartering" winds on a level that might be anticipated every sixteen years or so.

Since the engineer was the only person with this devastating knowledge, he had to make a choice: Say nothing and hope that such a storm did not occur, or reveal his findings, greatly embarrass himself and his company, possibly be sued, face bankruptcy, and perhaps even see a portion of Manhattan sealed off.

He took his findings to Citicorp's executives and openly pointed out the problem. Happily, it was found that structural corrections that weren't prohibitively expensive could be made to the building, and both the building and the engineer emerged relatively unblemished by the entire matter. Some might even say enhanced.

He actually received a little bit of *good* luck. A hurricane that was approaching Manhattan during this critical period suddenly changed course and veered out to sea. And throughout most of the period, New York was experiencing a newspaper strike.

You Have to Figure *This* One Out for Yourself

I would define the price of being ethical as similar to the price we pay for all the meaningful things in our lives. After all, we achieve a college education only at the price of years of hard work and self-discipline. We enjoy a fulfilling, lifelong marriage only with a certain sacrifice of self-interest and with hard work devoted to truly understanding another person.

We are rewarded with a successful business or academic career only after doing more than what is absolutely required.

We excel in sports only after many, many hours of training, conditioning, and self-sacrifice. And we achieve greatness as a nation only when we devote ourselves to a greater good.

As John Kennedy said about the Apollo program to send humans to the moon, "We do these things not because they are easy, but because they are hard."

I believe that what needs to be said to our friends, our employees, our colleagues, and our students is that by paying the price of being ethical today, we are actually investing for the longer good. We all know that nothing worth achieving is easily attained.

If we can strengthen our perception of ethical behavior, perhaps we will be on our way to a more ethical society. Those who say this is too great a task—that changing a society to make it more ethical is impossible—should be told the story about the great French Marshal Lyautey, who asked his gardener to plant a certain type of tree. When the gardener protested that the tree was slow growing and would not reach maturity for a hundred years, the Marshal replied, "In that case, there is no time to lose. Plant it this afternoon!"

And What Would *You* Have Done?

Here are a few scenarios I've used over the years with colleagues in the aerospace industry to illustrate the point that the world of ethics often presents a fuzzy array of choices.

In the aerospace business, when you're competing for a contract to make a new airplane, you often take out ads in the newspapers to display your design. But, in order not to help your competitor, the picture used in the ad is an artist's conception, never the plane exactly as it will look. Now suppose you're in the aerospace business, and one of your competitors makes a mistake and accidentally publishes its *real* design in the newspaper, and this becomes public knowledge.

Is it ethical to do some reverse engineering of their illustration and use their mistake to your advantage? Most people I've asked think that would be ethical. Do you?

Now let's change the situation just a bit. Suppose you're at the airport and you find the competitor's design laying at the top of a wastebasket. Say it had been thrown there accidentally (but you don't know that for sure). Is it ethical to dig it out of the trash and use it to your advantage? We know that newspaper reporters on occasion purposely go through the trash of someone they're interested in. If it's okay for them (and do you think it is?), is it okay for you?

Now suppose you're on an airplane. Two of your competitor's engineers are seated in front of you, casually discussing their design in voices loud enough that you can't avoid hearing what they're saying. Is it acceptable for you to sit passively and listen?

Or you're on the same plane and, by chance, the competitor's chief engineer is sitting right next to you *openly studying drawings for the new plane.* Is it okay for you to look? And then he gets up to walk to the rest room and leaves the drawings right there. Now is it ethical to look at them? To *touch* them?

Let me string this out a bit further. What if, in a mad dash to make a connecting flight, he leaves them behind when he gets off the plane? Are you obliged, ethically, to run after him and return the drawings? May you look at them under those changed circumstances?

How about going to the local bar where your competitor's employees hang out after work and listening to their conversations? Or perhaps going one step further and buying everyone in the bar all the drinks they want? Or, how about breaking into their plant and dynamiting the safe? (Okay, I'm getting carried away.)

In this continuum of choices, I've found large numbers of people who think of themselves as being quite ethical who nonetheless disagree over the point at which the boundary of propriety was actually transgressed—where, once again, the boa was hiding.

Enter Dilbert (Followed by Dogbert, of Course)

One of the most effective ways that we at Lockheed Martin have come up with to deal with ethical problems (in addition to our

Ethics Help Line) involves the expert assistance of Dilbert, the cartoon character so very popular with the American workforce. I can give a lecture on the philosophy of ethics, and two days later few who heard it could pass a simple quiz on what I'd said. But if I use our new video that stars Dilbert and Dogbert, people are still talking about it days and even weeks later. It all came about because Carol Marshall, an attorney who directs LM's ethics and business practices program, is a very imaginative person.

Carol noticed that wherever she went on her visits to our various operating companies she would run into Dilbert cartoons on the bulletin boards and in the cubicles. (Note: She says she never saw a picture of the CEO.) A lightbulb went off, and she got the bright idea of using this popular cartoon figure to help our employees focus on how to deal with some very real problems. She approached Scott Adams, Dilbert's talented creator, and asked for his assistance. Importantly, this assistance was not to teach ethics *per se;* it was to teach ethics awareness.

The result is a game, an interactive board game, in which teams of employees compete to see who can compile the most "right" answers to ethical problems (based on actual LM cases) outlined on a set of cards. And their judge is Dilbert! For example, they have to decide what is the most ethical way to respond when a customs official asks for an "expediting payment" to clear a much-needed package. (Dogbert says to make the payment and list it on your expense report as "oil and lube"!)

The reaction to the program, which we call the Ethics Challenge, has been overwhelmingly favorable. According to Carol, "Ethics behavior is great for teamwork. It'll help you get the right kind of employees, it's a great draw for customers, and it's good for business." The board game was *fun* too—especially for me, since I got to make a game-explaining video that starred Dilbert, Dogbert, and me. (That was the order in which we were listed in the video's introduction. Sort of a bummer to be behind a dog, and not even a real one.)

What's the Real Standard?

For most of us, when it comes to ethics, there is a personal Rubicon that, sooner or later, we have to cross. Our personal Rubicon may not be a matter of life or death, but nonetheless we have to recognize that ethical comportment comes before business, before winning, and sometimes even before loyalty.

Not long ago, I, an engineer and a Presbyterian, was hugely flattered to be asked to be the graduation speaker at Georgetown University, a great Jesuit liberal arts institution. But my pride came crashing down to earth when, as I sat on the stage in all my academic regalia and was being introduced, Father Leo O'Donovan, the president of the university and my greatly admired friend, leaned over and whispered to me, "What are you going to speak about?" Suddenly realizing the magnitude of my impertinence as I sat surrounded by Jesuits in their magnificent robes, I muttered, "Ethics—and if I go through with this, will you come out to Lockheed Martin and speak on mergers and acquisitions?" As I slowly rose to approach the podium, I explained to Father O'Donovan that this was covered by an old Jesuit term, "chutzpah"!

⊕   ⊕   ⊕   ⊕   ⊕

W. C. Fields, the heavy-drinking, sometimes rude, and almost always funny comedian of the 1930s and 1940s, once was discovered deeply immersed in reading the Bible just before a performance.

When a friend asked him what he was doing, Fields replied, with a wink, "Looking for loopholes!"

When it comes to ethics, there are no loopholes. There are no compromises. There are no back doors. But to be regarded as an ethical person may well be the ultimate reward.

Warren Buffett, addressing his son, put it this way: "It takes twenty years to build a reputation, and five minutes to ruin it. If you think about that, you'll do things differently."

And, to put it even more succinctly, the ethical life is its own reward.

2

Leadership

Sitting across the aisle from me on the flight from Washington to Havana was Richard Teerlink, the chief executive officer of Harley-Davidson, the motorcycle company. Earlier that same year, I'd gotten to know Dick when he and I had been the guests of General Gordon Sullivan, the top general in the U.S. Army, on another memorable excursion. General Sullivan had invited us to come along when he took half a dozen of his most senior generals on a field trip around the battlefield at Gettysburg.

The official tour guide was the Army historian, but it soon became apparent that the "guide behind the guide" was Gordie Sullivan. The "Chief," as he was called, had a very subtle way of underlining what the guide was pointing out, so there was no danger that the other generals would miss the point.

Just as in the past, there were lessons to be learned on that historic battlefield—lessons about how (and how not) to lead people. And he frequently drew parallels to the battles in Desert Storm in which they'd all participated in one way or another. General Sullivan was making sure his top officers got the message.

There's a very simple word for what Dick and I had witnessed that afternoon. The word is *leadership.*

⊕   ⊕   ⊕   ⊕   ⊕

A couple of years ago I received an award for leadership, which surprised me somewhat. As an engineer who had descended into management without much planning, I don't pretend to be much of an expert on the theory of leadership. In fact, a colleague once said I combine the inventive genius of an accountant with the conservatism of a rocket scientist! Once when confronted with the dilemma of having been asked to talk about leadership at the U.S. Military Academy at West Point, yet being far from an expert on the subject, I consulted with my number-one adviser, my wife, who offered some very sage advice. "Whatever you do," she said, "don't try to sound witty, intellectual, or charming. Just be yourself." Thanks, dear.

I also checked the dictionary for a definition of *leader*—and was not particularly enlightened, as far as my West Point audience would be concerned, to learn that it meant, "a short piece of cat gut."

Fortunately, when it comes to leadership I have had the opportunity to put into practice Yogi Berra's perceptive preachment that "you can see a lot by observing." So what follows comes under the gentle heading of Observations, and my intended point is to suggest ways in which you, the reader, can increase either your leadership potential or your leadership performance. Perhaps *leadership* strikes you as one of those words that are too big or too grand, but if your job includes motivating others, then you are in a position, like it or not, to exercise leadership. And the better you do it, the better off everyone is.

The Qualities of Leadership

During my career, I have had the privilege of observing and working with people I believe to be among the most outstanding leaders this country has produced. For each of these people, leadership took a unique form, depending on the challenges they faced. Some of the easily recognizable names from this list include David Packard, Jimmy Doolittle, Elizabeth Dole, Bo Callaway, David Kearns of Xerox, Jack Welch of GE, Bill Marriott, Warren Buffett, Mel Laird, General Omar Bradley, Supreme Court Justice Sandra Day O'Connor, astronauts Neil Armstrong and Jim Lovell, Don Rumsfeld, basketball's Wes Unseld, Colin Powell, Griffin Bell, Harold Shapiro, the president of Princeton University, several presidents of the United States, and a whole host of others.

What makes such people leaders? What are the qualities that enable one person to emerge from the pack, to seize the moment, to rally the troops, and, at times, even to change the course of history? That's the big question. And the answer to it, in my opinion, has at least five parts: inspiration, perseverance, courage, selflessness, and, most important of all, integrity.

Inspiration (or, in This Case, Inspired Management)

One quality that I have noted in leaders is inspired management. I suspect one can be an adequate manager without necessarily being a leader, but I think it's exceedingly difficult to be a leader if one cannot manage (with the assistance of lieutenants) the troops one leads. That is, leadership has to do with inspiring others to accomplishments that they themselves might not have considered even possible. It has to do with getting the most out of others—which is exactly what management is all about, too. Indeed, leadership concerns achieving important objectives through the efforts of others as well as your own.

In my forty-year management career I've learned one indisputable lesson: The key to almost any endeavor is *people*. I've noticed, over and over again, that when a project is in seemingly boundless trouble, if you put the right person in charge, the undertaking almost magically turns around. At Lockheed Martin, we truly believe what for some is just an empty phrase: "Our most important assets go home each evening." Ironically, that's an asset that doesn't even appear on the balance sheet.

GM executive Alfred Sloan, who for many years epitomized American industrial leadership, once said, "Take my assets, but leave me my [people], and in five years I'll have it all back."

The reverse of this notion was once expressed by a National Football League (NFL) quarterback who, during a particularly injudicious moment, said of his offensive line, "It's hard to soar like an eagle when you are surrounded by turkeys." (Throughout the subsequent season, he spent most of his Sunday afternoons on his back studying the sky above the nation's finer football stadiums. I wonder why.)

The challenge for any leader is to find eagles—individuals who aspire to that lofty goal in deeds as well as words. As Ross Perot once put it, "Eagles don't flock; you have to find them one at a time." However, I've noticed that if you treat people like eagles, pretty soon they start to *act* like eagles. If you treat your children like trustworthy people, they *begin to act* like trustworthy people.

I first became interested in this matter of identifying eagles many years ago. I was making a graph to compare the number of articles in a prestigious professional journal with the fraction of qualified people in the field in question who actually contributed those articles. About the same time, while watching professional football on television one Monday night, I noted that certain players seemed to score a disproportionate share of all the touchdowns scored by players in this position.

To my amazement, when I compared my "authors' graph" with the results for touchdowns scored by various running backs in the NFL, I found that the two graphs coincided within a pencil's width. So too did patents by employees of industrial firms, and a number of other such phenomena, and, in the spirit of total disclosure, I regret to report dutifully, even arrests by the Washington, D.C., police department!

My analysis led to one of the more obscure Augustine's laws, to wit: "One-tenth of the participants produce over one-third of the output, and increasing the number of participants merely reduces the average output." In fact, for a whole range of human activities, a small fraction of participants can be shown to produce a large fraction of the accomplishments. Why? Usually because these are the most highly inspired and motivated participants in the endeavor. In my experience, motivation will beat sheer talent every time.

This leads to my own theory of management, which can be summarized in just fourteen words (and can save you at least $40,000 in business school expenses): "Find good people, tell them what you want, and get out of their way." Or, as the great baseball pitcher Lefty Gomez put it when asked the secret of success, "fast outfielders."

If Lockheed Martin's predecessor, Martin Marietta, had done a better job of retaining "eagles" over the years, it is startling to think where our firm would be today. For example, a glance at a list of employees who worked on the early payrolls for Glenn L. Martin, the founder of the "Martin" part of our company, reveals such names as Dutch Kindleberger, who started the North American half of North American Rockwell; James McDonnell and his company's eventual partner, Don Douglas; plus a couple of fellows named Lawrence Bell and Chance Vought. And if that's not enough, how many people, even aviation people, know that Glenn Martin gave Bill Boeing his original flying lessons? (Now *there* was a strategic mistake!)

If Glenn Martin had hung on to those people, today our corporate aircraft would be a "Lockheed Martin 747"!

Perseverance

Another quality that I believe is absolutely essential for leadership is *perseverance.* Call it determination, call it what you wish, it's the willingness to dig deeper and demand more of one's self for a longer time than anyone else is willing to demand of themselves, and to do so day in and day out, to endure, to persist, to succeed.

(As a great example of perseverance, I'd like to offer my own mother, who is now approaching 104 years old. She says she believes in George Burns's theory of life: "Once you get to be 100, you've got it made. You almost never hear of anyone over 100 dying." Now *that's* perseverance.)

The reason that determination is so important is that in world-class competition, the margin between success and failure, accomplishment and disappointment, victory and defeat is usually very, very slim indeed. While visiting northern Alaska one February a few years ago on an extended dogsledding trip with my son, I learned of the finish to the Iditarod, a dogsled race over 1,049 miles of inhospitable terrain that had been taking place just to the south of us at the same time as we pursued our own more leisurely trek. The contestants in the Iditarod had encountered winds up to 100 miles an hour that year and temperatures down to 70 degrees below zero. But the important thing about the race (from the standpoint of this book) is that the person who finished second lost the grueling sixteen-day race by a mere three minutes and forty-three seconds.

That seemed like a narrow enough margin under the conditions until I learned that a few years earlier, in 1978, the difference between first and second place in this race was *one second!* Similar results have occurred at the end of the Indy 500 auto race. In one recent year, Al Unser, Jr., beat Scott Goodyear by 0.043 second—barely half a car length.

Moving to a different "track," Samuel Tilden would have been President of the United States if he had had *one more* vote in the Electoral College in 1876.

The difference between victory and defeat, between success and failure, is often a mere sliver. This is what makes Churchill's words so meaningful: "Never give in, never give in, never, never, never—in nothing, great or small, large or petty—never give in except to convictions of honor and good sense."

Courage

Courage is another essential element of leadership, because when one attempts great things the road will invariably be rocky. The movie *Apollo 13* (which I first watched sitting with astronaut Jim Lovell, the movie's hero, and his wife) was an excellent reminder of just how hard the struggle to achieve can be. Such struggles almost always involve a degree of personal risk and endurance. The story of the explorer Shackleton, memorialized in a book fittingly named *Endurance,* is another of my favorite examples. His indomitable will led him to save every one of the members of his sailing party who had become trapped in the Antarctic ice pack during an early expedition, in spite of the fact that all the odds were against him.

Those of us who've had the good fortune to play a role in the space program can attest to the difficulty of propelling highly complex, highly explosive objects into space. In fact, the task is so tough that fully two-thirds of America's early space launches *failed.* Ten of the eleven pre-Apollo moon probes failed; twelve of the first thirteen flights of one of America's most successful military space programs failed, as did the first thirteen test flights of the Sidewinder, which ultimately became one of America's most successful and durable missiles.

Did the people working on these projects give up? Absolutely not. In almost every case, there was a single individual who for a time stood alone against the legions of naysayers and Monday-morning quarterbacks.

Courage is a particularly vital quality in today's risk-averse world. You simply cannot accomplish great things without taking risks. As with the turtle, you only make progress when you stick your neck out.

A corporate advertisement by United Technologies Corporation offers food for thought. "R. H. Macy," one of the ads noted, "failed seven times before his store in New York caught on. English mystery writer John Creasey got 753 rejection slips before he published 564 books. Babe Ruth struck out 1,330 times, but also hit 714 home runs."

Another ad in the same series tells of a fellow who "dropped out of grade school. Ran a country store. Went broke. Took 15 years to pay off his bills. Took a wife. Unhappy marriage. Ran for House. Lost twice. Ran for Senate. Lost twice. Delivered a speech that became a classic. Audience indifferent. Attacked daily by the press and despised by half the country. He signed his name 'A. Lincoln.' "

But my favorite ad is the one on TV in which basketball great Michael Jordan walks slowly through a darkened hallway of an arena, saying that in his career he has missed 9,000 shots, he has lost almost 300 games, and 26 times he took the decisive shot at the end of the game and missed: "I have failed over and over in my life . . . that is why I succeed."

Selflessness

Great leaders subjugate their own personal interests to those of the team. They make sure their troops are "fed and bedded down" before they themselves seek comfort. They ask more of themselves than they ask of anyone around them. And they are consummate team players.

One of my favorite team play stories concerns the Chicago Bulls and their then-rookie forward Stacey King. As luck would have it, on a night when King managed to score one lone point, his teammate Michael Jordan scored sixty-nine points. When a reporter asked King after the game what he thought of the evening, he replied, "I'll always remember this as the night that Michael and I combined for seventy points." Now *that's* real team play.

Ironically, the best way to get ahead in business in fact seems to be to embrace selflessness. People resent those who are always seeking to take credit for everything that happens. (Casey Stengel once joked that management is the art of getting credit for the home runs your players hit.) In contrast, those who just do their job and seek opportunities to help others succeed are both appreciated by peers and noticed by superiors.

Integrity

The fifth important quality for a leader and perhaps the most essential is integrity. It is the enabling quality that has long been part of the American leadership profile.

My principal observation in regard to integrity is very simple: If people can't count on you, they won't follow you.

A compelling example of integrity concerns Theodore Roosevelt in his early years as a rancher out West. One day while Roosevelt and some of his ranch hands were rounding up stray cattle, they happened to wander onto a neighbor's property, where they found an unbranded calf. By western tradition, the calf belonged to the neighbor, but one of Roosevelt's cowboys started to put the Roosevelt brand on the calf. Roosevelt asked why he was doing this and was told, "I always put on the boss's brand."

Incensed, Roosevelt fired the man on the spot. "A man who will steal *for* me," he explained, "will steal *from* me." As a result of this incident, Roosevelt's reputation as one whose word was inviolable spread throughout the West and followed him throughout his life.

The importance of integrity in leadership was addressed by President Ronald Reagan during a commencement speech in 1993. He said, "The character that takes command in moments of crucial choices has already been determined. It has been determined by a thousand other choices made earlier in seemingly unimportant moments. It has been determined by all those 'little' choices of years past—by all those times when the voice of conscience was at war with the voice of temptation—whispering a lie that 'it doesn't really matter.' It has been determined by all the day-to-day decisions made when life seemed easy and crises seemed far away, the decisions that, piece by piece, bit by bit, developed habits of discipline or of laziness; habits of self-sacrifice or self-indulgence; habits of duty and honor and integrity—or dishonor and shame."

Of all the qualities an aspiring leader needs, to my mind, integrity is the most fundamental.

In the Right Place at the Right Time

When you look at the diverse qualities a leader must have, you can understand why so *few* people prove to be truly great leaders. But what has always struck me is how often, at a critically important juncture, a great leader suddenly emerges just in time to save the day. At the critical moment, Harry Truman appears on the scene. Or Winston Churchill. Or Norm Schwarzkopf. Or Colin Powell. Or Jim Lovell. Or Roger Staubach. Sometimes this individual is the last person you might expect to emerge as a great leader. I suspect that there is a lot more leadership in all of us than we realize—it just takes a major challenge to bring it out.

In science and engineering, there was Robert Goddard, the world's first rocket scientist, a Massachusetts college professor during the early part of this century. He endured widespread ridicule, including in the editorial pages of the *New York Times*, yet he built the first practical liquid fuel rocket. He said rockets would someday reach the moon, dismissing the scorn the media heaped on him by noting, "Every vision is a joke until the first [person] accomplishes it." Two decades later, German scientists paid the sum of thirty-five cents a copy for Goddard's patents, which became the basis for that country's advanced rocket program, which in turn became the basis for America's early space program.

If you'll grant me a moment of patriotic chauvinism, I'm

proud of the fact that my country has maintained its top rank in higher education and research, and has also provided technological leadership. (I think we've won 155 science-based Nobel prizes—in medicine, physics, and chemistry—in the last half-century.) And our colleges and universities continue to set the standard for the world, attracting by far the greatest percentage of students who study outside their own country.

In our military—I'm almost done bragging—we can see numerous examples of leadership. Admiral Hyman Rickover never won a sea battle, but he won a potentially more impressive contest by helping America be the first to develop the nuclear-powered submarine.

"One of the most wonderful things that happened in the *Nautilus* program," he once said, "was that everybody knew it was going to fail—so they left us completely alone [and] we were able to do the job."

Rising to the Occasion

During wartime, U.S. industry has demonstrated no less a sense of leadership and dedication when they were called on to back up our military. When the Patriot missile became a "superstar" performer in the Gulf War, very few people knew that most of the missiles fired against Iraq's Scuds did not exist *when Kuwait was invaded!* Lockheed Martin employees worked around the clock to build Patriot missiles capable of shooting down a Scud. The record was set when one Patriot, assembled in Florida, brought down a Scud over Israel just forty-eight hours later— talk about "just-in-time" manufacturing!

In business, world leadership is amply demonstrated by the size and diversity of the U.S. economy, the strength of our capital markets, the resurging competitiveness of U.S. goods abroad, the thrust of our technology, and the speed with which we recognize problems and respond to them.

On the other hand, and before I get carried away here, I have to admit that American business has made its share of mistakes, including getting caught in the sequence of developing the concept of quality, exporting that practice abroad, forgetting it ourselves, and then having to import it all over again from Japan. But learn we did—finally. Whenever I think of such lapses, I am reminded of Winston Churchill's observation that "Americans will always do the right thing . . . after they have exhausted all the other possibilities."

For every misstep, however, anyone can name ten success stories. In politics, America's impact as the world's only full-service superpower is self-evident. Democracy is sweeping the world, based to a large extent on the principles enunciated in the Declaration of Independence and the Constitution and demonstrated for all to see for more than two centuries.

I think Gamal Abdel Nasser got it just right when he said (in a somewhat convoluted compliment), "The genius of you Americans is that you never make clear-cut stupid moves, only complicated stupid moves which make [the rest of] us wonder at the possibility that there may be something to them [that] we are missing."

And, as Churchill said, we may not always do things right the first time, but in the long run our continual efforts growing out of individual accountability usually get us to the right place in the long run.

That, too, is a form of leadership . . . on a national scale.

It's hard to beat the advice of George Orwell, who wrote, during the darkest days of World War II: "The high sentiments always win in the end. The leaders who offer blood, toil, tears and sweat always get more out of their followers than those who offer safety and a good time. When it comes to the pinch, human beings are heroic."

Let's let the waste-no-words Harry Truman have the last few: "A leader has to lead."

3

Giving Value

Given the fact that I began as an engineer, I guess it won't surprise anyone to learn that one of my personal heroes is the great Leonardo da Vinci. If there was ever a true Renaissance man, it was Leonardo, a master of the arts *and* the sciences. That's why, excited as I was about all the destinations on the Time News-tour, I let slip a sigh of disappointment, knowing that we were flying so far north of Italy. Even though I have visited that wonderful country a number of times, it is never enough. I always welcome another chance to study the works of Leonardo first-hand.

Even a quick glance through his famous notebooks causes astonishment at the breadth of his interests, the extraordinary number of his inventions, and the multitude of scientific discoveries that he anticipated. Sketches for what would become major works of art are followed by designs for bridges and gears, and a few pages later come plans for flying machines and life preservers, dredges and diving bells. There are anatomical drawings remarkable for their detail and accuracy, and Leonardo's observations on the flight of birds were perceptive enough to enable him to write what was in all probability the first treatise on the subject.

While a few hundred miles to the east of Italy the great Polish astronomer Nicolaus Copernicus was still carefully working out his theory of a sun-centered universe, Leonardo was busily writing that "the earth is not the center of the circuit of the sun, nor the center of the universe."

Don't Be Afraid to Admit Your Strengths

Of all these many amazing accomplishments, however, what most impresses me is that Leonardo da Vinci, although best known for his artistry, was such a magnificent engineer. In fact, he was much more of an engineer than most people realize. Among the letters of his that have survived, one of the most intriguing is a job application he submitted to Lodovico Sforza, the ruler of Milan in 1482, a decade earlier than Columbus's epic voyage. In this letter, in order to get the boss's attention, Leonardo relied entirely on his skills as an engineer.

"I can construct bridges," he wrote with great confidence, "that are very strong and very portable, with which to pursue an enemy. . . . I can noiselessly construct to any prescribed point subterranean passages—either straight or winding—passing if necessary underneath trenches or a river."

Switching venues, Leonardo continued, "In time of peace, I believe I can give as complete satisfaction as anyone else in the construction of buildings, both public and private, and in conducting water from one place to another." Finally, almost as an afterthought, the master engineer suggested that he had other talents that might interest his prospective employer: "I can . . . execute sculpture in marble, bronze, or clay. Also, in painting, I can do as much as anyone else."

Lodovico was impressed, and Leonardo got the job. He kept it for sixteen years, until his patron was overthrown by an invading French army. Curiously, despite the ever-present threat of war, Lodovico never called on Leonardo to produce any of the major innovative military construction projects he described in his letter. When a plague killed about 50,000 of Milan's inhabitants, da Vinci, convinced the sickness had been caused by overcrowding and filth, drew up elaborate plans for wider city streets that would admit more light and air and for watercourses to carry off sewage. Lodovico wasn't interested. Instead, he ordered Leonardo to install an extra bath in his palace.

The Boss Doesn't *Always* Know Best

Lodovico frittered away much of Leonardo's time and talent on minor projects and frivolous court amusements. Odd as it may sound, among his other duties, Leonardo was expected to play the lute, sing, and tell stories! Had he not somehow managed to find time, during this same period, to paint his immortal *Last Supper*, this whole segment of his career might be written off as a tragic waste of genius.

The moral of this story—that we neglect the talent of our employees and colleagues to our own detriment—has a present-day application. Lodovico did not recognize his chief engineer for what he was or, more precisely, for what he could contribute. He underpaid him, he ignored his best ideas, and he demeaned his professional status. Yet in the end, Lodovico perhaps suffered more from his dubious treatment of Leonardo than did Leonardo himself. Why? Because it was Lodovico who lost the enormous advantages he might have enjoyed had he better applied Leonardo's enormous abilities.

Try to Learn From, Not Replicate, a Boss's Mistake

Lodovico of Milan's error in underestimating the potential value and importance of Leonardo da Vinci's engineering skills was a costly one, because this was a point in history when wind, water, and muscle provided the only power. And nearly all humanity had in the way of a computer was the human brain. Similarly, we pay an enormous price for underestimating the potential impact of the scientific and technical professions in today's era of nuclear energy, spaceflight, advanced telecommunications, and microprocessors that can store whole volumes of information on a silicon wafer the size of a thumbnail.

The advancement of technology continues at a record pace, as do the challenges our society faces, so we must move briskly just to stay in place. Today, we rely on engineers to keep us on the cutting edge of technology, maintain our leadership in space, and help solve a host of problems here on earth, such as pollution, urban congestion, air traffic control, our growing need for energy, and the crumbling with age of our dams, bridges, and highways. Yet, amazingly, the number of engineers being graduated in America each year is declining rather than increasing, and half the Ph.D.s granted by American universities in engineering and science go to foreign students.

You Can't *Give* Value If Your Work Doesn't *Have* Value

We also depend, to a very large degree, on these practitioners of the applied sciences to lead the way in meeting the challenge of global competition. The question of whether the United States can meet this challenge is going to be decided mainly by scientists and engineers, not by lawyers, not by investment bankers, not by stockbrokers, and not (I add this last category at the risk of sounding heretical) by corporate executives.

I cringe when I think about bright American students eyeing the stock exchange or walnut-paneled executive suites, and exclaiming, as the media reported one young business school graduate did upon visiting the floor of the New York Stock Exchange: "*This* is business. *This* is what it's all about. *This* is where it's at!"

Sorry, but this is decidedly *not* where it's at. "It" is not in the offices of the deal makers, the takeover artists, the arbitrageurs. "It" is not in the offices of the executives, the accountants, or even the lawyers. In my opinion, "where it's at," and *where it will be* in the critical years ahead, is in the research laboratories and the plants of American industry—which is right where it has been for the last hundred years.

America did not become an economic superpower and a technological pacesetter because of its excellence at *financial* engineering. We did not do it by the pointless restructuring of paper assets. We did it by *creating real wealth*—by investing in people, plants, and equipment and by making products and providing services *that people wanted to buy.*

Why (and How) I Became an Engineer

In my own case, it took me until I was actually in college to convince myself that engineering was "where it's at" for me. Again, there's a bit of a lesson here in the danger of too much long-distance planning when it comes to managing a career. Prior to that, I wanted to be—are you ready for this?—a forest ranger.

My ancestors had emigrated from Germany to Ohio in 1834, where they farmed for more than fifty years before moving west, in the late 1880s, to Buena Vista, a tiny town high up in the Colorado Mountains (at the foot of Mt. Princeton—named after another place that would become important in my life). Colorado was truly a frontier in those early days. Grandfather Augustine eventually left the mountains and opened a small grocery store in Edgewater, Colorado (then also a small town; today it's a Denver suburb). His son, my father, was in a related line of work, the wholesale fruit business. Both men loved the mountains, and I do too, so it must be in the genes.

My mother, whose people had also originally emigrated from Europe to the Midwest, was born and raised in Denver. However, she had friends—whom she, at age 103, still remembers clearly—who crossed the prairies in covered wagons. (She has also met friends of mine who've walked on the moon. If any of this fazes her, I've yet to see signs of it.)

My father, who was born in 1894, learned to read by the glow of a kerosene lamp in a cabin in a small mountain community high up in the Rockies. He once told my son, an electrical engineer who at the time was helping to train America's astronauts for the first "human satellite"—free-flight in space— mission, that the most important technological development of his lifetime had been the tubular wick for oil lamps (which, apparently, gave off much more light and thus extended the useful hours of the day).

My dad passed three loves on to me: One was his love of the great outdoors, another his love of sports, and the third his devotion to scouting. Chiefly because of my father's influence, I became an Eagle Scout, as did my son after me.

From the time I was nine until I graduated from college, I took not dozens but probably hundreds of camping trips in the breathtaking moutains that fill so much of my home state. On these trips I learned several important basics: the need to be able to care for one's self, to appreciate the land and the wildlife I encountered, to help and be helped by others, and to strive to do the very best at whatever I did since survival could some-times hinge on exactly that. In the Rockies, it is not uncommon to be caught in a snowstorm above timberline on the Fourth of July. So, through my early high school days, and despite my earning quite respectable grades (which meant I'd have a rea-sonable chance at a college scholarship), what I really wanted to do was to work in those glorious mountains.

Go East, Young Man

In 1952, during my junior year at East High, a huge public school in Denver, one of my teachers, Justin W. Brierly, called me into his office and asked me what I intended to do after graduation. When I told him I thought I'd like to be a forest ranger, he threw me out of his office. But I wasn't kidding. I really meant what I said.

But Mr. Brierly wasn't kidding either! A few months after he'd thrown me out of his office, he summoned me once again. This time, rather than ask me my plans, he simply handed me a pair of envelopes. One contained information about Williams College in Williamstown, Massachusetts, and the other about Princeton. A friend of mine who had recently graduated from Princeton had been urging me to "think about it." Mr. Brierly told me I should apply to both schools for need-based scholar-ships (my family would not have been able to afford to send me to either one of them).

In those days, the early 1950s, I had virtually no knowledge of the eastern United States. To me, the East was pretty much what began on the other side of the river that ran through Mt. Hope, Kansas, where my aunt and uncle had a farm. South was Pueblo, Colorado. North meant Cheyenne, Wyoming, and West was Salt Lake, which I had visited once. Except for one brief foray into the, for me, uncharted eastern region (namely, Washington, D.C.), that was about the extent of my travels. Nonetheless, I filled out the applications I had been given, and, seemingly, the next thing I knew I was on a train that was pulling into a railroad station about fifty miles from New York City in a place called Princeton, New Jersey. I was wearing blue suede shoes and a necktie prominently featuring a hand-painted horse. It became immediately clear that my roommates weren't ready for me.

While I learned early on from going through the application process that Princeton did not exactly have a lot to offer in forestry, I wasn't prepared for the degree or amount of humor that my initial choice of major had provoked. Finally, in desperation, I had asked someone what was the closest thing to forestry that Princeton deigned to teach and was told geological engineering. I promptly signed up for that.

A Quirk of Fate, and a Quart of Beer

After a year of "Busting Rocks," our semiaffectionate term for our course of studies in geological engineering, I was returning to Princeton on a train from a weekend outing in New York City (because we usually hitchhiked, I guess I must have just won the lottery) when I ran into a Princeton senior who had also gone to East Denver High. Clearly he had been "overserved" during his weekend in the Big City, for he was hanging over the railing on a platform between two cars of the train, seeking relief from the discomfort his overindulgence had caused him. Afraid he might actually fall off the train, I grabbed the back of his belt and hung on to him for (his) dear life.

A most unusual conversation took place, as his waves of discomfort rose and fell, so to speak. He told me, with great enthusiasm, that his course of study, aeronautical engineering, was definitely "taking off." Oddly enough, despite his condition, he made a great deal of sense, at least to me. The very next day, I became an aeronautical engineering major.

Not the least of the reasons why I thoroughly enjoyed my new course of study was the growing awareness, as I progressed from one level of knowledge to another, that when it was all over, I would be able to get a *real* job. I would be doing something truly exciting. I would be building things. I wouldn't be dealing with paper profits, or some ethereal theory of economic redistribution or self-actualization. Because I would be making something that had intrinsic value, I would be giving value.

In the meantime, during my summer vacations, I had a job that was also very real: I spread tar on roofs. (You could, I suppose, say I started in business at the very top.) Years later, the *Washington Post* asked me to list the most important lessons I learned from my first "real" job, and I gave them three. One, there are a lot of fine people who make their livings spreading tar on roofs; two, the key to getting *off* the roofs is education; and, three, it takes an awful lot of tar to cover a roof!

Another Quirk of Fate (Minus the Beer)

In our last undergraduate semester at Princeton, seven of us went to the Philadelphia Navy Yard to take our physicals in order to become Navy pilots. We were a bit dismayed at the confusion evidenced by the young sailor who had been assigned to take our blood pressure readings, but other than that, everything seemed to go off quite well. We returned to campus confident that in six weeks or so we'd be notified of our acceptance, and begin our careers boring holes in the wild blue yonder. In fact, the news did come in six weeks, but it was not what we'd expected. *Every one* of us had failed the Navy's entrance exam. We all had—high blood pressure!

In fact, we did not have high blood pressure (from then to now mine has always been the same, about 105 over 70). But, not knowing for sure that the young sailor had read all seven of us wrong, but aware that time was running out, we each fell back on Plan B, which was already in place: to go to graduate school. In my case, it was aeronautical engineering (again, or still), and two years later, master's degree in hand, I said good-bye to what had become to me the very friendly East, and headed back West, this time for sunny Southern California, where I had a job—a *real* job—with Douglas Aircraft.

But that quirky fate wasn't finished with me just yet. I took my first step on the road to a career in the missiles and space business because someone in the personnel department had, by mistake, routed my application there instead of to the airplane division, where I had wanted to work. Sometimes you just have to go where fate sends you, or as Yogi counsels, "When you come to a fork in the road, take it." More on that later.

Don't Microplan Your Career

I believe that one of the biggest mistakes a person can make in a career is to plan it too carefully. I have seen this error made by people on all levels: coworkers, employees, and even bosses. The problem is that when you stare so hard at a distant prize, you are likely to overlook something that is lying at your feet.

It's just not useful, in my experience, to try to plan an entire career in detail. There are just too many changes ahead, too many things that are going to happen that you can't anticipate. I think that, instead, it's useful to have a general sense of direction, and then to be well prepared, and to be extremely opportunistic. When those opportunities appear, jump at them.

Here are a couple of examples that I believe support this point. The first was told to me—on the Time Newstour—by Don Fisher, who founded the chain of clothing stores known as The Gap. The second, which I don't believe has ever been in print before, is the story of how Omar Bradley came to join the Army. And I know it's true because it was told to me by the general himself.

Some years ago, Fisher, who was in the real estate business, went to a store and bought a pair of Levis. In too much of a hurry to try them on, when he got home he discovered they were an inch too short. He took them back, but the store where he'd bought them had such a small selection that they couldn't accommodate him. Knowing that the ubiquitous Levis had to be stockpiled somewhere, he became so frustrated that it gave him an idea.

He called the company at its headquarters in San Francisco and offered them a deal: If they would agree to supply him, he would open a store that had the largest selection of their products ever offered for sale in one spot. Fine, said the company, and thus The Gap was born. Don later told me, "If my pants had been an inch longer, I'd still be in real estate instead of owning The Gap!"

My other example of the importance of seizing an opportunity, the one that relates to General Omar Bradley, has a different twist to it.

One fine Saturday when Omar Bradley was a high school senior back home in Missouri, he and his friends had planned a day of playing baseball. Much as he would have preferred to play ball with his friends, the young Bradley had been instructed by a teacher to take an exam—offered only once a year—to see if he could get in to the military academy at West Point. Thus, on the day in question, while his friends headed off to the diamond, Bradley found himself in a stuffy classroom. The teacher who was proctoring the exam handed out the test papers.

General Bradley told me, many years later, that after he'd taken a look at the questions, he was convinced there was "no way I'd ever pass that exam." The thought of wasting the whole morning *failing* an exam when he could be playing baseball was too much for him, and before he'd even begun the test, he got up and walked to the front of the room, past the curious eyes of all the other candidates, to hand back the exam. The elderly teacher sat at her desk, head down, absorbed in the book she was reading. Because she was wearing bifocals, her gaze was so lowered that she did not notice him.

"In those days," he explained, "you didn't interrupt a teacher. You stood until you were recognized." So Bradley stood . . . and stood . . . and stood. Pretty soon the other students saw him and began to chuckle.

"Eventually," he said, "it got more embarrassing to stand there than to go back to my seat and take the exam."

So that's what he did—and the rest is history, including the considerable impact General Omar Bradley had on the outcome of World War II.

The Values Shared by Those Who Give Value

What continues to impress me about the type of people I've been describing in this chapter—the value givers—is how similar they all are in so many ways: professional, ethical, innovative, competent, motivated, energetic. And, perhaps above all, they exhibit the quality of staying focused on the job at hand.

Over my years in business, I've seen too many people who spend too much time worried about "the next step," about how they're going to "get ahead in life." To me, the people who give the best value are those who treat each and every job as if it's the last job they're ever going to have—and do it the best they know how. And not only do they do their own job well, they help others do their jobs. They don't divert their energies scheming how to make certain their efforts are noticed.

All of us only have so many hours a day to think, and only so many calories of energy to burn, so we ought to devote as little of that time and energy as possible to plotting how to get ahead. Do your current job so well that everyone will notice you and *want* you to move up.

I've seen so many people wreck careers because they were like the football player running down the field about to catch the game-winning touchdown pass, and just before it gets to him, he looks up into the stands to make sure everyone's watching. The ball hits him in the back of the head—or, worse, he runs into the goal post! His team loses the game.

Two other points on the subject of busted careers have to do with the concept of giving value. I've noticed that, generally speaking, the people who have serious problems or fail early in their careers are people who are not well equipped in the basics of their own profession. When you get right down to it, they really don't understand accounting, or thermodynamics, or plumbing, or the law, or whatever else the case may be.

In contrast, late in a career, the problems stem, in my opinion, from one central difficulty of a quite different kind (and it's one younger managers and executives should be particularly mindful of). The so-called Late Failure has nothing to do with not knowing the basics, the fundamentals. By this point people who hold fairly senior jobs have been promoted six or eight times, so the question is not one of competency. They've been through all kinds of filters, and obviously they wouldn't have gotten through them if they didn't have *some* degree of basic capability. What I've seen as the problem that surfaces later in careers, and sometimes even in the most senior careers, is a very simple *sounding* problem: personality conflicts. These concern people who just can't seem to get along with other people.

I've also noted that it is usually not one's strongest quality, or even the average of one's overall qualities, that counts in selecting talent to take on greater responsibilities. What counts is how strong is the *weakest* of one's relevant attributes. This is, of course, the place to focus self-improvement efforts. It's a little like playing doubles in tennis: Usually the team with the stronger of the weak players wins. But overall, we at Lockheed Martin have learned that the best way to pick talent is based on past performance. What someone has done before seems to be the best predictor of what that person is likely to do in the future.

That may seem simplistic, but it also happens to be true, and it's one of the reasons that I'm such a strong proponent of outside activities, especially sports.

There's no better place that I know of to learn, and in a crucible of intense but tolerable outcomes, to get along with people—both people who disagree with what you are doing and people who are trying to help you with what you are doing—than sports. There is also no finer place to learn leadership.

As a highly successful football coach once said, "I'm just a plowhand from Arkansas, but I have learned how to hold a team together. If anything goes bad, then I did it. If anything goes semigood, then we did it. If anything goes real good, then you did it. That's all it takes to get people to win football games." As some wise soul once said, it's amazing what you can accomplish if you don't care who gets the credit.

Of course, life is life, and not a football or a basketball or a baseball game, but the similarities, especially when it comes to working with others and wanting to give real value for one's efforts, are undeniable.

I think there is no other feeling quite like that of joining forces with like-minded others in order to produce a result that once seemed impossible—a result that gives true value.

There is a poem that I often share with business colleagues because it pretty well lays it on the line. It goes as follows:

> *Every morning in Africa a gazelle wakes up.*
> *It knows it must outrun the fastest lion or*
> *it will be killed.*
>
> *Every morning in Africa a lion wakes up.*
> *It knows it must outrun the slowest gazelle or*
> *it will starve.*
>
> *It doesn't matter whether you're a lion or a gazelle—*
> *When the sun comes up, you'd better be running.*

SECTION TWO

Management

AROUND THE WORLD IN EIGHT DAYS, II

At 1:00 A.M. on Sunday, October 8, we landed in Gander, New-foundland, to take on fuel. As usual, my timing was off. I have been in Gander many times but still have yet to see it. For some reason, I always seem to arrive in Gander in the middle of the night. The temperature was about fifty degrees lower than it had been in Havana just a few hours earlier. I could hardly wait for Moscow.

The people from Time, with their customary thoroughness, had overlooked nothing. In this case they had somehow managed to get the ice cream counter in the airport to open, and free ice cream cones were being passed out to anyone who wanted one. Soon we were all standing around eating ice cream. This struck me as kind of humorous, as I doubt if, left to our own devices, any of these CEOs would have bought ice cream in Gander, Newfoundland, at one in the morning in freezing weather. But, hey, they were free! (I had two.)

Finally, up and away we went on our way to Moscow. Because Fidel Castro had given each of us a carton of Cuban cigars (and three bottles of Cuban rum), there were some miscreants who broke the otherwise-firm no-smoking rule. I was not one of them; as a matter of fact, I thought about posting a sign above the emergency exit door near my seat saying, "If you must smoke, please step outside."

When we landed in Moscow, it was 2:00 P.M. (But that was "clock time"; according to "body time," it was only 6:00 A.M.) It was a perfect Moscow day, overcast with a cold rain. Once inside the city limits, we passed the original Russian McDonald's, and, as usual, despite the rain, there was a long line of people standing outside waiting, placidly, to get their burgers (on a sesame seed bun) and fries.

Taken directly to Red Square for some instant acculturation, we strolled around St. Basil's, Lenin's Tomb, and the Wall of the Kremlin. I had last been in Moscow two years earlier, and I could see that even Red Square had changed: There were no lines outside Lenin's Tomb. Indeed, it seemed that these days Ronald McDonald was a much bigger draw than Vladimir Lenin.

Another sign of change appeared around the next corner. A very attractive, small church near the end of Red Square was newly reconstructed. It hadn't been there on my last visit. In fact, the area it occupied had primarily contained a public rest room.

To my surprise, our hotel, the Oktobraskaya, or October Star, was the same one where my wife and I had stayed many years before on our first trip to Russia, then the Soviet Union. At that time, the hotel was where the government put visiting members of the communist party's Central Committee—and a few wanderers from abroad such as ourselves. The hotel's name had been changed. It was now the President, and the high steel fence that surrounded it made us feel quite secure from the crime that has become rampant on the outside. (On our first trip, we got the feeling that the fence and guards were to keep us *inside!*)

As we toured Moscow that day, we began to get the revised lay of the Russian land. Had the area still been the Soviet Union, it would have had 300 million people, but Russia today is only half that number. Unemployment was said to be very low, less than 2 percent, but the definition of unemployment is very flexible. Once again I heard the comment from Russian workers: "We pretend to work, and they pretend to pay us."

Except for a lot more goods in stores and people wearing more attractive clothing, the principal change since my last visit appeared to be the increase in crime. Sadly, that affliction all too often seems to follow the gift of freedom. (The former president of Singapore once told me that the difference between Singapore and America was that Singapore puts the rights of society above the rights of the individual, and America puts the rights of the individual above those of society.)

Just in case we needed a warning, a piece of paper in each of our hotel rooms notified us of our personal code number, which we would need to get back into the compound "in the off (and highly unrecommended) chance that you wander outside the grounds." That was good enough for me.

Evidence of the national sense of humor resurfaced at lunch. A Russian businessman told us a story about a peasant who'd been caught scrawling "Khrushchev is an idiot" on a wall. The peasant was given twenty years in prison: "Five years for defacing public property, and fifteen years for revealing state secrets."

At the meal's end, one of the Russian guests remarked, "We always hope that things will turn out for the best, but unfortunately they always turn out as they do."

What was perhaps the highlight of our visit to Moscow was the chance to meet and talk with Prime Minister Viktor Chernomyrdin, then the second most powerful person in Russia, except during Yeltsin's many illnesses, when he was probably the most powerful. He spoke at some length about business relations between the United States and Russia, the bottom line of which was that there were still too many barriers on both sides, "particularly on the American side." U.S. attitudes toward Russia, he said, still reflected the Cold War era, in that America was still treating Russia as if it were a communist nation. He said that the United States doesn't treat East European countries that way. Why are we prejudiced against Russia? It struck me that we'd also heard that line before, in Cuba when Castro had pointed out that America had fought wars with Germany, Italy, Japan, North Vietnam, and a host of others, then turned around and helped them. "We didn't even fight you, and look how you treat us. What's wrong with us?"

Prime Minister Chernomyrdin wrapped up his remarks neatly by noting the difficulty of producing change: "It can never be that you go to bed in one system and wake up in another." I could relate to that.

That night, the visit was capped by a gathering at the presidential guest house, where we met informally with the Russian cabinet. Interestingly, the dinner was laid out on three long parallel tables with a head table at one end. But there were no chairs. As in Cuba, we "grazed," which actually turned out to be a much more effective way of conversing with people than if we'd been seated and limited to conversations (usually through an interpreter) with the guest on either side.

I spoke with the Prime Minister briefly and mentioned that Lockheed Martin was in a partnership with Russia's Krunischev Industries to launch spacecraft using the Russian-built Proton launch vehicle. I was relieved to learn that the Prime Minister was not only quite familiar with Krunischev but also somewhat familiar with our project. I ended up feeling a bit sorry for the Prime Minister, a pleasant but not exactly outgoing man, because everyone wanted to talk with him, and thus he hardly had a chance to eat anything at all. (The members of the cabinet made up for him!)

When we got back to the hotel at 11:00 P.M., we were told to have our bags packed and in the hall by midnight. That would leave just enough time for a few hours of sleep before our "passage to India."

My overall assessment of Russia was that things seemed to have improved since my last visit. And, contrary to my earlier predictions, it appeared they did have a *chance* of "making it." Of course, the jury is still out, but there *is* a ray of hope. I cannot help but recall a comment made some years ago by a Russian economist friend of mine. He chastised me for my pessimistic view that Russia *would not* be able to get on its feet with a free economy and free society.

"Mr. Augustine," he remonstrated, "you forget that we are very good at suffering."

Who knows, perhaps this may yet turn out to be Russia's secret weapon.

Visitors to Russia cannot help but be struck by the immense human and natural resources the country possesses. Today Russians even have a degree of freedom and a budding free enterprise system. What they seem to lack the most is *management*—people who can pull all the pieces together.

⊕   ⊕   ⊕   ⊕   ⊕

In this section of *Travels,* we'll be dealing with a variety of management issues, all of them central to the difficult, yet fascinating, challenge of being a manager or corporate executive in today's business world (I almost typed *whirl!*).

These issues include competition, that quintessential business activity; mergers and acquisitions; reengineering; crisis management; and the changing nature of corporate management that affects everyone from CEOs and directors to employees all up and down the chain of command. First up is competition.

4

Competitiveness

The only thing harder than changing is paying the price for
not changing.

During one of the many trips to one of the many airports we
used on the Newstour, I found myself sitting next to the CEO of
Sears and across the aisle from the CEO of J.C. Penney and the
chairman of General Motors. Interestingly, each of these people,
as well as several others who joined in the conversation, spoke
of their company's having at one time been on top of their respective fields, subsequently failing to recognize a changing environment, and, as a result, being severely threatened by
competitors.

Most of these individuals had been brought in from the outside to try to get their respective companies moving again, to
make them competitive in the changing markets they had encountered. Although they were not with us, I suspected that the
heads of IBM, Kodak, Chrysler, and many other fine companies
would have said that at one time their companies had caught the
same disease. The only thing harder than changing is paying the
price for failing to change. And the only thing more likely to
make you overlook the need to change, other than human nature
itself, is to be on top—that is a successful product of the status
quo.

To an ever-increasing extent, changes in technology (and the knowledge base that underpins it) determine the quality of the lives we lead and the success of the businesses we manage. As economist Paul Romer has noted, "In the long run, it's clear that ideas drive growth."

But it is axiomatic that growth cannot occur without change, and change is something about which we all have mixed feelings. It is a sometimes agonizing, but almost always necessary, aspect of life that, incidentally, will probably be opposed by practically everyone. It's like having a cavity filled; it's no fun, but it may just be preferable to a root canal down the road. Or, as the American businessman Charles Keating once said, "The world hates change, yet it is the only thing that has brought progress."

The failure to embrace change can lead to altogether irrational behavior, as the owner of a professional basketball team seemed to recognize when he offered a two-year contract extension to a losing coach. He explained, "He's committed to us, and we're committed to him. We probably all ought to be committed."

Economic change has traditionally encompassed a relatively slow, deliberate process, carried out over a period of years, held back by such difficulties as raising sufficient capital to put change into effect. Today the dynamics are radically different. Instantaneous communications, rapid transportation, the advent of worldwide marketing techniques, and a much more sophisticated capital formation process have increased the velocity of economic change to a point unprecedented in human history. We live in an era when time itself seems to be stuck on fast-forward. Indeed, change is apparent in virtually every aspect of human experience.

In business, change is as frequent as the latest market report. A recent Business Roundtable study found that the labor market is more volatile today than ever before, with jobs being created and destroyed at record rates. The Business Roundtable estimates that there is in the U.S. workforce a turnover rate of nearly 10 percent a year. And about 7 percent of the largest companies in America—those shown on the Fortune 500 list—disappear each year.

According to a *Forbes* article entitled, "What Happened to All Those Blacksmiths?" only eight of the top thirty occupations in 1900 are still in the top thirty today. In fact, even such familiar occupations as assemblers, textile workers, machinists, and packers, which were still on that list as late as 1960, have dropped off today. Significantly, in 1960 only three of the thirty most abundant jobs required substantial education. Today, twelve of them do.

What this means—and especially from the standpoint of competition—is that the marketplace has been totally transformed in a very short period of time. Whereas a few years ago the United States was considered to be noncompetitive in world markets, today we are selling semiconductors to the Koreans, computers to the Japanese, satellites to Brazilians, telephones to Saudi Arabians, and even high-tech, power-generating windmills to the Dutch! And as far as Lockheed Martin is concerned, the greatest change is that we are now partners with our former Soviet adversaries in the selling of rockets used to launch commercial telecommunications satellites.

In medicine, many operations that used to require major invasive surgery can now be performed endoscopically through small incisions, allowing patients to go home in a fraction of the time previously required. Advanced drugs, vaccines, and treatments have greatly extended average life spans. In 1850, the average life span was thirty-eight years. In 1900 it was forty-five years. And today it is seventy-seven years—a doubling of the average American's life expectancy since the time of the Civil War.

So what we have is not so much simply a revolution in a few fields such as economics, technology, and politics as it is a broadly based *knowledge explosion*. And today this jarring expansion of knowledge rumbles through the world, producing tectonic shifts, leaving in its wake some individuals who were unequipped for the future. What can we do in such a world to give us greater control over our lives—and our businesses?

I read an observation recently that suggests the answer. The president of a major university was quoted as saying, "We live in a time of such rapid change and growth of knowledge that only [the person] who is in a fundamental sense a scholar—that is, a person who continues to learn and inquire—can hope to keep pace."

The speaker was the president of Harvard, and the year was 1963, a third of a century ago. Of course, Dr. Nathan Pusey's observation is even more relevant today.

Keeping Pace With a Whirling Globe

Price Pritchett, the internationally recognized management consultant, wrote a little book that deals with how to survive in the knowledge-driven twenty-first century. (The book is "little" only in terms of its being terse and to the point; it is "big" in the sense that it has sold more than a million copies.)

In this book—*New Work Habits for a Radically Changing World*—Dr. Pritchett gives expanded meaning to the expression "stay in school." He argues that "today's world takes no pity on the person who gets lazy about learning. . . . It doesn't take long for skills and knowledge to get outdated in a fast-changing world. Lifelong learning is the only way to remain competitive. You should invest in your own growth, development, and self-renewal [because while] your employer may help out with this, ultimately the responsibility is yours. Your future depends on you having a relentless drive to update credentials, acquire new skills, and stay abreast of what's happening in your field."

It is not possible to compete with outdated skills.

GM Can Recall a Car; LM Can't Recall a Rocket

On March 11, 1968, a subcontractor for the National Aeronautics and Space Administration (NASA) shipped a cryogenic oxygen tank to a California assembly plant, where it was installed in a spacecraft for an upcoming mission. Hidden inside the oxygen tank was a flaw: A 65-volt heating element contained a thermostat that was designed to handle only 28 volts. Later, the impact of this defect was exacerbated by a ground procedure that inadvertently overheated the tank and destroyed some of the insulation meant to protect its internal wiring. The spacecraft would be some 200,000 miles from the earth before this combination of errors was detected.

When astronaut Jack Swigert switched on the heater, a spark ignited the insulation material, and the resultant fire raised the temperature and pressure to the point where the tank failed. The mission was aborted, and the three-man crew barely made it back to earth.

This life-or-death example of quality control was retold in the movie *Apollo 13*—a gripping story that reminded all of us in the aerospace industry how extraordinarily demanding are the requirements of the work we do.

Can You Modify "Quality"?

Similarly, a few years ago, as the quality process was making its way into manufacturing facilities, a debate arose over terminology. Was the phrase "high quality" an appropriate way to describe the products that were made in those facilities?

Some objected to the phrase, saying that quality is not a relative term. Since no one would ever introduce a "low-quality" process, to call something "high quality" would be redundant. Implementing the "quality process" implied that every aspect of an organization should and would be the very best that employees could make it.

At the company I serve, the generic name we use for this concept is "mission success." Actually it is far more of a culture than a process. What specifically do we mean by that? As far as Lockheed Martin is concerned, it means the *daily* commitment to providing customers with quality products and services. It means underpromising and overproducing. It means giving the customer what has been agreed upon.

More concisely, the term could be defined as total customer satisfaction—meeting the customer's expectation. *Every* time. *On* time. In terms of the broad range of activities in which Lockheed Martin is involved, mission success might mean delivering aircraft that perform flawlessly in their stated missions; engineering electronics that fully meet the customer's specifications;

managing energy and environmental facilities in ways that optimize their performance and output; creating information systems and providing technological services that fulfill our customers' requirements well into the future; manufacturing launch vehicles and spacecraft that perfectly carry out highly complex missions in the demanding conditions of space. In short, it means being intensely and unwaveringly customer oriented.

We Have Met the Enemy, and It Is Complacency

Like the debate about whether the term "high quality" was appropriate, I suppose that some might question the continual need to reemphasize mission success. They might observe, "We're already doing these things. That's the way we stay in business." William Wrigley, Jr., was once asked by a fellow passenger on a train why he kept advertising his chewing gum when everyone in the world knew what it was. He answered, "Why not remove the engine from this train? It's moving along just fine."

The truth is that the qualities that enable any company to achieve mission success are extremely delicate and subject to rapid deterioration if not constantly nourished. The lesson that complacency is one of our most dangerous adversaries was brought home vividly to the entire nation in such incidents as the *Challenger* failure, coming as it did on the heels of twenty-four successful shuttle flights. We must continually remind ourselves of the thought expressed by the British statesman Benjamin Disraeli: "The secret of success is constancy of purpose."

Mission success is not a slogan. It is a very real commitment to achieving success for customers—*their* success—in every task. It is critical for the future of any company that everyone, labor and management alike, succeed in their individual tasks. In this regard, a corporation is truly no stronger than its weakest link.

The history of the aerospace industry is replete with tales of companies that have endured enormous setbacks because a single individual improperly installed a turbine blade, omitted a symbol in a software code (one costly spacecraft was lost in space because an engineer forgot to include a *hyphen* somewhere in several hundred thousand lines of code), or made an error on an electrical wiring diagram. But the aerospace industry is by no means unique in this regard. The extent to which any American company will enjoy success in the highly competitive global marketplace will depend on the intensity with which it commits itself to mission success.

The chance to display that commitment to one's employees is high among the reasons I jump at the chance to do such things as go down on the first dive of a new nuclear submarine of which our company has built significant parts, fly in our new Block 50 F-16 fighter aircraft, and the like. (Because I am not an aviator, the company's chief test pilot came along on that latter venture to help handle routine administrative matters—like taking off, aerobatics, and landing.) I first learned this lesson from David Packard, the cofounder of Packard Bell and my boss when he was Deputy Secretary of Defense during my first tour in the Pentagon as a civilian during the Vietnam war. When I complained that some of the equipment being used in Vietnam was not working well, Dave promptly shipped me off on a visit to Vietnam to see firsthand what sort of problems the troops were having. It is for a related reason that at Lockheed Martin we try to have astronauts and test pilots spend a lot of time walking through the factories and talking to the workers who are building the machines they will fly. It is called commitment.

Competitive Today, Here Tomorrow

In fewer than five years, Lockheed Martin has reorganized its businesses throughout its product lines and consolidated what used to be seventeen predecessor companies or major parts of companies into a single corporation. The steps we took to do so were often painful, and the fact that they were necessary didn't make them any more palatable, but after years of turbulence, it's increasingly clear to us that we took the right path. We passed the test of Yogi's fork, if you will. And by taking the necessary steps to become more competitive in a changing marketplace, we greatly improved our long-term prospects.

One of our successful tactics is useful in any business, no matter what its size. It is noteworthy that our vision over the last few years was not to achieve a certain size or standing in the marketplace. We were not seeking a "state of being"; we were seeking a "state of becoming." The hockey great Wayne Gretsky once said, "I skate to where the puck is *going* to be, not where it's *been.*" Thus we have tried to act in anticipation of where our industry will be five, ten, and even twenty years from now.

We want LM to distinguish itself as the world's premier systems engineering enterprise, and we've been going about achieving this in two ways. The first is to build our competitive strengths to grow our existing businesses, and the second is to explore opportunities to make inroads into new markets that are closely related.

We are trying to achieve what I call the "power of corporate diversity." That means our company is far more competitive today than its individual heritage companies could ever have been alone. And we never forget—because it can help to motivate us, as an analyst from Lehman Brothers pointed out recently—that every major competitor in our industry is hard at work making plans to knock us off because for the last several years we have represented the vanguard of the industry.

We like being in that position. As the saying goes, only the lead dog gets a change of scenery. But we are not forgetting for a moment that we have to keep our eye on where the puck *will be.*

Here are three critical goals that we emphasize, goals that I believe can be transferred easily to any company (especially if that company, too, has undergone restructuring):

1. Acquiring new businesses through mergers and aquisitions
2. Integrating different businesses in a way that realizes even greater savings, synergy, and success than previously had been the case
3. Completing consolidation plans without business disruption and in a manner that delivers projected savings

The extent of a company's success in the worldwide marketplace will depend on the intensity with which it pursues new business and the excellence with which it executes the business that it has won. How successful a company is in today's competition will in large part define what it can be tomorrow. Most will be up against competitors that are committed, hungry, and in some cases even desperate. Some of these competitors must win these contests if they are to survive at all. Whether we win or they win will quickly boil down to whether we are willing to commit greater intensity, energy, and dedication to the tasks before us than they are willing to commit. It's that simple.

Because of the effort American business has put forth over the past half-dozen years, we now have control of our future. What we do with it depends on us, for truly, in the demanding free market system, only those who are competitive today will be here tomorrow.

How Did We Get So Global . . . and So Soon?

More and more often these days, companies small, medium, and large find themselves involved, as if by magic, in a global rather than a local, regional, or national market. This globalization of the marketplace has been made a reality by two extraordinary developments.

The first of these is modern transportation, and especially the modern jet aircraft that can move people and products around the world in hours. It is now commonplace to find fish from Nova Scotia being sold the next day in Los Angeles, flowers from the Netherlands being marketed in Buenos Aires, strawberries from California being found on store shelves in Tokyo, and tomatoes from Israel being retailed in New York.

The second key development affecting globalization has been the advent of worldwide, instantaneous telecommunications. We take for granted the live CNN interview with a prominent chief of state halfway around the world or the real-time coverage of a war in Baghdad. In fact, then President Ozal of Turkey once told me, and I think he was at least figuratively correct, that the collapse of communism "was caused by CNN." But we often overlook that the same communications infrastructure that makes possible the electronic movement of more than

$2 trillion around the United States every day also creates a shareholder base for which geopolitical borders are becoming increasingly transparent and irrelevant.

I hope that this globalization will not be accompanied by the spread of unrestrained governmental intervention, particularly in the form of direct government ownership of companies, a practice that causes grievous distortion of the marketplace. Nonetheless, the possibility of such intervention will certainly intensify as new product sources come on-line, with, for example, wheat from Ukraine overwhelming Kansas farmers and software producers from Bangalore displacing engineers in Silicon Valley.

In the United States, we have already seen a willingness of the Congress to legislate limits on the tax deductibility of CEO pay. While the amount in question is one on which most people can presumably survive, what's at stake is the *principle* of the thing! And, according to the same practice, if one happens to sell defense products to the government, the "allowability" of such pay in the cost of one's product is lowered even further. One of the main reasons for Europe's foundering economy today is the excessive government intervention it has experienced in recent decades.

I suspect that the business environment of the future will be characterized by:

A single labor market, in which a worker's geographical location is far less important than the skills possessed by that worker and the wage for which he or she is willing to apply those skills. The impact of a single worldwide labor market, which we have only begun to experience, will have particularly adverse repercussions for unskilled U.S. workers when they find themselves competing, day in and day out, with, for example, workers in parts of Asia earning twelve cents per hour.

A single market for products, where quality and price are the key determinants and loyalty to one's fellow citizens is an afterthought. We have already experienced the dichotomy of American workers' seeking more pay and fewer hours, then going home to become consumers who want more products and lower prices. Precisely this point was made by a prominent U.S. automobile union leader who criticized his members for driving imported cars to the factory.

A single owner's market, serviced by stock exchanges throughout the world that are interconnected via real-time electronic media. Over the past two decades, Americans have been raising their stake in foreign securities from less than $20 billion in 1980 to nearly $500 billion today. And as trading has become more convenient and markets more volatile, the stability of ownership of U.S. corporations has gradually declined to where the shareholder base of a Fortune 500 firm turns over on the average of every two years, a trend that is likely to continue, and perhaps even accelerate.

This swift turnover in shareholders greatly increases pressure on management to produce short-term results at the expense of investing for the long term—a strategy that is almost always wrong.

Some years ago an opportunity appeared for Martin Marietta to increase substantially its spending on applied research, and by so doing open major new product opportunities. So pleased was the management with the promise of this investment that the company's president held a special meeting with investors and analysts in New York to inform them of the news.

At the close of the meeting, the audience literally ran from the room . . . and sold the company's stock. The price of our shares dropped 12 percent in five days, and then dwindled slowly downward thereafter.

Later they explained why they'd sold: "Everyone knows it takes ten to fifteen years for research to pay off, and we didn't want to have our money in a company with such shortsighted [their words] management." (To the credit of the company's leadership at the time, they went right ahead with the project—and it paid off handsomely.)

In addition to globalization, there's a technological explosion that is also unprecedented. The cost of information storage has been cut in half virtually every year for the past quarter century. America's fastest-growing industries are those devoted to creating and selling "brain products," such as computers, the software to run them, and the telecommunications to interconnect them. As another example of this technological revolution, New York Stock Exchange chairman Richard Grasso recently noted, "The Exchange will soon have a global clock to its trading, giving us a 16–18-hour trading day."

What Happens When You Have to Compete Globally, and What You Need to Know in Order to Do It

If my views on foreign competition (especially in regard to how you respond when a foreign competitor doesn't play by the rules) seem quite strong, it probably has to do with the fact that the company I run has over 25,000 employees in the United States, and another 6,000 overseas, whose jobs depend directly on our ability to sell our products abroad, and to do so in an ethical and legal fashion against all global competitors.

One vital part of our infrastructure is our base of information and understanding about foreign markets. We need to know:

- What companies participate in those markets?
- Who is poised to enter?
- With what products?
- What foreign laws and regulatory schemes apply?
- What special procurement rules apply?
- What resources and support are available to U.S. companies considering a leap into a new market?
- What technological breakthroughs have been achieved abroad?

U.S. companies of all sizes in all industries obviously need access to reliable information of this type, which can often be derived from publicly available sources in order to make reasoned decisions about what foreign markets they should attempt to enter—or not enter.

America's understanding about foreign markets is *uneven*—we know more about trends and opportunities in some geographic areas than others—and we wish we knew more about *emerging* technologies, before they show up in competing products. Individual companies collect and analyze information about foreign markets only at great cost and with great duplication of similar efforts by other U.S. firms.

Cold War Tactics in a Warmer World

Each company's needs are different, although we can assume that smaller companies and those just starting to market their products abroad will be the ones with the most to gain from some kind of organized effort to collect data about worldwide markets.

Increasingly we measure national power and national security in economic as well as military terms. We also measure quality of life, at least in part, in terms of America's competitiveness. The position of the United States on the cutting edge of technological innovation makes us a primary target for technology theft. The trend of state-sponsored espionage that targets the business decisions and technologies of U.S. corporations apparently has become more widespread in the past decade, but it could potentially become the predominant form of foreign espionage as we move away from the Cold War era into the economic war era.

As Alvin Toffler stated in his recent book, *Powershift*, "Spying, to a greater extent than at any time in the past century, will be pressed into service in support not only of government objectives but of corporate strategy as well, on the assumption that corporate power will necessarily contribute to national power."

What to Do When the Others Won't Play Fair

I believe that the intelligence agencies have a role to play in *combating* economic espionage and illegal and unethical business practices . . . a role wherein U.S. industry can do relatively little to protect itself. Correspondingly, I believe that there is no role in the business world for covert intelligence-gathering activities.

I suggest that Congress consider asking both the U.S. intelligence agencies and other agencies of the federal government to contribute whatever in-the-clear (that is, available from public data) information and analyses they have about foreign companies and industries, foreign products, foreign regulatory regimes, and foreign markets to a unified national information database where it can be accessed more readily by U.S.-based companies (including foreign-owned U.S.-based companies). This would include the translation of selected publicly available technical reports.

While the present focus of U.S. intelligence agencies is properly on military and political affairs, even this information, to the extent it is unclassified, can be of help to many companies.

Public information about local and regional political events, specific foreign markets, opportunities, and resources available to assist U.S. companies competing abroad, and even information about the state-sponsored economic espionage activities being practiced by other governments and companies against U.S. industry, could be provided.

Lead by Example

The provision of counterintelligence services and foreign open source information would certainly help U.S. firms, but I would also hope that the United States could set a good example for other nations by *not* using U.S. intelligence agencies to gain private commercial information for the benefit of U.S. companies. We should set a good example of free and honest commercial relations and continuing to encourage other nations to abide by these same free trade principles.

To Compete or Not to Compete Is *Not* the Question; It's *How* to Compete in a Swiftly Changing World

There are many ways of competing in a business world in which the only constant seems to be change. Here are a few:

To Market, to Market

The first technique is one we at Lockheed Martin call "creating the 'virtual company.' " We're a huge company, which gives us certain strengths in terms of breadth of technology, efficient use of facilities, and staying power. But large companies tend to lack one great advantage enjoyed by smaller companies, and that is not the *ability* to market but the *agility* to market.

The challenge we have taken on is to build a large company with the advantages of size yet possessing the ability to act as a small company in the marketplace. In order to do that, we create—for each of our major projects—a virtual company within our larger organization. The people who comprise that virtual company are selected because of their ability to contribute to that specific undertaking. They are located throughout our organization, sometimes many thousands of miles apart, and they are linked together with state-of-the-art computers and telecommunications.

The essense of the concept of the virtual company is in fact to bring together all those resources that are needed for a particular undertaking—and no more. In our personal lives, we do not bring along all of our possessions every time we set out on a trip. A corporation must take the same selective approach.

Share and Share Alike

The second concept we've been pursuing involves sharing critical resources with other corporations. My favorite example of this is our access to 20 percent of General Electric's Corporate Research Laboratory (which I happen to think is one of the best industry labs in the world). This combination of talents enables us to increase substantially the productivity of that facility *and* in addition gives us exclusive access to any discoveries that come within GE's 80 percent, providing we don't use them to compete in the marketplace where they compete. And the agreement is reciprocal, under the same terms, for the discoveries made within our 20 percent. We actually closed two of our own major (and quite good) corporate research labs in order to throw in our lot with GE.

So as to take advantage of this unique arrangement, we have had to overcome the "not invented here" syndrome, which is advisable for any corporation of any size. We encouraged our managers to regularly look beyond their own company ID badges, and accept what other people—even people from other companies!—can do. Sometimes the phrase, "It can't be done," simply means, "I won't do it any way except my own way." That can be a death knell for a corporation.

A Three-Cornered New Hat

A third concept we use to encourage competitiveness has to do with creating and using specialized coalitions between and among the following three entities: our company, select academic institutions, and, where appropriate, government.

The underlying beauty of this approach is that it forces us to reach outward. No matter what your size, you *have to* look broadly for new ideas, new approaches, new products. Lockheed Martin used this approach in a surprising manner when it set out during the height of the Cold War to make stealth aircraft and missiles. The technical idea came from research done at the Institute of Radio Engineering in Moscow in the 1960s that was published, and publicized, quite openly in the academic media.

Despite the great contrasts among government, academia, and private business, we have found ways to work together that have produced very positive results, not the least of which is our ability to compete on a global scale.

Don't Price Yourself Out of the Market

The real challenge for American business in the global marketplace of the twenty-first century will be how to remain competitive with a labor cost structure that is anything but competitive. We have already seen the exodus of much of the work performed by unskilled persons to the Pacific Rim and to Mexico. And we are now faced with the reality that even in the high-tech end of the employment spectrum, talented software engineers can be hired in India for about one-tenth of what they are paid in

America and in Russia for about one-tenth of what they are paid in India. The question to be answered is whether we can offset such huge wage disparities with greater innovation and productivity. Our standard of living in the years ahead will depend largely on the answer to this question.

Simply stated, America is unlikely to be able to attract global customers to our marketplace if we offer prices that are not on a standard with the rest of the world's suppliers.

It's like a story of the new bartender his first day on the job. His first customer turns out to be a huge bear, who walks into the bar, throws a five dollar bill on the bar, and asks for a beer.

Not certain how to handle the situation, the neophyte bartender hastens to the back room and asks the bar's owner, who has had decades of experience, what to do.

"That bear," says the owner, "is probably not very smart, so go ahead and give him a beer, but just give back a quarter in change."

The new bartender does as he's told, placing a cold beer and a single quarter on the bar. Then he watches with curiosity as the bear calmly sips his beer.

Finally, the bartender, unable to restrain himself any longer, leans over and says, "You know, we don't get many bears in this bar."

"It's no wonder," replies the bear, "at $4.75 a beer!"

5

Mergers and Acquisitions

or "These People Are Professionals . . . Don't Try This at Home"

"Draw up your chair close to the precipice and I'll tell you a story."

F. Scott Fitzgerald

Any number of scholarly books have been written on the topic of mergers and acquisitions, and the authors of many business school treatises go to great lengths to explain such arcane business terms as *dilution, pooling, exchange ratios,* and *purchase accounting.* But relatively little has been written or said about what *really* happens in huge business deals, what takes place *behind* the scenes—not the headline stuff, but the scar tissue stuff.

This, however, is the story of roughly, and that is exactly the right adjective, a dozen years of business transactions, all as viewed from *behind* the headlines.

Gunfight in the CEO Corral

This story begins one beautiful fall morning a dozen or so years ago when Tom Pownall, then the president of the Martin Marietta Corporation, received by messenger a letter from Bill Agee, the chairman and CEO of the Bendix Corporation. This was not a friendly letter inquiring about Martin Marietta's health. Rather, it indicated that Bendix was lusting after Martin Marietta's corporate body and, in fact, as of that very moment was busily initiating a hostile takeover of the company.

Over the weeks that followed, a number of improbable, even seemingly impossible, situations occurred, including a Bendix shareholder meeting that was chaired by the general counsel of Martin Marietta and the midnight purchase of a Fortune 100 corporation that took less than sixty seconds. How did all this happen?

Read On, Macduff

It was like this. A few weeks after firing the first shot in the takeover war, the Bendix Corporation informed its shareholders it would be scheduling a special stockholders' meeting. But following a series of tactical moves and countermoves by the two companies, Bendix's management decided it no longer wanted to hold the meeting. Under the corporate rules, there wasn't enough time to cancel the meeting, so Bendix continued to prepare for it, on the presumption that it would be easy, once they'd convened the session, simply to adjourn it.

Convinced the entire matter would be routine, Bendix's management overlooked one important detail: They neglected to make sure they had enough votes to prevail in case someone contested the motion to adjourn. Perhaps equally important, they were apparently unaware that among their corporations' shareholders was an individual who just happened to be Martin Marietta's general counsel. As it happened, he owned a few shares of Bendix stock in his personal account, so he attended the Bendix meeting as a private stockholder. Along with the other shareholders present, he was informed that the meeting would be perfunctorily adjourned, and thus when the motion to adjourn was made, he was ready.

Rising to his feet, he challenged the action. Then he suggested the meeting should address what he termed the "inappropriateness" of Bendix's hostile action. Seemingly stunned, the Bendix management responded by preemptively declaring the meeting adjourned, whereupon they stalked out of the room.

Going to the podium, the Martin Marietta counsel pointed out that the Bendix management did not have the votes necessary to adjourn the meeting legally and announced that in the absence of any Bendix officials he, as a Bendix shareholder, would chair the meeting for them. And so he did!

The discussion progressed, and, not surprisingly, it took a course not particularly to the liking of the Bendix management, which by this point was listening from the hallway. Suddenly the hotel ballroom was plunged into darkness, the electric lights having apparently been tripped by a Bendix official with powerful connections (or should that be powerful *dis*connections?). The meeting continued in the dark for a period of time, but soon retired to a hotel across the street for the completion of business under more "enlightened" circumstances.

But in spite of this tactical "victory" by Martin Marietta against the forces of darkness, Bendix, having struck first in the takeover war, enjoyed the benefits of surprise and soon managed to accumulate 72 percent of Martin Marietta's shares. For all practical purposes, Bendix owned Martin Marietta lock, stock, and barrel.

The Pac Man Defense and the Mighty Minute

Martin Marietta, led by its president, and CEO-to-be, Tom Pownall, was, however, singularly unimpressed, and adopted a defensive strategy never before tried, at least not on the scale of these two giant corporations: Martin Marietta set out to *buy Bendix* in retaliation! Never mind that Bendix already owned Martin Marietta—the torpedos be damned! (Tom was a former naval officer.) The media quickly dubbed the strategy "The Pac Man

Defense" after the video game cartoon figures that run around the screen gobbling one another up.

The problem with implementing the Pac Man defense stemmed from the existence of two regulations, which, given the fact that Bendix did own a majority of Martin Marietta's shares, severely limited the latter's latitude to act. One of these regulations precluded the company from buying Bendix shares prior to a certain date, and the other precluded the company from buying the shares on or after that date.

For a time it seemed that Martin Marietta's future was behind it.

Some very imaginative legal research by one of Martin Marietta's lawyers soon revealed, to the ecstasy of the company's management, that the definitions in one of these regulations stated that a "day" ended at midnight, whereas in the other regulation, a "day" began at 12:01 A.M. Thus, during that one magical minute between 12:00 P.M. and 12:01 A.M. on September 23, 1982, carefully wired into the Naval Observatory to ensure the accuracy of the time (Mickey Mouse watches are not recommended in such circumstances), Martin Marietta retaliated and purchased a majority of the shares of the Bendix Corporation. A gaggle of lawyers furiously signed the necessary documents as the minute ticked by.

The resulting stalemate was one wherein each company literally owned the other. Watching them, an independent observer probably would have been reminded of the dog that *caught* the car, or its own tail.

Each corporation considered that it was entitled to occupy the other's boardroom, and each believed it was entitled to receive a majority of the dividends declared by the *other* firm— since it "owned" it. For those managers in the operating companies of the two organizations who were competing against each other for business, a particularly perplexing question arose: "If each side is best served by the *other's* winning, what strategy should be adopted to ensure that you always lose when your competitor is also trying to lose?!" It was truly a case of malice in wonderland.

Of course, this all added up to a feast for many of the nation's better-known law firms.

At one point, Martin Marietta alone had hired fourteen major firms and was litigating in eleven federal district courts, three federal courts of appeals, and three state courts, including the Supreme Court of Delaware. Smelling opportunity, three other Fortune 100 companies jumped into the fray, turning the event into no less than a five-ring circus. One judge, exasperated with Bendix and Martin Marietta alike, summarized her sentiments by quoting Shakespeare: "A pox on *both* your houses."

A Seven-Year Itch . . . and Then More Bad Luck

The eventual outcome was that Martin Marietta escaped, thereby maintaining its freedom. Bendix, no longer searching for the cheese but simply wanting out of the trap, agreed to be absorbed by the Allied Signal Corporation, which had entered the fray as a sort of "White Knight." Earlier, Harry Gray, the CEO of the UTC Corporation, had sought unsuccessfully to play this same role, and the media dubbed him merely a *"Gray Knight"*!

Unfortunately, Martin Marietta's freedom had its price: an 82 percent debt-to-total-capital ratio. This represented a burden seldom survived by any major corporation.

In order to dig itself out from under this overbearing debt, Martin Marietta sold its aluminum, chemical, and cement companies, retaining only its crushed rock operations and its aerospace business.

It took a full seven years for the firm to emerge financially from this stifling debt, during which it reconcentrated on aerospace/defense. And then the Berlin Wall collapsed, followed shortly after in similar fashion by the Soviet Union and the United States' defense budget.

The U.S. aerospace industry began to shed employees at a rate of one every thirty seconds and quickly found itself saddled with an excess plant capacity nearly two-thirds greater than that which was needed. Over a million employees lost their jobs, and the *combined* market value of the four largest aerospace firms tumbled below that of McDonald's. One European aerospace executive summed up his company's situation by saying, "We're already dead. We just don't know it yet."

Diversity, Schmiversity

The majority of the academic community having any interest in the matter, and much of the Congress and media, promptly advised the industry's leaders that they should simply diversify into altogether new fields. The only problem with this seemingly attractive "the-grass-is-greener" notion was that it had been tried many times before in earlier down-cycles and the industry's record in pursuing this approach was largely unblemished by success.

Notwithstanding all the prior problems, the scramble to find new markets began in earnest, with the hope that a few individual companies might be salvaged even as the overall industry collapsed. The lesson we had missed in our earlier efforts was that you can in fact diversify away from your current products, but *not* from your current competencies. As the saying goes, it's important to know one's *in*competencies.

As an alternative to the "diversify-at-any-cost" approach, Martin Marietta adopted a contrarian strategy and set out to build market share in its existing area of expertise—all while enhancing efficiency through the tactic of combining with other companies that were similarly suffering from a lack of critical mass, and then shedding that part which was unneeded.

At one point during this precarious period, the company found itself engaged in an international "war" of sorts. This was triggered when Martin Marietta teamed with the Lockheed Corporation to buy LTV Aerospace, whose parent firm had by now found itself in bankruptcy. The effort to acquire LTV was met by an aggressive bid from a French company largely owned and strongly backed by the French government, including a bank the company and the government just happened to have acquired together.

The domestic part of the corporate battle quickly broke into a two-theater confrontation: a northern front, located in the bankruptcy court in New York City, and a southern front, fought in the corridors of the U.S. Congress in Washington, D.C. The Pentagon, wanting nothing to do with the matter, watched from a safe distance . . . barely leaning forward in their foxholes.

A long-time friend of mine, who had attended the same college as I and who later served as Secretary of Defense prior to joining an investment banking firm, represented the other side. We argued our respective cases in the media and testified against each other's views in heated congressional hearings (and on one occasion, together with my colleague from Lockheed, Dan Tellep, shared a sandwich and soft drink as we ran from the House to the Senate to initiate still another assault on each other's positions).

Although the Martin Marietta and Lockheed arguments prevailed in Washington—ultimately by a vote of ninety-four to four in the U.S. Senate—the bankruptcy court in New York was far less impressed, and LTV ultimately went to another (U.S.-based) company, which submitted a higher bid, the Loral Corporation. In bankruptcy court, money talks.

Although we didn't realize it at the time, the training we had received, sort of a corporate equivalent to the Spanish Civil War, would prove to be invaluable experience for what was about to occur.

Time to Choose a Partner

The dust had barely settled on the transatlantic battle over LTV Aerospace when Martin Marietta set out to find another partner with which we hoped to prosper as the aerospace industry began what the company's management believed to be an inevitable implosion. The objective was straightforward: to be among the first to select partners so as not to be stuck with the industry's leftovers as the pace of industry consolidation accelerated . . . as we expected it would. Also, this appeared to be a good time to be a buyer, as prices were relatively low. I've always believed in keeping an eye out for contrarian opportunities.

The problem was that, for largely ethical reasons related in part to the company's Bendix experience, we did not believe it appropriate to initiate hostile takeovers. (I should confess that I view hostile takeovers as the business equivalent of nuclear war, but without the dignity.) Thus, our latitude to act was considerably constrained as we sought to find a partner of like mind.

A rather extensive review conducted by a small team of Martin Marietta's leadership, which had been gathering for several months in a series of secret meetings away from the headquarters, concluded that in the case of an acquisition, the preferred partner would be General Electric's aerospace company and, in the case of a merger, the favored choice was the Lockheed Corporation.

There were only two problems with this conclusion. First, Lockheed was pursuing its own acquisition strategy, and there was little evidence, if any, that it might be interested in a merger. Second, General Electric was over ten times the size of Martin Marietta, a circumstance that posed a considerable hazard since if approached with the idea of selling its aerospace business, General Electric's CEO, Jack Welch, might simply decide to solve *his* critical mass problem by purchasing Martin Marietta with his firm's petty cash account!

At this point luck stepped in to play its often critical role. I had a chance encounter with Jack during a Business Council meeting, and he remarked that our two companies' aerospace businesses faced similar challenges, which they might be better able to confront as partners than as separate entities. He went on to assure me that General Electric's interests in Martin Marietta were altogether "friendly," a commitment I took at face value, given my conviction that Jack's word is as good as his bond. This was a conviction that in the months and years ahead proved entirely warranted.

Within a few days, a handshake was struck to undertake a $3 billion-plus transaction, one of the largest in the history of the aerospace industry. The negotiations leading up to this good-faith agreement were conducted in great secrecy, initially involving only a handful of people hidden away in New York City, and soon to be known as the "Hole in the Wall Gang." There were no investment bankers or outside law firms included until after the essentials of the deal had been settled. The original features of the transaction had been sketched on a paper napkin late one evening—an exhibit that is now framed and proudly displayed on my wall of memorabilia at home.

Trying to Keep a Big Secret

As the negotiations progressed, my colleagues and I made three secret, overnight trips from Florida to New York in as many nights, meeting with Jack and his associates for several hours before returning to Florida in time to resume business as usual early the next morning with about one hundred of Martin Marietta's senior executives who were gathered for an off-site meeting on Captiva Island and were as yet unaware of the transaction being explored. One night during the hectic weeks that followed, Tom Young, Martin Marietta's president, slept in a New York hotel for three hours, which costed out to $80 an hour simply to sleep!

In spite of all the precautions taken, secrecy was a never-ending concern. Negotiations were mostly held on the fifty-third floor of Rockefeller Center, with the hope that the representatives of the two companies could lose themselves in the chaos of Manhattan. Work continued literally around the clock, with meals brought into the work area at all hours of the day and night. Concern over security reached a peak one morning at about 3 A.M. when the chief financial officer of General Electric left the meeting to grab a few hours of sleep at a nearby hotel. As he walked out onto the empty streets of Rockefeller Center, a stranger suddenly emerged from a manhole and said to him, "Oh, the meeting on the fifty-third floor must be over!" The man then disappeared back into the manhole, just as quickly as he had appeared. To this day, we do not know who that person was or how he knew where we were meeting or why he cared.

Jack Welch and I frequently found it necessary to telephone one another at home in order to resolve various problems that cropped up as the negotiations at Rockefeller Center proceeded. By happenstance, the Assistant Secretary of the Air Force during that period also bore the name Jack Welch, and he had been a friend for a number of years. On those occasions when General Electric's Jack Welch would telephone, my wife, who was, of course, unaware of the GE negotiations, would, after his intentionally brief greeting, presume she was speaking to the "Air Force" Jack Welch, and would invariably ask, "How's Patty?"

This would always evoke the same noncommittal, "Just fine, thank you." A few days after the proposed merger was publicly announced, I inquired as a footnote to a letter I was sending to GE's Jack Welch, "Incidentally, who *is* this Patty?"

And Only One Leak!

Speed is absolutely crucial in transactions that have so many moving parts if there is to be any chance at all of maintaining secrecy and completing the deal. From our first serious discussion of the combination to the announcement of the contract between the two companies, a total of twenty-seven days elapsed. Toward the end of that period, perhaps 200 people were involved in the negotiations, including a number of investment bankers, lawyers, accountants, and, of course, the boards of directors of both companies.

The only leak known to have occurred bubbled to the surface in the middle of the night just prior to a planned morning press conference at which the transaction was to be announced. A *Washington Post* reporter had somehow gotten wind of what was taking place. Being a true professional, the reporter spent several hours trying to confirm his suspicions, and the time lost in this process was such that only the final papers to come off the press carried the story. As luck would have it, all of these copies were loaded onto a single truck for delivery, and those papers all went to the neighborhood where many of Martin Marietta's executives lived. This led to a very disconcerting beginning to their day! When later asked what it was that led him to the conclusion that a transaction was imminent, the reporter would only respond, "My wife figured it out . . . and you would die if you knew how!"

A few hours later, the official announcement was carried on the front page of newspapers throughout the country, several of which inadvertently interchanged the photographs of Jack Welch and myself. Having seen one of them, my then 100-year-old mother called from Colorado with a firm instruction, "Norman, you need to get more rest." Jack, for his part, complained even more vociferously!

The day of the announcement revealed once again one of the reasons that it is so important such transactions be kept secret: The stock of the two companies jumped by $2 billion in the first four hours. The opportunities for unethical insiders, or simply hangers-on, to make huge sums of money from illicit trading are an inherent danger in such undertakings.

Four months later, after a thorough review of the transaction by the Department of Justice's antitrust lawyers, the deal between General Electric Aerospace and Martin Marietta was formally consummated.

Next . . .

The two organizations immediately began to function as a single entity, with a good deal of attention being devoted to preempting the so-called cultural issues that are supposed to plague mergers and acquisitions. One incident did occur when a group of employees tracing their heritage to General Electric Aerospace arranged to have a videoconference with a group of their counterparts from the heritage of Martin Marietta. As the videoconference began, the participants silently took note of the fact that those in attendance from Martin Marietta were dressed in coats and ties, and corresponding attire for women, whereas the General Electric participants were all wearing sport shirts, sweaters, or the like.

In spite of the disparity in dress, the meeting that ensued proved extremely successful, and it was agreed that a follow-on videoconference should be held the next week. When the appointed time arrived and the television screen came to life, everyone on both ends of the circuit spontaneously burst into laughter. The "General Electric people" were now dressed in coats and ties, and the "Martin Marietta people" were wearing sport shirts and sweaters!

Once again it had been demonstrated that, left to their own devices, the great majority of people will try very hard to overcome so-called cultural impediments. In any merger or acquisition, such differences must be viewed as assets to be built upon, but never tolerated as excuses for nonperformance.

Only a few weeks after the completion of the General Electric transaction, we learned that General Dynamics' space business might be available for purchase. Inasmuch as General Dynamics had a half-full factory in San Diego manufacturing space launch vehicles and Martin Marietta had a half-full factory in Denver building space launch vehicles, it seemed eminently sensible that the two companies be combined into a single entity with a single full factory. The result would be a huge cost savings to the principal customer, the U.S. government, a savings estimated to equal nearly half a billion dollars over the first five years alone. But before this could become a reality, it would be necessary for Martin Marietta's shareholders to invest a considerable sum of money to purchase General Dynamics' space business and to move one or the other of the factories.

In spite of congressional and media opposition, the General Dynamics space group acquisition was finally completed, and Martin Marietta's management looked forward with relief to a period of simply tending the store, free from the added workload of mergers and acquisitions.

A $50 Million Windfall

This hope was promptly crushed during a conversation with Renso Caporali, the CEO of the Grumman Corporation, an individual with whom I had originally become acquainted because many years before we had attended the same graduate school. It seemed that he wanted to explore the possibility of folding Grumman into the "new" Martin Marietta—which by now had established itself as one of the clear survivors in the shakeout that was rapidly and profoundly reshaping the aerospace landscape. Grumman and Martin Marietta did in fact appear to be a quite reasonable fit, so the necessary steps were put into motion to turn the proposal into reality.

A major obstacle, however, loomed over the likelihood of successfully completing the deal. Martin Marietta's management had come to suspect that the Northrop Corporation might seek to upset the transaction. Because of this concern, Martin

Marietta demanded and received from Grumman a guarantee of $50 million plus expenses should the deal fall through.

Immediately after Grumman announced its intention to combine with Martin Marietta, Northrop submitted a higher bid of its own.

Although Martin Marietta never budged a penny from its initial bid, Northrop, in the heat of the battle, further increased its offer, thereby seemingly bidding against itself. This was almost exactly the same thing that had happened during the Bendix episode some years earlier, when Bendix also raised its then-prevailing bid. Martin Marietta seemed to have a propensity for entering two-person auctions and having the opposition submit both the first- and the second-place bids!

Whatever the case, the morning that Grumman was sold to Northrop, a lawyer from Grumman dutifully appeared at Martin Marietta's headquarters in Maryland and delivered a $50 million check. My rather stunned secretary, Jean Ross, not accustomed to being handed checks for $50 million, wisely concluded that the proper thing to do was to deposit it, and to deposit it fast! Jean has not been seen since (just kidding).

There was one final chapter to the Northrop Grumman story that was chronicled in the proxy statement issued by Grumman following the final round of bidding. It seemed that on the Sunday afternoon that Grumman's board required both Northrop and Martin Marietta to submit best and final bids, Martin Marietta's investment banker, Bear Stearns, annoyed over Northrop's intervention into what had theretofore been a done deal, sent a messenger to sit outside the Grumman boardroom and prominently display not one but two large brown envelopes, the first conspicuously marked with an "A" and the second with a "B."

It was to be presumed by all who observed the envelopes that if Martin Marietta were not considering raising its bid, there would be no reason for a second envelope. Northrop once again raised its bid! Both envelopes, of course, contained *identical* letters—letters declining to raise Martin Marietta's bid from what had already been publicly termed the "full and fair price" offered weeks before. The investment bankers had their revenge.

That Should Have Been It for a While

Late on a Saturday afternoon, as the final piece in the abortive Grumman-Martin Marietta consolidation fell into (or, more precisely, out of) place, I packed my briefcase and reflected on the years of essentially nonstop mergers and acquisitions, all of which had occurred on top of trying to manage a business in a collapsing market. My thoughts of our team's enjoying a more normal and less turbulent period of conducting the corporation's affairs this time were interrupted by the ringing of the telephone on my desk.

I was greeted by the cheerful voice of my friend and colleague from the LTV wars, Dan Tellep, the CEO of Lockheed. After a brief discussion about an upcoming tennis tournament in which we would be opponents, Dan explained that he and his colleagues had been considering their company's options as the industry further downsized and had concluded that it would be in the best interests of our two companies to consolidate in a merger of equals.

Drawing on the analysis Martin Marietta had performed some two years earlier, it took about one microsecond for me to concur.

Following the conversation, I walked into the office adjacent to mine to tell Martin Marietta's President Tom Young what had just transpired. I began by saying, "Tom, fasten your seat belt. Here we go again!"

"Wait a Minute, That's My Code Name!"

Mergers are much more difficult than acquisitions since in a merger, particularly a genuine merger of equals (which this was in every respect), each detail demands complete, mutual agreement between the parties involved, an acid test of the goodwill and trust of all the participants. Some five months of secret negotiations were therefore required to complete the deal. This prolonged period placed even greater demands on efforts to maintain secrecy than had been the case in our earlier transactions. Thus, our strategy for maintaining secrecy involved not only the normal precautions but also entailed the intentional creation of "planned confusion." For example, notes were openly passed through the company mail asking detailed financial questions about companies of no particular interest to anyone, in the hope that if accurate leaks did occur, they would be lost in a sea of rumors.

Meetings between Lockheed and Martin Marietta managements rotated around the country in various cities such as Phoenix, New York, San Francisco, Cincinnati, Washington, D.C., Dallas, and Denver, never returning to the same place a second time. Each company took a code name that was frequently changed. The individuals involved in the transaction also adopted pseudonyms of their own. Mine was "Mr. Kent," selected not because of any resemblance to the bespectacled Clark, but because it was the first name of the Northrop CEO, my friend who had so thoroughly disrupted our previous transaction!

It turns out that engineers who through some quirk of fate become CEOs—as was the case for the people involved in each of these deals—are not very good at subterfuge. For example, one day when telephoning my office from a pay phone, a Lockheed colleague who had placed the call was startled to hear an unfamiliar voice answer and inquire of him, "Who is this calling?" Panicking, the executive blurted out, "I can't remember my name!" and hung up.

On another occasion, Lockheed's CEO, Dan Tellep, telephoned my office and suddenly realized that he too had forgotten his code name. Retreating to a hastily conceived backup plan, he told my secretary *he* was "Mr. Kent," thinking I would realize who was calling and accept the call. But when my secretary, catching me at a rather preoccupied moment working at my desk, advised me that a "Mr. Kent" was on the phone, I absent-mindedly responded: "It can't be Mr. Kent. *I'm* Mr. Kent!"

After a series of such mishaps, representatives of the two companies gathered in Cincinnati, a location chosen principally because neither of the firms had plants in that city, although the General Electric Corporation did happen to have a large aircraft engine facility there. As luck would have it, the Lockheed and Martin Marietta corporate airplanes were parked at the airport

side by side! Other than the pilots' eyeing each other suspi-
ciously, it appeared that no harm had been done—at least not
until the next day when the Cincinnati newspaper, apparently
misinterpreting this same piece of evidence, carried a front-page
story proclaiming that Martin Marietta would be buying General
Electric's aircraft engine division!

We did nothing to try to correct that story since confusion,
in all forms, helps provide cover under these difficult circumstances. Further, our company's policy had long been not to
comment on rumors regarding business transactions. This
stance did not, however, enhance my relationship with one of
our board members who happened to be president of General
Electric's aircraft engine division, or, for that matter, with Jack
Welch himself, whose company owned 25 percent of Martin
Marietta as part of the payment from the prior transaction. The
newspapers made it appear that he was in effect buying himself—and at a healthy price, too!

From that time on, meetings were scheduled only in cities
that had *two* airports. But that didn't solve the secrecy problem
either. Having traveled to Dallas soon after the Cincinnati scare,
the leaders of the two companies arranged to eat dinner sepa-
rately prior to a series of planned meetings in a hotel room in
order not to draw attention. No sooner was the Martin Marietta
contingent seated at the restaurant it had selected than a group
of visiting Martin Marietta employees from our Orlando plant
was spotted enjoying their dinner at the very next table. It turned
out they happened to be in Dallas for a meeting with Texas In-
struments Corporation. Those of us involved in the Lockheed
transaction mumbled a quickly improvised but in retrospect
rather implausible explanation of why we too happened to be in
Dallas.

Just Wait in the Hall

After several months of intense work, it became increasingly im-
perative that the Secretary of Defense be advised of the proposed
merger in order to verify that the Department of Defense would
have no fundamental objection to our plans. Dan Tellep, Lock-

heed's CEO, and I agreed that he would make the initial contact with the Secretary but would not reveal the name of Lockheed's partner company, Martin Marietta, unless the Secretary was willing to have us do so. This seemed only courteous since the Secretary might prefer not to become an insider to our specific transaction. Thus, it was planned that if the Secretary indicated he wished to know the identity of the other partner, I, until then waiting inconspicuously in the Pentagon hallway, would join the meeting. If he preferred not, I would simply evaporate from the scene without having been observed. That was the plan. But as the saying goes, General Custer had a plan too.

The needed appointment with the Secretary of Defense was scheduled without a hitch, and a few days later Dan began the meeting by explaining that a proposed merger was being contemplated with an unnamed mystery partner. While this opening conversation was taking place, I was at my assigned post, loitering stealthily in the hallway outside the Secretary's office, trying with all my might to appear inconspicuous. This proved to be exceedingly difficult, since I had worked in the Pentagon for some ten years, and it seemed that everyone who passed the Secretary's office stopped to visit with me. Further, as I appeared to be roaming aimlessly, most of these people were very insistent that I tell them what I was doing so that they could be of help.

At one point during my sojourn in the hallway, the Secretary's special assistant burst into the busy corridor and, spotting me, called out, "Well, I can tell what the next big merger in the aerospace industry will be. The CEO of Lockheed is in there right now with the Secretary!" I tried to hide behind a flag.

Planning proceeded apace for the announcement of the merger. Night after night was spent seeking to resolve seemingly mundane but nonetheless important and often intractable details. For example, how do you call a press conference and attract a good turnout of a skeptical media when you can't say who is calling the conference or what the subject is? And what do you do when your employees, your shareholders, your customers, most members of Congress, and your wife—all scattered around the globe in twenty-four different time zones—each believes, and with some merit, that they should be the very first to hear the news?

In spite of our many missteps, secrecy was somehow maintained until, as in the case of the General Electric transaction, just hours before the planned announcement. In this case, the leak occurred at about midnight before the scheduled press conference. Since it appeared that the media were hot on our trail, we decided to go ahead and make our news release about nine hours earlier than we had intended. Better to have the correct story on the wire a little prematurely than to spend the next three months explaining all the erroneous speculation that was sure to result from a story based on leaks.

This time there was less danger of the media's interchanging the pictures of the principals of the companies involved in the merger because the *Economist* magazine simply carried its story under a cover adorned with a photograph of two exceedingly ugly camels copulating! A bit tasteless, I thought.

A few weeks later, the two companies issued the requisite proxies—253,000 copies of documents, each some 200 pages long, a pile of paper over one mile high. (This resulted in yet another of Augustine's less-remembered laws: "If all the proxies over ten pages long were piled one on top of one another at the bottom of the Grand Canyon . . . it would probably be a good idea.") No one appeared to read the proxies, except, of course, for a few lawyers seeking grounds to sue one or the other of the companies involved—or, better yet, both. It was a bad day for the forests of America.

As in all our previous transactions, the stock market reacted very favorably, and the usual set of law firms throughout the country began filing suits against both companies for one reason or another. As is the case in most such transactions, the companies involved "confess" to almost anything that might settle a suit without producing costly delays in the transaction, sometimes even simultaneously "confessing" to contradictory "transgressions"!

Bureaucracy blossoms in the environment surrounding large business transactions, and this one was, in terms of size, a new record for the aerospace industry, far eclipsing the previous all-time record holder.

It *Seemed* Like a Good Idea

Dan Tellep and I thought it would be a nice gesture if we were to open trading in the new company's stock by personally buying enough shares to pay for the college education of the first two children born to employees of the new company. This well-intentioned notion almost instantly generated a three-week exercise involving gaggles of lawyers, accountants, auditors, and P.R. experts.

The lawyers advised that the gifts would be viewed by the Securities and Exchange Commission as a "sale" of stock, and Dan and I would be in violation of Section 16(b) of the securities laws. The accountants reported that such a gift might preclude the "pooling of assets" accounting treatment so essential to the transaction and, as a consequence, both companies would be grievously harmed. The Human Resources department posed a long list of concerns: What if the "winning" child were born out of wedlock? What if someone unwisely induced birth simply to win the prize? And the outside lawyers told us that we would be violating the prevailing contest laws in no fewer than thirty-two states.

It was at this point that I actually had a nightmare in which the company's public relations coordinator of our so-called contest inadvertently stated on television that the prize would go not to the first child *born* after the new company was formed but to the first child *conceived!*

Dan and I dropped the whole thing as a bad idea whose time would never come.

Overwhelming Approval . . . and a Few Squawks

In spite of all the obstacles and distractions, the Federal Trade Commission, after a thorough review, blessed the deal. The transaction was then approved by the company's shareholders at a special meeting held a few days later in Chicago. At the meeting, in spite of a five-year record of bettering Standard and Poor's market average by a *factor* of three, about eight out of ten of those who rose to comment at the meeting spoke vociferously against management and its plans. The formal vote by the company's 30,000 shareholders, on the other hand, was ninety-nine to one in *favor* of management's plan to merge the two companies! Apparently those who speak at shareholders' meetings don't have a lot in common with a company's owners as a whole. But that's another story.

The most vocal opponent at the shareholders' meeting turned out to be the head of a labor union who had led a 107-day unsuccessful strike against the company several years earlier. Much of the media's attention following the gathering was focused on this "unbiased" source.

Hey Buddy, Can You Spare a Dollar Six?

The final obstacle to the merger arose minutes before the new company was to begin operation. It seemed that the million-dollar deposit made with the Securities and Exchange Commission to cover the costs of the mandated official reviews had, in the final tally, fallen short of the actual costs by $1.06. The commission thus denied the approval needed to begin operations of the newly formed company until the shortfall was rectified, "in cash or cash equivalent, please."

After several hectic telephone calls to the SEC from partners of the New York law firm handling this aspect of the merger, the SEC agreed that the newly formed $23 billion company and its law firm might be good for the $1.06 until a messenger could be dispatched across Manhattan with the necessary funds, "in cash or cash equivalent," and the closing was thus approved. It seemed a fitting conclusion to the entire episode. The next day, Lockheed Martin's stock went on sale under the ticker symbol LMT. Within two months, the price of the stock increased another 30 percent.

Not *Another* One!

My new best friend, Dan Tellep, and I spent the entire month of April 1995 explaining to the people who worked for us why we had merged the two companies. During that single month, we spoke to sixty-two groups of employees at a large number of locations throughout the country. Individual audiences ranged in size from 50 in a conference room to some 4,000 gathered in the mile-long factory in Fort Worth, where the F-16 fighter was being assembled.

We were asked hundreds of questions by employees who stepped up to the microphones placed here and there in the crowds. "Is my pension safe?" "Why do you get paid so much?" And my favorite, asked by a man who'd just been transferred to a plant in New York with a business base that was, unfortunately, quite tenuous: "If *you* had just moved here, would you rent or buy?" I advised him to lease with an option to purchase (which turned out to be pretty good advice).

As Dan often noted, the issues to be dealt with as we created a brand-new corporation—which on Day One had 195,000 employees—ranged from the cosmic to the comic. One moment we'd be discussing which plants would have to be closed (an overall total of some 16 million square feet were ultimately shed, which, together with other actions, produced recurring savings of about $2.6 billion per year—but at a loss of a large number of jobs), and the next moment we'd be discussing whether we should take away executive cars (we did).

Apparently we managed to get a number of the answers right because the company got off to a great start, adding some $13 billion of shareholder value by the end of its second year of operations, which far eclipsed the performance of the market as a whole.

Lockheed Martin had been operating only about six months when opportunity knocked once again. It was, of course, not a particularly propitious time for the infant company to take on yet another major challenge; however, one doesn't tell opportunity to go away and come back at a more convenient time. Struggling with a business is like wrestling a gorilla; you rest when the gorilla wants to rest.

To Repeat (for Emphasis): Don't Microplan a Career—Just Be Ready to Jump on a Good Opportunity

This time opportunity appeared in the form of the Loral Corporation, which for several years had been the other principal consolidator in the aerospace/electronics industry. No one had even imagined that Loral might be prepared to switch its strategy and become a seller; thus, when this possibility was raised by Dennis Bovin and Mike Urfirer of the investment banker Bear Stearns, Dan Tellep, CFO Marc Bennett, and I and the small group of our colleagues involved in such discussions all viewed it as an extraordinary opportunity. (In Dennis's words, in a perhaps overly effusive reference to our earlier activity, "You have already won the chess game. Here's your opportunity to pick up the board and the table and carry *them* home too.")

Throughout most of its existence, the Loral Corporation had been led by Bernard Schwartz; under his guidance the company had grown over a two-decade period from a $20 million near-bankrupt business to a thriving $7.5 *billion* enterprise, a truly remarkable accomplishment. Bernard was widely known for his business acumen and his negotiating skills. Over the years, I had had the occasion to know him as both a competitor and, on occasion, a partner, and had come to have enormous respect for his capabilities, as well as to count him as a friend. We had called one another numerous times to offer congratulations when one of our firms had prevailed over the other in a competition for some new contract. He and his associates were effective competitors. It would be great to be on the same team.

Thus, on September 14, 1995, as Bernard and I walked down the ninth corridor of the third floor of the Pentagon between the C and D rings during a break in a meeting we had both been attending in the Secretary of Defense's conference room, I raised with Bernard the possibility of combining our two companies. He indicated a willingness to discuss the subject, and about two weeks later we met over lunch at the Marriott Hotel near Newark Airport.

This session led in turn to a series of meetings among Bernard, Dan, and myself, bouncing back and forth between New York and Washington, with most of the discussions being held late into the evening or wee small hours of the next morning at the pricey Waldorf Towers in mid-Manhattan, chosen because of the relative inaccessibility of its lobby and the privacy of its layout. (Dan and I always managed to stick Bernard with the bill—for dinner *and* for the room—which must have bothered him a lot, but when we eventually paid $9.1 billion for his company, those bills were of course offset in the assets we received, so we paid for the rounds after all! As I said, Bernard is known for his business acumen.)

After a four-month period of roller-coaster negotiations, we finally reached a handshake a few days before Christmas, with the agreement that we would seek formal approval of our respective boards immediately after the holidays.

A Late Leak Beats an Early One Every Time

We planned to announce the transaction at a press conference in New York on a Tuesday morning a few days after New Year's. In preparation for this event, we held a meeting in midtown Manhattan to coordinate things on the Friday prior to the scheduled media event. Late that afternoon, while our meeting was underway, we were interrupted by an urgent message from the investment bankers we had assigned to monitor the options market for any unusual trading in Loral or Lockheed Martin stock, somewhat analogous to the "shark watch" we routinely had maintained for years to warn of corporate raiders. The report we received suggested that, indeed, someone seemed to be on to the fact that we had a transaction underway. Trading of this type, if based on insider knowledge, would, of course, be illegal, not to mention stupid (since it is usually relatively easy to track). Nonetheless, it was quite apparent that we had a leak.

We made the spot decision to move the announcement forward from Tuesday morning to Monday morning, with the stock market now (fortunately) closed for the weekend. Once again, we had managed to keep a secret for months, only to have it spill a few hours or days before the big moment. The principal problem this created, aside from requiring that three days of intensive work be packed into two, was that Lockheed Martin had scheduled its board meeting to seek final approval of the deal on Sunday afternoon in Washington, D.C., and the weather forecasters had been warning all week that the storm of the century would be smashing the East Coast of the United States throughout the weekend.

Having received indications of this possibility (based on the long-range forecast derived, in large part, from data gathered by Lockheed Martin–built weather satellites circling high above the earth), we had rented as many four-wheel-drive vehicles as we could lay our hands on in Washington, D.C., reserved as many rooms as we could obtain in the Marriott Hotel down the street from the Lockheed Martin headquarters, purchased a bundle of train tickets each way between Washington and New York, stuffed our desk drawers with crackers and pretzels, and stood by for the onslaught. These logistical preparations proved to be fortunate indeed when on Saturday evening the storm struck Washington with a vengeance. *Nothing* moved.

The board meeting, planned for the next afternoon in Washington, was quickly changed to a videoconference around the country, with each board member proceeding to a Lockheed Martin location near his or her home, avoiding the East Coast insofar as possible. In preparation for this critical meeting, the video network was checked out over and over on Saturday, and it performed beautifully. But when the moment of truth arrived on Sunday, absolutely nothing worked, not even the sound, proving once again that the likelihood that a rocket will fail is proportional to the number of VIPs at the launch site. (If I don't have a law about videoconferencing, I soon will.)

We finally reverted to a telephonic conference, which proved quite satisfactory since we faxed the charts to be discussed to the various locations. Over the next week, the video circuit was retested again and again, and never repeated the failure. Electronics fail only when it matters; it's the Fourth Law of Thermodynamics.

When the announcement of the Lockheed Martin–Loral deal was made on Monday morning, chaos consumed the business television networks since few commentators who had the background needed to analyze and explain the complex transaction had been able to make their way through the snowbanks to their stations. The transaction did in fact have an unusual number of moving parts, which added to the confusion, a not unintended consequence of our efforts to dissuade interlopers from jumping into the fray, as had occurred during the LTV and Grumman episodes a few years earlier.

One of the first letters I received following the announcement of the combination of the two companies was from a top general in the U.S. Air Force, who enclosed a bogus "press release" that had been circulating around the Pentagon hallways stating that Lockheed Martin would next be acquiring the Air Force! I promptly wrote him a note in reply, assuring him that the rumor was false, explaining, "We looked into the possibility, but your current owner has too much debt on the books."

An interesting aspect of the deal was that we, the former Lockheed and Martin Marietta, would finally be obtaining LTV Missiles and Space, albeit a couple of years after the battle royal that had erupted following our earlier attempt to do so and had ultimately resulted in LTV's purchase by Loral in the New York bankruptcy court. Apparently, with companies as well as people, it's wise to treat everyone well—you never know who you are going to meet the next time around. And, as the saying goes, what goes around comes around.

On Being Born at a Young Age

The government's blessing to proceed (which this time took three and a half months to get) was finally granted, and on April 23, 1996, the "new" Lockheed Martin opened for business with a backlog of $53 billion—and a debt requiring interest payments of $4 million per day, not to mention the need to bring in $1 million of new business *every three minutes* simply to keep all the doors open. We had created a machine with a voracious appetite for backlog!

To finance the acquisition, an initial commercial paper borrowing was put in place involving a consortium of forty-seven different banks. This was followed by a long-term debt offering of which Goldman-Sachs, the investment banker, stated, "This is the largest high-grade unsecured debt financing for a U.S. corporation ever. Only federal agencies or countries have had larger debt issues or asset-backed issues." Pretty sobering for a fellow who began his career spreading tar on roofs for $1.69 an hour.

Nonetheless, the new corporation had prodigious capabilities, and there was every reason to believe it would soon generate nearly $2 billion of free cash annually, not to mention disposing of the billion dollars of unneeded real estate it owned, along with a few noncore businesses. (Within the next year we sold thirteen businesses.) The proceeds of all this could be used to pay down in rather short order the debt that had been incurred. This in fact seemed to be the view of the financial markets, for the debt offering was quickly oversubscribed by those seeking to lend the corporation money.

The story of the building of Lockheed Martin illustrates once again the importance of timing. Had we waited until the industry began to get back on its feet before undertaking the transactions that we completed during the window of opportunity when the prices of aerospace companies were low, it would have cost us an additional $14 billion at then-prevailing prices. If, indeed, anything would still have been for sale.

One Last Story (I Promise)

Perhaps it had something to do with all the turmoil and tumult that had been in the air recently, but when Lockheed Martin's first-ever annual meeting took place—just two days after the Loral transaction closed—it gave new meaning to the word *bizarre.* Let me tell you about it.

Unfortunately, annual meetings—about which I have very little to say that is good—have become a true anachronism in corporate America. They have devolved into an exercise in democracy at its worst and futility at its finest. Aside from the fact that it costs a major corporation at least a million dollars to put on an annual meeting, barely a handful of shareholders show up. In the case of Lockheed Martin, out of 41,737 shareholders, we typically have a couple of hundred who attend. Most of the people who attend fall into one of six categories: retirees, disgruntled employees, local union representatives from tiny obscure places, rebels with a cause (that is usually unrelated to the corporation), would-be thespians who love a captive audience, and what have come to be called "corporate gadflies."

Because of the circus-like atmosphere that surrounds such meetings, serious shareholders have little opportunity to ask serious questions, and no institutional shareholder or legitimate buy-side analyst would be seen dead at such a carnival. At Lockheed Martin's first annual meeting, the question period was totally dominated by a shareholder who held less than 0.000001 percent of the outstanding shares of Lockheed Martin.

The proceedings began with Evelyn Y. Davis, corporate gadfly extraordinaire, bursting through the crowd of people waiting to pick up their entry passes and accidentally knocking over a potted palm—which set off the metal detectors guarding the entrance to the meeting room. (That such devices are necessary at annual meetings serves only to strengthen my case against these meetings; I'm told that in Japan all annual meetings are scheduled at the same time so as to make it more difficult to attend more than one, and that proceedings are cut off after ten or fifteen minutes. Hmm.)

For once, someone beat Ms. Davis to an open microphone. It was another regular of annual meetings by the name of John Gilbert. Before making his welcoming speech to the audience, Mr. Gilbert pulled a clown's nose from his pocket and donned it for all to admire.

Ms. Davis then stood and demanded an immediate answer to a rather arcane financial question. Our chief financial officer, stumped by the question, politely responded that he would find the answer by the end of the meeting and personally report back to her. Evelyn sneered. "I do not talk to flunkies," she said. "I only deal with Dan or Norm." Sensing blood, the crowd roared.

The next act featured an older gentleman who stood up and announced (with no relevance whatsoever) that he was wearing the same suit he had worn at his wedding fifty years earlier. And *then* he announed he was "eighty-two years young and looking for a girlfriend."

Up on the podium, we thought that would be the end of it, but suddenly we could see a tiny woman who appeared to be nearly as old as the gentleman, and who was wearing an enormous hat that drooped almost to her shoulders, rise from her seat and charge down the aisle.

She actually leaped on the elderly gentleman, threw her arms around his neck, and held on for dear life. Unfortunately, all this commotion caused her oversized hat to become dislodged and fall to the floor. This would not have been so bad were it not for the fact that her wig had been attached to the hat.

As Dan and I stood at the podium, trying courageously not to smile, the crowd went wild.

Finally, the motion to adjourn was met by thunderous applause, led by us, and thus ended the nation's twenty-second largest employer's first exposure to the highest level of corporate governance. But whatever the character of the annual meeting, everyone present agreed that Lockheed Martin's first year had been the finest in its history. Of course, it had also been the *only* one!

Reviewing the Troops

Following the annual meeting, the work of combining Loral with Lockheed Martin began in earnest with yet another round of plant visitations so as to welcome this newest group of employees to the corporation. We toured seventeen locations and spoke in twenty-six sessions to more than 10,000 employees in factories, auditoriums, parking lots, and courtyards from coast to coast. Again, we fielded whatever questions anyone had for us.

Amazingly, the company now included seventeen organizations that only a few years earlier had been strong, independent entities in their own right. These were Ford Aerospace, GE Aerospace, most of General Dynamics, Goodyear Aerospace, Gould Electronics, Honeywell Electro-Optics, IBM Federal Systems, LTV Missiles, Lockheed, Loral, Martin Marietta, RCA Aerospace, Sanders, Unisys Defense Systems, Xerox Electro-Optical Systems, Fairchild West Systems, and Librascope.

It was possible that *maybe* the Fat Lady *still* had not sung, but to us it sure sounded as if we could hear her humming.

What Was That Dog's Name, Again?

That's pretty much the story from behind the scenes. It's not always pretty, but this is a story of how a company in a precipitously declining market managed to increase its size through consolidation and internal growth by a factor of five, while producing a five-year shareholder return exceeding by a factor of two that of the stock market as a whole. The organization that resulted was without question one of the world's leading high-tech firms, with nearly 200,000 employees, ranking as the sixth largest employer and twenty-second largest corporation in America.

It is a story of hard work by many, many individuals, only a few of whom got the headlines. It is a story of setting into motion the exchange of billions of dollars literally on hand-shakes. And, yes, it is from time to time the story of dumb luck.

A notice I saw years ago posted outside the bunkhouse of a ranch in Wyoming pretty well sums it all up: "Lost Dog. Missing left ear and tip of tail. Large scar on right side. Recently castrated. Goes by the name, 'Lucky.' "

A Twelve-Step Program to Better Negotiating

I don't consider myself a very good negotiator (I'm too much of a "what-you-see-is-what-you-get" personality; in negotiating, it is often necessary that you play your cards close to the vest), but I have done a great deal of it. In fact, thanks to my travels, I have wrestled with some world-class deal makers in places like Saudi Arabia, Egypt, Panama, Korea, and Japan. The following twelve points are the result of hard-earned lessons that came from those experiences. I think you'll find them useful:

1. Make a list of your objectives and prioritize them.
2. Write down *in advance* your walk-away position. The hardest thing in negotiating is not to get caught up in the spirit of the chase.
3. Understand your counterpart's emotional issues.
4. Understand your counterpart's *real* objectives.
5. Never bluff! Be prepared to back whatever you say. (Bluffing is a short-term, dead-end strategy that can destroy credibility.)
6. Be patient.

7. If things are going badly, try to involve a neutral third party—preferably one that is respected by both sides.
8. Never permit debate and disagreement to become personal—stick to the issues.
9. Try to find items to trade that are more important to the other side than to you.
10. Don't be constrained by the specific scope of what's being negotiated—bring in peripheral items that could be traded to bring about a solution.
11. Never give up (some of the best deals we completed were ones that jumped off the embalming table).
12. Negotiate only with individuals having at least as much authority to make an agreement as you have (to avoid bait-and-switch tactics).

Oddly enough, my favorite negotiating story does not involve any one of these world-class opponents, yet it remains the most unusual negotiation I ever witnessed. It involves a street merchant in Mexico and my then 5-year-old daughter.

We had been on a family trip to San Diego, and decided to visit nearby Tijuana one Sunday afternoon. Our daughter had been saying that she wanted a pocketbook, and knowing there were lots of leather goods stores along the main street, we told her this was the time and place to find one. We also hoped perhaps she might learn a little bit about bargaining, so we gave her a basic explanation of the fundamentals of negotiating.

We soon found a leather goods store, and René soon found a purse she liked, and asked the store owner its price. So far, so good.

Upon being told, "six dollars," she gave it some thought and then in a firm voice made her counteroffer.

"Nine dollars."

A look of puzzlement crossed the face of the store owner, followed by the faint glimmer of a smile.

"Three dollars," he demanded.

My daughter thought this was fair, and the deal was struck.

As I paid the bill, I told the gentleman that what he had just done showed a lot of class. He answered that he had been in business in Tijuana for twenty-five years, and that was a technique he had never seen before.

⊕   ⊕   ⊕   ⊕   ⊕

Among the lessons we learned in the deals we did, the one that was most critical was never to become discouraged—no matter how badly things appeared to be going. In each of our transactions, there was a point where everything appeared lost. But with the help of a few champions, we were able to achieve each of the goals we had set for ourselves. If we'd let down our resolve and given in, and given *up*, we'd have lost everything we eventually won.

The other even more fundamental lesson was always to do business with people you feel you can trust. Life is short.

6

Crisis Management

Don't wait 'til the river's rising.

Anyone interested in learning how to plan constructively for the unavoidable should pay close attention to the events of August 1989, when a joint federal-state emergency disaster team of some 1,000 officials tested an earthquake reaction plan in San Francisco. A scant six weeks later, the powerful Loma Prieta earthquake struck the city, collapsing buildings and starting fires and floods. It is likely that many lives were saved as a result of the relatively smooth handling of evacuations and medical emergencies.

Elizabeth Dole, the president of the American Red Cross (an organization with a long history of alleviating the human suffering that results from disasters), points out another important advantage of planning for crises: "The midst of a disaster is the poorest possible time to establish new relationships and to introduce ourselves to new organizations. When you have taken the time to build rapport, then you can make a call at 2:00 A.M. when the river's rising, and expect to launch a well-planned, smoothly conducted response."

⊕   ⊕   ⊕   ⊕   ⊕

117

Some years ago, business writer Robert Heller noted, "The first myth of management is that it exists. The second myth of management is that success equals skill." I came to a very similar conclusion in *Augustine's Laws*. Mr. Heller's assertion is directly supported by Law #29: "Executives who produce successful results hold on to their jobs about five years. Those who do not produce successful results are gone in half a decade."

In sum, the notion that one person, sitting atop the corporate hierarchy, can regularly and successfully guide the daily actions of tens of thousands of individual employees is a pleasant confection created, some would suggest, by the abstractly inclined, or by those leaders themselves, to make sense out of the rough-and-tumble world of business. Only the truly brave (or the truly foolish) would claim that there is a rigorous scientific discipline at work here, with management "cause" unwaveringly yielding some sought-after bottom-line "effect."

However, there is at least one aspect of management where a chief executive's influence is measurable; indeed, the very future of the enterprise often depends on how expertly he or she handles the challenge, and that is in the area of *crisis management*.

"There *Is* a Tide . . ."

Crises tend to be highly formative experiences, watershed experiences, sometimes even life-threatening experiences, for a business. Nowhere else is the leadership of a chief executive more apparent or more critical to the long-term prospects of an enterprise. It is a passage that demands the continued individual attention of the CEO—a true challenge in itself given that most CEOs have the attention span of a tsetse fly.

Webster defines a crisis as "a turning point in the course of anything; decisive or crucial time, stage, or event. A time of great danger or trouble whose outcome decides whether possible bad consequences will follow." At the same time, crises can afford unprecedented opportunity. As Shakespeare wrote:

There is a tide in the affairs of men,
Which, taken at the flood, leads on to fortune;
Omitted, all the voyage of their life
Is bound in shallows and in miseries.

As regular as the tide are headlines that yet another business has "managed," if the word may be used in that fashion, to stumble into a crisis situation, often without warning and occasionally due to no direct fault of management. An organization in Louisville is said to maintain a data bank of some 85,000 negative stories about businesses, each a potential crisis in the making.

Not too long ago a single day's copy of the *Washington Post* reported the following crises: the almost unprecedented series of apparently unrelated crashes that American Eagle Airlines had suffered; the flight restrictions placed on two of the aircraft involved, which were built by the French firm Avions de Transport Regional; the Orange County bankruptcy stemming from speculation in leveraged derivatives; and Intel's travails with its most advanced semiconductor chip, the Pentium. All in all, a good day for bad news. "Business as usual," skeptics might say.

Shortly after, a story appeared in the *New York Times* about a very large and well-respected mutual fund having admitted that a $1.3 billion *gain* it had reported was actually a $1.3 billion *loss*. According to the firm, an accountant had inadvertently reversed a minus sign in making a calculation of the year's results. (As Everett Dirksen once remarked, "A billion here . . . a billion there, and pretty soon you're talking about real money.") But the end truth is that this unfortunate mathematical misstep simply verified the observation of the nineteenth-century American diplomat Edward John Phelps, who noted, "The man who makes no mistakes does not make anything."

Interestingly, the Pentium incident caused a great deal of embarrassment for its maker, while the mutual fund error seemed to vanish from our television screens with relatively little corporate flagellation. Why should such a contrast in treatment be the case? This is one of the mysteries that make crisis management much more of an art than a science, mysteries this chapter shall seek to unravel.

The airline, computer, and mutual fund industries are not, of course, alone in facing crises. In virtually every human endeavor, there is potential for the sudden cascade of starkly negative events that are associated with the word *crisis*.

On the international scene, the United States seems to face at least one major crisis every year. In the last decade or two, there have been the Soviet invasion of Afghanistan; the hostage taking at the embassy in Tehran; the bombing of the Marine barracks in Beirut; the armed conflicts in Panama, Grenada, and Somalia; the hostilities in Bosnia; and, of course, the Iraqi invasion of Kuwait, to name only a few of the more prominent incidents.

In medicine, there has been the AIDS crisis. In engineering, TWA flight 800. In sports, the cacophony of off- and on-field misdeeds by prominent players. In charitable work, the United Way crisis. And in nature, earthquakes, floods, hurricanes, and tornadoes.

In politics, a crisis looms for every public official every time he or she ventures to give an off-the-cuff remark to a reporter. (In my case, it was when I was worrying in front of a hostile reporter about a terrorist's sneaking a nuclear weapon into the United States. Apparently disbelieving, the reporter asked, "How in the world would you do that?" to which I unthinkingly replied, "Well, I suppose you might hide in it a bale of marijuana.") And, of course, individuals face crises as well, whether they be the loss of a job, a divorce, or a serious illness.

"I Prefer to Profit From Others' Mistakes and Avoid the Price of My Own" (Bismarck)

Looking back in history, there has been no shortage of business crises. In the late 1970s, a number of large insurance companies faced possible bankruptcy as a result of the Equity Funding scandal, during which the insurance companies found they had been paying off large sums for nonexistent policyholders. In 1959, the Food and Drug Administration seized a tiny part of the nation's cranberry crop because it contained a small residue of weed killer, causing the bottom to drop out of the entire cranberry market just before Thanksgiving. In 1906, the San Francisco earthquake devastated the city and its banking community, except for A. P. Giannini, whose small Bank of America continued making loans during the crisis and went on to become one of the world's largest banks.

I do not have an advanced degree in crisis management, nor have I published scholarly articles on the subject. There are no parchment diplomas hanging in my office declaring (in Latin) that I am an expert in "crisisology." In fact, with regard to crisis management, I am merely a graduate of the school of hard knocks. But I have acquired a generous collection of scar tissue over the years, somehow having had, as I pointed out ruefully in the Preface, an impeccable sense of timing that has frequently served to place me in exactly the wrong place at precisely the right time.

I have thereby assembled ample evidence that an underlying lesson concerning crisis management is that there is no magical "911" to call to extricate oneself from such predicaments. One gets oneself into a fix; one gets oneself out of it. It's that simple. There is no way to run the sausage machine backward and get pigs out the other end. After all, if the solution were easy, we wouldn't call it a crisis.

In this era of burgeoning technology, crises stemming from engineering failures will almost inevitably represent a growth industry. I still recall vividly in the hours after the explosion of the space shuttle *Challenger*, agonizingly studying, over and over, the initial flight data, which *seemed* to suggest that our company's hardware was reponsible for the failure. As it turned out, the huge orange-colored external fuel tank—a product of our Manned Space Systems division—was *not* the culprit. But the soul-searching was an experience that those of us who were involved will never forget.

Among the most prominent of business crises are, of course, those that in their wake create public relations catastrophes—for example, placing incendiary devices in automotive crash-test vehicles; putting glass marbles in soup to make it appear thicker in television commercials; allowing a heavily laden oil tanker to run aground in a pristine Alaskan waterway; or having a customer find a dead mouse in your firm's premium beer.

Then there are the marketing crises that occur when promising products fail their makers' expectations, including such well-publicized products as Betamax, the Edsel, and New Coke. There are crises associated with labor disputes such as the ones encountered by Kohler, International Harvester, Caterpillar, major league baseball, and the nation's air traffic control system. There are sudden market shifts like, for example, the one the airlines and telecommunications industries experienced with the introduction of deregulation.

In studying this gamut of business crises, it is possible to view the anatomy of a crisis in terms of six basic stages.

Stage I: Avoiding the Crisis

The first stage, not surprisingly, has to do with prevention. Amazingly, although this is the least costly and most logical way to control a potential crisis, this stage is usually skipped altogether. Perhaps this is due to the fact that crises are simply accepted by many executives as an unavoidable condition of everyday existence. Indeed, Henry Kissinger was once heard to remark, while serving as Secretary of State and confronted with still another international flare-up, "There cannot be a crisis next week. My schedule is already full."

Chronic inattention to preventive measures must to some degree be attributed to a type of blind spot that seems to afflict business executives. This blind spot has one redeeming virtue in that on occasion it proves to reawaken the executive's humility. I am reminded of the remarks the chairman of New York's Consolidated Edison made during a television interview in July 1977, when he reassuringly announced, "The Con Ed system is in the best shape in fifteen years, and there's no problem about the summer." Three days later, the entire New York metropolitan area was plunged into twenty-four hours of darkness in the legendary Blackout of '77.

This phenomenon was specifically addressed in my book of laws in Law 37, which states, "Ninety percent of the time things will turn out worse than you expect. The other 10 percent of the time, you had no right to expect so much."

Unfortunately, the fact that one may not have control over the origin of a problem does not exempt one from living with its consequences, as some of my engineering colleagues discovered when the spacecraft project on which they were working was canceled as a direct result of a period of unusually intense sunspot activity, an activity presumably not altogether under their control. The project on which they were working was intended to build a "space tug," which would rendezvous with a very large and then-defunct spacecraft orbiting the earth and guide the latter to a safe impact in the ocean. But the unusual sunspot activity increased the air density at high altitudes such that the inoperative spacecraft crashed of its own account before the rescue tug could be finished. Fortunately, the crash landing occurred in a sparsely populated area of Australia, and no one was hurt.

When wondering why major corporations do in fact seem to encounter so many crises, it is useful to recall that General Motors has about the same number of employees as San Francisco has citizens, AT&T is about the same size as Buffalo, and Lockheed Martin is the size of Spokane. The real dilemma for an executive is that potentially almost any one of those employees can, and occasionally does, plunge an entire corporation into a crisis, either through misdeed or oversight, as became abundantly clear in the 1995 collapse of the venerable Barings Bank, reputedly the oldest merchant bank in England, at the hands of a young, risk-taking employee.

Given the frequency of crises, managements live highly precarious existences, but existences in which they can minimize their organization's exposure by making very clear to their employees what behavior the company expects of them. The preventive phase is where an executive must seek to minimize risks and be certain that those risks that must in fact be taken are commensurate with the returns to be expected—and that the risks that cannot be avoided are properly hedged.

Some years ago my wife and I attended a course in which the lecturer made this very point. On that occasion the lecturer sought out a volunteer from the audience and posed the following question: "If I were to place an I-beam on the floor in front of this podium, would you be willing to walk across it for twenty dollars?" The person in the audience indicated that he would in fact be prepared to take on such a challenge. The lecturer continued, positing that the imaginary I-beam had now been suspended high above the ground between the roofs of two separate forty-story buildings. He again asked the gentleman in the audience if he would walk across the I-beam for twenty dollars, and the respondent indicated that he would not.

Having made his point, the lecturer should have quit. However, he plowed ahead, reaffirming that the I-beam was still poised between the two forty-story buildings, but now asking, "If I were on top of one of the buildings and was holding one of your children over the edge and you were on the other building, and I said to you that if you don't come across the I-beam and get your kid, I'll drop 'im, would you then cross the beam?"

There was a moment's hesitation, after which the man in the audience inquired, "Which kid have you got?"

Most of the potential business crises that are successfully dealt with in the prevention phase never receive public scrutiny and are, therefore, not widely known. For example, having successfully maintained and serviced the airplanes that transport the 1.3 million passengers in America who every day board one of 21,300 domestic airline flights, the airlines' overall safety record is noteworthy but not newsworthy. It is only on the rare occasion when a plane crashes that a crisis develops. Similarly, the elevators that transport millions of people successfully every day, the restaurants that safely feed many more millions, the nuclear reactors that provide megawatts of electricity to millions of customers, and the electronic systems that move trillions of dollars in business transactions generally do not create crises because the preventive systems that have been put in place work. These accomplishments are largely taken for granted.

The real problem, however, is that perfect prevention is perfectly unattainable in a world occupied by humans.

One of the darkest moments of my own business career occurred about midnight during a 1993 meeting a few days before Martin Marietta was to close on its $3 billion purchase of General Electric's aerospace business. On the evening in question there suddenly appeared considerable evidence that the Justice Department might not approve pivotal elements of the transaction because of alleged antitrust concerns. Were the transaction to have cratered at that point, it is likely that General Electric and Martin Marietta stockholders would have lost, overnight, the $2 billion in market value that had been gained when the combination was originally announced.

Despite all the meticulous preparation of the two companies to ensure that there would be no cause for the merger to fall off the track, Martin Marietta's senior executives learned, to their chagrin, that the term *high probability* is subject to a variety of different interpretations. To a dozen or so lawyers from some of the nation's most prestigious (or at least most expensive) law firms, "high probability" meant "over fifty-fifty; perhaps even a 70 percent chance of success," whereas to those of us who were engineers, "high probability" meant more like 99 percent—or better.

Thus, the leaderships of the two companies suddenly found themselves plunged into a predicament that, until that moment, had been considered by most to be extremely remote. Fortunately, the companies were able to put together the evidence needed to resolve the questions that the Justice Department had raised and thereby avert a major crisis at the eleventh hour. When the merger finally won approval, someone quoted Winston Churchill's remark that "nothing in life is so exhilarating as to be shot at without result."

As Gerry Myers, former head of American Motors and the author of the aptly titled book, *When It Hits the Fan*, recently observed, "There are two kinds of crises: those that you manage and those that manage you." He went on to say, "Crises do not appear out of thin air. There is always a pre-crisis period. The trick is to detect crises early and then control or even prevent them."

Stage II: Preparing to Manage the Crisis

The second stage in the anatomy of a crisis has to do with preparing for that circumstance when prevention *doesn't* work—

that is, preparing a plan to deal with whatever circumstances might reasonably be anticipated when disaster does in fact strike. Remember, Noah started building the ark *before* it began to rain.

In his book *Crisis Management*, Steven Fink wrote that every person in a position of authority "should plan for the inevitability of a crisis in much the same way that [one] views and plans for the inevitability of death and taxes: not out of weakness or fear, but out of the strength that comes from knowing you are prepared to play the hand that fate deals you."

Fink included a survey of CEOs of Fortune 500 companies in which it was found that CEOs, while often suffering from a severe lack of crisis preparedness, certainly do not suffer from a lack of *crisis confidence*. Eighty-nine percent of those surveyed said that crises in business are "inevitable," yet 50 percent said they did not have a plan for dealing with them. Nonetheless, fully 97 percent felt abundantly confident that they would respond well to any future crisis. These are the kind of CEOs who hide their own Easter eggs.

But the fact that you don't control the source of a crisis does not mean that you can't plan for dealing with the crisis. Crises fitting this category include the one that followed the Six Day War, when the energy supply from the Middle East was suddenly disrupted and the repercussions were felt almost immediately in Detroit, where there were huge stockpiles of gas-guzzling cars. Suddenly the demand for small, gas-frugal cars skyrocketed. Chrysler's Lee Iacocca observed, with his usual incisiveness, "The American motorist wants economy so badly they will pay almost anything to get it."

Most airlines have crisis teams at the ready along with special telecommunications and detailed contingency plans. Almost all companies today have backup computer systems in case a natural disaster or other catastrophe should disrupt their on-line system. (At Lockheed Martin, all the supplies needed to communicate in writing with every member of key constituency groups are maintained at a central location, so that, for example, a letter can be at the homes of each of nearly 200,000 employees and 40,000 shareholders within two or three days. As it happens, there have been occasions when this system was used.)

Preparation for crises must always include a search for subtleties—the second-order effects. The devil *is* in the details. For example, in the aftermath of a recent major hurricane, some telephone companies found that one of the principal shortages impeding reestablishment of telecommunications was, almost implausibly, not the lack of poles, wire, or switches but the lack of day care centers for children. It seemed that many of the companies' field operations employees were members of single-parent or two-working-parent families, and when day care centers were destroyed by the hurricane, someone had to stay home to care for the children, thereby significantly reducing the workforce at the very moment when it was needed the most. The problem was eventually solved by soliciting retirees to tend ad hoc day care centers, thereby freeing working parents to assist in restoring the telephone network.

An inspection of past experience suggests that among the useful preparations to undertake for dealing with an upheaval are establishing a crisis center, preparing contingency plans, identifying in advance the members of the crisis team, designating a spokesperson, providing ready and redundant communications—and, importantly, testing those communications.

Stage III: Recognizing the Crisis

The third stage of crisis management is often the most challenging—and has to do with recognizing that in fact there *is* a crisis.

In the most Machiavellian version of the crisis recognition dilemma, a company may be presented with an altogether unfounded and unfair challenge, a challenge that the mere act of recognition may make worse. For example, one of the nation's great consumer product firms has for years been unjustly accused of promoting satanic pursuits, apparently because of symbolism the critics read into the corporation's more-than-a-century-old logo. Another well-known firm, a fast-food chain, recently reeled from rumors that mice had been found fried along with the chicken it had sold. Clearly any response to such unsavory rumors may merely serve to draw additional attention to the scurrilous claims that the firm is seeking to erase from the public conscience in the first place. It is much like being told that under absolutely no circumstances should you think of polka dot elephants.

But even in these egregious cases, a company cannot simply move away and hide. The fact that 90 percent of all accidents occur within ten miles of one's home is not resolved by moving to a new home. One fairly successful approach has been to establish "800" lines, so that consumers who harbor genuine concerns can discuss them with knowledgeable representatives of the company, and the company can avoid splashing the gory details all over the newspapers any more than is likely to happen anyway.

Gauging how the public will react to a business crisis is, of course, not easy. This was vividly explained by Norm Ornstein, the extraordinarily perceptive Washington political pundit. He once told me that he had conducted a public opinion survey, the kind where a question is asked and the public can call one of two "900" numbers and pay seventy-five cents to record their response to whatever might be the question at hand. The question in Norm's provocative survey was, "Would you pay seventy-five cents to answer a telephone survey?"

For the record, it turned out that 92 percent of the respondents who called the "900" number said they would *not*.

Further to the point, one morning not long ago a Baltimore TV station that conducts a daily viewer call-in poll to address some question of current prominence forgot to pose a question at the outset of the program. Not to be deterred, a substantial number of viewers called to cast their ballots anyway. (For the record, the opinions expressed were roughly equally split between "yes" and "no.")

So much for predicting public reaction.

But sometimes there are even stronger warnings of impending crises that go unheeded. For example, nearly a decade prior to the launch of the Hubble Space Telescope, two different tests conducted by the telescope's optical manufacturer indicated something very major was wrong with the primary mirror. Shortly after the launch, the entire project was tagged with the "Trouble with Hubble" sobriquet, and likened to the near-sighted Mr. Magoo by the media when the spacecraft was discovered to suffer from severe nearsightedness. So confident in their design had been the mirror manufacturer's engineers that they simply disregarded the test results. Which raises the question, Why conduct tests if you are willing to disregard their results? (In this case, a set of corrective eyeglasses was later added to the spacecraft, and it worked magnificently.)

Prior to the space shuttle *Challenger* failure, a series of memoranda to the solid rocket booster company's management from various of their engineers contained such impassioned statements, highly unusual for technical documents, as "HELP! The seal task force is constantly being delayed by every possible means." Another memo implored, "If we do not take immediate action to solve the problem with the field joint, we stand in jeopardy of losing a flight along with all the launch pad facilities." As history records, these pleas went unheeded.

Lessons derivable from past experience in this phase of crisis management suggest that no one should rely on the corporate establishment as the only source of information about a problem. That establishment may, in fact, *be* the problem. Asking the people who were responsible for preventing a problem whether there *is* a problem is like delivering lettuce by rabbit.

There are, of course, costs associated with this independent investigative approach, but as one of the great crisis managers of all time—Red Adair, the oil well firefighter—is said to have pointed out when talking to prospective clients, "If you think an expert is expensive, wait until you hire an amateur."

Stage IV: Containing the Crisis

Stage IV of crisis management has to do with triage, stopping the hemorrhaging, the phase in which the tough decisions have to be made, and made fast. For example, should the area surrounding the Three Mile Island nuclear reactor be evacuated, with the almost certain chaos that would entail, or should people be told to remain in place and accept the risk of a nuclear catastrophe? Should all Tylenol pills be immediately recalled, at great cost, or should executives wait for more conclusive evidence? In this phase, decisiveness is critical. That is, *some* reasonable, decisive action is almost always better than no action at all.

The problem facing executives in this phase of a crisis is that typically they are ignorant of the extent of their ignorance. It has, of course, been wisely stated that when you reach the bottom of a hole, you should stop digging—but how do you know when the bottom has been reached? Many years ago, General Motors violated the "stop digging" principle when, bedeviled by the public criticism of a bright young antagonist (and college acquaintance of mine), rather than try to disprove his charges, they hired private detectives in an effort to tarnish his reputation— and by so doing merely succeeded in making the name Ralph Nader a household word.

Part of the predicament faced by management in the early phases of a crisis is that saying too much too soon can later prove to be devastating to credibility. The report of the Kemeny Commission investigating the Three Mile Island incident included the following statement: "During the first few minutes of the accident, more than 100 alarms went off, and there was no system for suppressing the unimportant signals so that the operators could concentrate on the significant alarms. Information was not presented in a clear and sufficiently understandable form."

Unfortunately, this characterization might well describe the development of most crises. Crisis situations tend to be accompanied by conflicting advice, with the legal department warning, "Tell 'em nothin' and tell 'em slow," the public relations department appealing for an immediate worldwide multimedia press conference, the shareholder relations department terrified of doing *anything*, and the engineers all wanting to disappear into their laboratories to conduct confirmatory experiments for a few years. It has been my experience that in such circumstances, it is preferable to err on the side of overdisclosure, even at the risk of damaging one's legal position. Credibility is far more important than legal posturing.

James Lukaszewski, a specialist in communications, counsels, "Say something. If *you* aren't prepared to talk, reporters will find someone who is."

Similarly, "No comment" is an unacceptable response in

today's instantaneous world of telecommunications. So, too, is, "We haven't read the complaint," or "A mistake was made." (When my son was four years old, he stumbled on to this latter theory of "detached responsibility" by explaining, when asked if he knew how the shoe polish got all over the living room wall, "Sometimes that happens.")

There is, of course, the question of what specifically is the principal message the corporation wishes to convey in its communications. It has been wisely said that "the world is not interested in the storms you encountered, but did you bring the ship in."

A word to the senior executives who are reading this: It is at exactly this point, I believe, that you must call on your own conscience. You must set aside for a few minutes the voices of trusted advisers and, in as calm and dispassionate a manner as possible, evaluate in *human* terms the real issues and the real messages. By so doing, you will at least have the comfort of defending a position that *you* believe to be correct.

It seems that organizations and individuals who best manage crises are those who, well in advance of the crisis itself, have thought through what it is they stand for. Then, when all seems to be crashing about them, they have something to fall back on. Jim Burke, the CEO of Johnson & Johnson, told me that his company's highly regarded response to the Tylenol murders was based on actions that were preordained by the firm's corporate credo; that is, given the widespread attention the credo had received, no other response could even be considered.

Another conclusion I've gleaned from studying crises is that a company is almost always best served by immediately dispatching the senior responsible individual to the scene of the problem. Usually this means the CEO.

The CEO may know less about the details of the situation than the local management, but his or her physical presence sends two messages: "I care" and "I am accountable." This was the courageous approach the CEO of Union Carbide pursued during India's Bhopal tragedy when some 2,000 people died as a result of a chemical leak at the company's Indian subsidiary.

The immediate, and obviously unexpected, result in this instance was that the CEO found himself in jail. Again, good decisions do not necessarily guarantee good outcomes. Nonetheless, traveling to India was the proper course on his part. The delicate balance to be struck is that if the CEO enters into the union negotiation with the head of the local, the CEO is not likely to be particularly effective in subsequently resolving with the head of the national union any impasse that arises. But in cases that truly are existence threatening or reputation threatening, the CEO belongs on the front lines.

Four other lessons can be learned from the triage stage. First, it is wise to have a dedicated group of individuals work full-time containing the crisis; others, it must be remembered, still have a business to run. Further, a "fire wall" should be built between the crisis management team (led by the CEO) and the business management team, led by an appropriate senior operating designee.

Second, a single individual should be identified as the spokesperson for the company with regard to all public comments. This stems from another of my laws, which states, "If enough layers of management are superimposed on top of one another, it can be assured that disaster is not left to chance."

Third, a company's own constituencies—its customers, owners, employees, and communities—should not be left to ferret out their information from the public media. With all the pressures on management to respond to news reporters, management must not neglect those who have special needs for information.

And fourth, it is helpful to have a devil's advocate as part of the crisis management team, someone who can in no uncertain terms tell the king (or queen) when he (or she) is wearing no clothes.

An interesting question arises as to how, in the spotlight of intense public scrutiny that goes with a crisis situation, executives can obtain the legitimate privacy needed to weigh sensitive alternatives, discuss the performance of specific individuals, and discreetly conduct any necessary planning. But, obviously this sort of secrecy must be distinguished from any attempt to cover up wrongdoing—which is the third rail of crisis management.

It has been my experience that it is best to assume that every word you utter will appear in the newspapers (as well as some words you don't utter). The fundamental physical law governing such matters is derivable from any basic course in hydrodynamics, namely, "Everything leaks." You may as well plan on it.

Stage V: Resolving the Crisis

Stage V in the management of a crisis has to do with resolution of the problem. Speed is once again of the essence. As Will Rogers aptly stated, "Even if you're on the right track, you'll get run over if you just sit there." A crisis simply will not wait.

Two years ago, the supermarket chain Food Lion suddenly found itself thrust into the public spotlight when it was accused by ABC's *Prime Time Live* of knowingly selling spoiled meat. The company's stock plummeted, eventually bottoming out at slightly greater than half its precrisis value. The firm responded quickly, offering public tours of stores, putting large windows in meat preparation areas, increasing levels of lighting, putting workers in new uniforms, expanding employee training, and offering large discounts to draw customers back into stores so they could see what had been done. It eventually earned an "excellent" rating from the Food and Drug Administration, and at least in areas where the company had previously been well established, sales quickly returned to normal. The company also won a substantial court judgment from the news network (because of the way the information was gathered, not because of the veracity of the reports, one way or the other).

Similarly, when accusations were made that the electromagnetic fields accompanying the use of cellular telephones caused brain tumors, the manufacturers of these devices quickly sought out independent experts who took the facts directly to the public, and the concerns that had been created promptly subsided. Pepsi-Cola used a corresponding approach when syringes were found in cans of soft drinks. The company quickly and publicly demonstrated that the foreign objects would have to have been planted in the containers by the purchaser. Once again, the furor quickly passed.

Stage VI: Profiting From the Crisis

The sixth and final stage in a crisis is that of seeking to make lemonade from the lemons in which you very likely will have been engulfed by this time. One example of this process of turning negatives into positives was the Army's handling of the highly volatile situation that arose when munitions left from the World War I era were found buried in what is now the residential community of Spring Valley, Maryland.

A number of homes had to be evacuated, and emotions in the community ran understandably high. The Army General having overall responsibility in the area took charge of the situation personally, meeting each evening throughout the crisis with local citizens in a community forum. The media were always invited, and questions were answered willingly and candidly. When the crisis had subsided, the local citizenry named a street in their community in honor of the General.

The canonical example of turning around an emotion-charged, highly visible crisis is Johnson & Johnson's handling of the Tylenol case. Responding to the series of deaths that resulted from cyanide adulteration of Tylenol capsules, the company's CEO, Jim Burke, reasoned that forceful measures were needed to ensure the safety of the public as well as to restore trust to its top-selling product. With full-page ads and television spots announcing its intentions, the company pulled 31 *million* capsules from store shelves and home medicine cabinets around the nation. Within three months, Tylenol had regained 95 percent of its precrisis market share.

This was not accomplished without cost, but the cost of repurchasing a reputation is infinite. From a business perspective, the end result of the Tylenol case was that Johnson & Johnson displayed its care for its customers and its commitment to the corporation's ethical standards. Although the situation was tragic, the company was even more highly regarded by the public after the episode than it had been before. It showed that the company cared.

I took the liberty of showing this account of the Tylenol problem to Jim Burke and asked him what he would add to it.

He said he would emphasize two points. First, he cited the axiom that many somehow seem to overlook, namely, "If you run a public company, you cannot ignore the public." Second, and these are Jim's words, "Institutional trust is a lot more important than most people realize. And the operational word is *trust.* Whether people will take one's word when one badly needs them to do so will depend on how much confidence has been built in the organization over the years before the crisis occurs."

In other words, what is in one's bank of goodwill will, not surprisingly, depend on what one has deposited there before that precious commodity had to be called on.

This is, of course, not particularly good news for American business as a whole. A recent Gallup poll ranks the American public's confidence in big business only slightly ahead of Congress and about equal with the newspapers. (Faint praise.)

But there may be a silver lining in this cloud. When, for example, two spacecraft that had been built by another company just prior to Martin Marietta's purchase of that same company failed, Martin Marietta publicly took full responsibility and voluntarily returned $22 million of profit to its customer. To the company's utter surprise, it was given great accolades by the public and the media for this seemingly obvious act. Apparently expectations for business are so low that a company will be given effusive credit simply for doing what is right.

Yes, there are many lessons to be learned from a crisis.

A Final Observation

Those are the six stages through which most crises seem to evolve. But I cannot leave this topic without touching on one other important ingredient that affects all crisis managers from time to time: It's called luck.

Borrowing once again from the experiences of Martin Marietta, bad luck was having a division that manufactured clothing dyes work for years to develop a foolproof, nonfading version of martin blue, the dye then widely used in blue jeans. The successful results of this marathon technological *tour de force* arrived on the market at precisely the moment when a sudden shift in consumer demand occurred: to the desire for *prefaded* jeans!

As John Chalsty, who runs Donaldson Lufkin Jenrette, once said of an experience of his own firm, presumably with apologies to Ralph Waldo Emerson, "We had built the perfect mousetrap. Trouble was, that mouse was already dead."

7

"Reengineering? Been There. Done That."

A Reengineering True Story

He that will not apply new remedies must expect new evils;
for time is the greatest innovator.

Francis Bacon

Reengineering—the pet business theory *du jour* in political circles and scholarly journals, and also on factory floors—has been
analyzed and dissected by countless ivory tower theoreticians,
media mavens, and armchair pundits for nearly a decade. A
quick search I made of four major business periodicals revealed
more than 500 articles on the subject published in the past five
years alone.

Given this vast collection of opinion, one might assume that
everything that *could* be written on the subject *has* been written.
However, all too many of the articles I read, while eloquent in
their expression and admirable in their theory, have been, ah,
devoid of practicality. In other words, they don't reflect the real
world.

It's like the comment Yogi Berra made one night after he was thrown out of a game while arguing an umpire's call at the old Crosley Field in Cincinnati. At that park, a wooden barricade sat atop a concrete wall in left field. If a ball hit the wooden barricade, it was a home run; if it hit the concrete wall, it was still in play. On the night in question, one of Yogi's players hit a ball against the left field wall, and the sound the ball made convinced Yogi it was a home run. Unfortunately, the umpire heard it differently and ruled the ball was still in play.

Yogi discussed the point so heatedly that he was sent prematurely to the showers. Later, when he met with reporters, he explained his logic: "Anybody who can't tell the difference between the sound of a ball hitting wood and a ball hitting concrete must be blind!"

How It Was, I'm Sorry to Say

Similarly, I've often found myself shaking my head at some of the theories proposed for reengineering—or, more often, for *not* reengineering—large corporations. Like Yogi Berra, my inner voice says: "That just doesn't look right." So I have taken the opportunity, having just had the experience of living through a reengineering of a magnitude not often paralleled in American business history, to set down some thoughts on how the process occurred and to offer some prescriptions to others should they have the occasion to find themselves in a similar predicament.

I have borrowed unabashedly from conversations with many of my colleagues and a handful of other CEOs (including some of those with whom I traveled on the Time Newstour) who generously shared their experiences and lessons learned with me prior to our undertaking our own corporate reengineering. In this sense, this chapter is less a "how to" than it is a "how it was," with all the accompanying details.

Included are the startling nosedive in the marketplace (in our case a 23 percent decline in acquisition outlays for national defense between 1991 and 1995 alone) and the dramatic growth of the company that is now the Department of Defense's biggest supplier, which, despite the nosedive, has seen its stock price increase more than two and one-half times and seen the company diversify its business to the point where only half is now with the Department of Defense.

"How Did They Do That?"

Some might well be puzzled by certain apparent contradictions, such as the notion that large corporations are often created by *down*sizing. But the logic is unassailable: The first rarely occurs without the second. One grows while one shrinks. By becoming more efficient, one wins more business. With more business, the bottom line grows. And with a single-minded focus on efficiency, even the announcement of layoffs by a company in recent years usually brought a jump in stock price. Are investors happy to see people lose their jobs? No, but the market is predisposed to "reward" a management that takes steps to become more competitive in the world marketplace. Such an action reassures investors that the company is not comatose and intends to be a survivor. It is very painful to see people in a company lose their jobs, but it is even more painful to see *everyone* lose their jobs in a hopeless attempt to salvage the jobs of the 20 percent who truly *aren't* needed.

This is not to say that management is immune to an equal and opposite backlash over its efforts to streamline for the longer term. A *Newsweek* cover story blamed "in-your-face capitalism" for mass layoffs and labeled several CEOs as "hit men" indulging in "trendy" corporate firings. And in the *Wall Street Journal*, one of the leading gurus of the reengineering movement admitted that too much emphasis had been placed on trimming workforces. "The real point of [reengineering]," he is quoted as saying, "is longer-term growth on the revenue side. It's not so much getting rid of people. It's getting more out of people." Of course, behind the headlines, while American business was undergoing its much-scrutinized "downsizing" over the past decade, few seemed to notice that it was actually *adding* 18 million jobs, net. Or that in the last quarter-century the United States has added five times as many new jobs as all of the countries of Europe combined—many still suffering from their earlier socialistic tendencies.

Some might inquire what an engineer such as myself possibly knows about reengineering, a pursuit presumably more suited to business schools than engineering schools. Arguably any engineer worth his or her salt would get it right the *first* time—so that there would be no need for reengineering! It will even be pointed out that I made exactly such a point in another of Augustine's "less-well-remembered" laws, which stated, "One should expect that the expected can be prevented, but the unexpected should have been expected."

Reengineering has to do with change—something which the corporations I have served have developed considerable familiarity with over the past dozen or so years. Franklin Delano Roosevelt once said, "In a changing world worthy institutions can be conserved only by adjusting them to the changing time."

There are only two kinds of companies: those that are changing and those that are going out of business.

There are of course numerous interpretations of the term *reengineering.* In fact, there are a number of overlapping definitions. *Restructuring,* for example, has mostly to do with redrawing organization charts and rearranging the assets they represent, or, alternatively, reorganizing the balance between debt and equity on the balance sheet. *Downsizing* implies reducing the size of the workforce, layers of management, and plant space. *Empowering* means letting the people who know the job best have a greater role in deciding how to perform the job: a concept that took modern American industry about a century to figure out. *Reinventing* typically means starting with the desired product or service, then working backward so as to keep only those functions actually needed to produce the desired end product or service. This concept is vaguely analogous to what used to be called zero-based budgeting in government financial circles.

Reengineering is probably the most encompassing of these terms. It includes streamlining processes, reducing labor content, refocusing management, eliminating layers of management, emphasizing the use of technology, increasing the effective use of capital, moving into new markets, improving training, and much, much more.

Change is, of course, painful—sometimes very painful. New expectations and new priorities can be very unsettling. As Woody Allen has remarked, "Ours is a world with too many moving parts," and the fact that change is necessary in a free enterprise–based global economy makes it no more pleasant for the individuals involved. But as former British Prime Minister Harold Wilson once observed, "[The person] who rejects change is the architect of decay. The only human institution which rejects progress is the cemetery." Or as automotive executive Charles Kettering said some years earlier, "The world hates change, yet it is the only thing that brings progress."

Even a well-established giant like General Motors is trying to ensure its competitiveness in a constantly changing marketplace, most recently by announcing a goal of cutting the time it takes to design, test, and build a new automobile by 40 percent. Trimming development time to twenty-four months will save millions and allow GM to respond rapidly to changing consumer tastes. GM, under Jack Smith's leadership, seems to have understood the saying, "If you always do what you've always done, you'll always get what you've always gotten."

What If You Don't *Want* to Change?

The penalty for *not* changing to reflect external reality is not only painful but often lethal to organizations as well as individuals. Western Union had the opportunity to purchase the rights to a new invention called the telephone but declined to do so, saying it saw no reason to adapt to such an unproven device. The passenger railroads in the 1940s and 1950s didn't take the upstart airlines seriously—and paid the price.

In contrast, IBM *didn't* pay the price (just $75,000) when offered a revolutionary new operating system to run its line of personal computers. The young man who located the operating system while acting as IBM's agent recognized its potential and bought the system now known as DOS for his own start-up software company. Yes, the name of the start-up company was Microsoft, and the name of the young man was Bill Gates.

Equally instructive is the experience of Xerox, which, having invested significantly in the development of a commercial copying machine, sought to sell the technology in the late 1950s for an infusion of much-needed cash. No takers emerged after independent marketing research concluded that there was no substantial need for a fast, cheap copying machine. Xerox held on to its creation in hopes that a market would emerge. It did, confirming the observation by personal computer guru Alan Kay, "An important technology first creates a problem, then solves it."

Unfortunately, head-in-the-sand thinking has not yet been reengineered out of the earth's lexicon. On our Time Newstour, in Havana Fidel Castro told us that the bicycle is the transportation of the future. Apparently Fidel has yet to meet Henry and Orville. The moral of such illogic seems to be, "If at first you don't fall behind, try, try again." Interestingly, as markets change, the established market leaders are often blinded by their past successes, not to mention their disproportionate stake in preserving the past.

Part of the problem, of course, is that, as the saying goes, it is difficult to make predictions—especially about the future. Even some of America's finest businesspeople have fallen victim to this problem, including IBM's legendary founder Tom Watson, who once forecast that "there's a world market for about five computers." On the other hand, it is sometimes fortunate that businesspeople are not perfectly prescient, as was the case when appliance mogul Alex Lewyt predicted in the 1950s, "Nuclear vacuum cleaners will be a reality within ten years."

As the World Shrinks

The Information Age has made the global economy a reality, forcing firms to compete not just with neighbors on the other side of town but with companies literally on the other side of the globe—with different pricing structures, different standards of living, and, as we have seen, even different ethical standards.

As already noted, India pays its world-class software engineers about one-tenth the going wage in the United States. And with today's technology, it is a trivial matter to flash software around the world at the speed of light.

The Shelf Life of Excellence

We live in Darwinian times: Our companies are subjected to the unforgiving pressures of the marketplace and the unrelenting spotlight of public opinion. When the Dow-Jones industrial average recently marked its hundredth anniversary, only one of the original companies survived to join in the celebration. A close reading of the Fortune 500 list of America's largest companies reveals an attrition rate of 7 percent per year. Even the forty-three companies highlighted in the much-acclaimed book of the 1980s, *In Search of Excellence,* have taken their lumps. A follow-up article just two years after the book appeared asserted that no fewer than fourteen of the companies had already "lost their luster," in the sense that they had suffered serious profit reversals.

Apparently excellence is a constantly moving target—which is what Darwin may have had in mind when he observed, "It is not the strongest of the species that survives, nor the most intelligent, but rather the one that is most adaptable to change."

How does a business manager or executive become aware that such a battle for survival is imminent? Samuel Johnson once remarked, "Nothing concentrates the mind like a hanging." It used to be that the hanging was the threat of bankruptcy, a threat such companies as Commodore, Wang, Cray, Drexel Burnham, W. T. Grant, Penn Central, Pan American, Woolco, and even New York's Rockefeller Center apparently did not foresee.

In today's highly competitive marketplace, the hanging might simply be a poor quarterly earnings report. Or it might be a product reliability problem. Or it might be a technological breakthrough by a competitor. Or it might be a political event halfway around the globe. The Information Age has narrowed the margin for error, a phenomenon such companies as Harley-

Davidson, Sears, Kodak, and GM all recognized in time to save themselves from the corporate graveyard.

Harley's CEO told me the story of how his once-proud company had been bedeviled by a series of quality problems, which caused the business to suffer. Having been brought in from the outside to fix things, he began a two-front campaign: one, to fix the problems, and, two, to communicate that the problems *had* been fixed. To do the latter, he ran a series of ads showing a group of *very* tough-looking motorcyclists hanging around their Harleys, with this simple caption: "Would you sell a bad bike to *these* guys?" Soon business was booming, and everyone was once again happy with his "Hog." An important point here was that it was necessary to deal with both the *substance* of the problem *and* the intangible part, the *image*.

But even healthy companies have reengineered themselves. Why? That's easy: because they wanted to *stay* healthy. As a recent article in the *Wall Street Journal,* entitled "Jobs Die So Companies May Live," stated, "When markets demand that companies restructure, action cannot be delayed. It is customers, after all, who are defining markets and industries." It is of little solace that the same employees who would like to earn more for working less go home in the evening and become consumers who want to purchase more while paying less—witness our ready willingness as American consumers to create a $100 billion annual trade deficit. Or that union pension funds that invest in the stock of corporate America are among the least tolerant of a period of financial nonperformance. Or that the same government officials who chastise American industry for downsizing, demand—as they should—that those who sell to our government offer highly competitive prices. What's more, these same officials then take credit for the increase in competitiveness and jobs that those very corporate policies they criticize have produced! Or that public employee pension funds demand steady increases in the value of their investments in America's corporations while criticizing management's actions to become more competitive so as to produce those increases in value.

Thus, healthy firms such as General Electric, Intel, Procter & Gamble, and Lockheed Martin—as well as innumerable others— have discovered that enduring some pain today is often the only way to ensure a viable tomorrow. In a recent survey of 2,000 industrial leaders employing 18 million people around the world, 94 percent say they have been through a reorganization or downsizing in the past two years. Fully 66 percent of these predict the pace will continue or accelerate.

The Last Supper

America's aerospace industry offers a striking example of what happens when a company—or an entire industry—suddenly is confronted by a vastly smaller and more competitive market—in our case, smaller than at any other point in a half-century. You might say that as American industry as a whole has been going through a wrenching downsizing over the past decade, prompted in considerable part by the *presence* of Japan on the world scene, America's aerospace industry has experienced a similar process of "rightsizing," prompted in considerable part by the *lack* of a Soviet Union on the world scene.

Several years ago, Defense Secretary Les Aspin invited a dozen or so aerospace CEOs to the Pentagon for dinner, after which he served us a rather unappetizing but highly prophetic fortune cookie: He and Deputy Secretary Bill Perry stated that within five years, about half of the companies we represented would not be needed by the Department of Defense. Period. Over and out.

Secretaries Aspin and Perry spoke with great credibility; those of us in that room knew only too well that, for example, the number of prime manufacturers actively producing new tactical combat aircraft had already declined from eleven in 1950 to two in 1992.

During the course of that Pentagon dinner, at one point I exhibited the impertinence to refer to the gathering as "The Last Supper," much to the chagrin of everyone present. But perhaps an element of candor was not altogether inappropriate at a moment that would mark the redefining of an entire industry, an industry that in the past couple of decades had placed men on the moon, helped build the global village by providing jet air travel and space telecommunications, explored the planets, and, in just forty days, helped defeat the fourth largest army in the world—not to mention giving quality jobs to several million American workers.

As if a reiteration of the message were necessary, Perry, when later Secretary of Defense, reasserted, "We expect defense companies to go out of business. We will stand by and let that happen."

One industry executive, searching for a ray of hope, countered this point of view by stating his belief that you could still make a small fortune in the aerospace business, "but only," he admitted, "if you started with a large one."

By far the most imaginative strategy for dealing with the evolving crisis was offered by the CEO of what was then the Northrop Corporation. His strategy, as described in *U.S.A. Today*, was as follows: "CEO Kent Kresa also said that Northrop will continue to sell non-productive assets. Last year it sold its headquarters in Los Angeles."

In the most fundamental form of reengineering, many firms simply left the field, either by design or by the unyielding forces of the marketplace. Estimates suggest that only about one-quarter of the 120,000 firms that once supplied the Department of Defense still serve in that capacity. The U.S. defense industry has sustained a far greater rate of market loss than any other industry in recent times, and a huge conglomeration of human tragedy as well—ironically, all brought about by the welcome news of the end of the Cold War.

A Baker's *Half*-Dozen Painful Lessons of Reengineering

In lieu of some fabled, easy, and painless rules of reengineering yet to be discovered, I offer seven (a baker's *half*-dozen, according to my slide rule) pretty good, but difficult and painful, rules that represent the best practices we had derived from among the seventeen major companies that have combined to form today's Lockheed Martin, as well as those of several other prominent companies with which I have some familiarity. The latter include Procter & Gamble, Phillips Petroleum, and Black & Decker.

These rules are not based on elegant or esoteric theories; they are derived from real-world experiences. Bismarck once observed, "If you like laws and sausages, you should never watch either one being made." The same is true of reengineering. It is not fun, and it most assuredly is not a spectator sport. There is a saying in the world of corporate economics that every time we try something that works, the practitioners of the media and politics invariably raise the criticism, "Yes, but would it have worked in theory?" In this case, the rules offered did work in practice, whether or not they are very solidly grounded in theory.

1. Read the Tea Leaves

To some, the task of recognizing that change is in fact needed may seem rather rudimentary, yet many executives find this the most challenging step of all. It would seem that the hard-and-fast lesson to be learned from most reengineering examples is that there is usually some warning that problems lie ahead. The trick is to recognize those warnings and then be opportunistic in acting on them. And whether there is a warning or not, every manager, and especially every CEO, should have a personal list of "the worst things that could happen to me," backed up with contingency plans. One of my newest "laws" states, "Tornadoes are caused by trailer parks." Every manager should maintain a constant inventory of where the trailer parks are in his or her business.

2. Have a Road Map, Even When There Are No Roads

As the saying goes, if you don't know where you are going, any road will get you there. Embarking on any major reengineering effort is doomed in the absence of a well-thought-out plan or vision of where you wish to venture. Especially avoid the false hope of unrealistic goals and assumptions. As Dan Tellep, my colleague at Lockheed Martin, is fond of saying, "Hope is not a strategy."

In specifying a vision and a strategy to reach that vision, it is profoundly important to recognize one's core *in*competencies. Remember Michael Jordan, the *baseball* player? Try to build on what you already understand. And when undertaking tectonic change, allow for the unexpected, providing reserves in the form of money, time, and alternative approaches. Often, the difference between a good manager and a *great* manager can be summarized in one word: *reserves.*

In every reengineering effort, the forest and the trees at first seem indistinguishable. Some years ago, Martin Marietta was challenged by NASA to cut the weight of the external tank, the huge fuel tank that forms the structural backbone of the space shuttle—by several thousand pounds. A great deal of progress was made, but the effort temporarily stalled out when it came to the last 800 pounds.

As the engineers focused on new and exotic lightweight materials—some seemingly derivatives of "unobtainium"—one of the factory workers, *not* one of the engineers, incidentally, suggested a detail everyone had overlooked: Stop *painting* the tank. We had been using 200 gallons of white paint on the tanks for the early launches to cover the rust-colored insulation. The process was time-consuming as well as adding—you guessed it—800 pounds of unneeded weight to a fuel tank whose useful life span in flight is only about eight minutes and whose intended fate is to end up at the bottom of the Indian Ocean. So we stopped painting the tank. Sometimes the best way to "think outside the box" is to ask someone who *is* outside the box.

3. Do It Fast

Among other things, the great Mae West was famous for pithy sayings, one of which was, "He who hesitates is last." As usual, Mae was onto something. In business, after establishing a strategy, the most important rule is almost always, "Faster is better." If you have made the decision to reengineer, then announce an ambitious schedule for doing so, and stick to it. If you don't, you may find yourself emulating the Evil Knievel syndrome of "trying to leap deep chasms in two bounds."

It is vastly more beneficial to get the reengineering done fast and 80 percent correct than to get it 100 percent correct but too late. It is not acceptable to say, as did one professional football player after his team had lost a close game, "We didn't lose; we just ran out of time."

One of the greatest challenges to timely consolidation in American business is posed by the antitrust laws, which, of course, were enacted to perform a very important and necessary function. In my experience (which is more extensive in this area than I care to recall), the antitrust review process has invariably been competently administered and smoothly executed, but you could never confuse it with being fast. Each review involved months of painstaking and time-consuming work during which the firms involved were essentially placed in suspended animation, a sort of time warp. And there is nothing more debilitating to morale and efficiency than a prolonged process that all employees know will determine what their benefits will be, whom they're going to work for, where they will work, or even *whether* they will work. Customers have their own set of questions.

In the case of the review of Boeing's proposed acquisition of McDonnell Douglas, more than five million pages of documentation were submitted to the government's regulators.

I sincerely believe that our government has extraordinarily principled and knowledgeable professionals serving in the antitrust area, but I also believe we need to revise further our antitrust review process to reflect better the pace of the highly competitive world marketplace of the twenty-first century. As the CEO of Sears told me, "Don't cut off the cat's tail one inch at a time."

4. Keep Score—That's What the Big Leaguers Do

It is essential to be able to monitor progress throughout the reengineering process and point to quantifiable improvements at its conclusion. Strenuously avoid being placed in the fog of ambiguity in which one unfortunate Marine Corps official found himself when asked to quantify the expected cost of a new helicopter. He confessed, "The estimate is based on an estimate."

Keeping score begins with setting forth the indexes that are important—from financial results to process measures—and then recording those indexes consistently and sharing them with the affected part of the workforce. GE frequently uses cycle time. Others measure scrap and rework. Still others measure touch-labor content or yield. Whatever the case, it is also essential to survey outside constituencies, including, of course, customers, to determine how they think you match up with the indexes that are important to *them,* and to learn what the benchmarks are of world-class performers. No one would watch a football game where no one kept score, so why would anyone try to manage a business without keeping score throughout the contest?

There is a story of a blast furnace in a steel mill where some years ago the supervisor of each shift would record on a mani-fest the number of batches of metal produced during that shift. A seemingly unending number of "sixes" were recorded, until one day the day shift turned out *seven* batches. In order to get the point across, the supervisor wrote a big "7" with chalk on the floor in front of the furnace. Sure enough, the workers on the night shift saw that number and, stepping up the challenge, redoubled their own efforts. The next morning when the day shift arrived, they found—not a "7"—but a huge "8" on the floor. A few weeks later, there was a "9" and eventually a "10." Bringing out the natural competitiveness of people is a great way to enhance efficiency, while instilling pride and teamwork. This can work wonders even when the "competitor" is one's self, as is so vividly evidenced by the durability of the game of golf.

5. Communicate, Communicate, Communicate

A reengineering effort is a lifeboat in which every employee's participation is critical. One cannot have employees dismissing obvious problems by saying that the leak is not in their end of the boat. Every member of the team has to understand and *be-lieve* why the status quo is unsustainable. This requires using every means at one's disposal to get the word out, including visits to plants and offices, letters mailed to homes (they are more likely to be read than letters passed out at the workplace), employee newspapers, videotapes, magazines, and, perhaps most important, face-to-face visits with the entire workforce. As the oracle Pogo declared, "The certainty of misery is better than the misery of uncertainty."

Management has the obligation to be totally candid, despite pressures from the media, shareholders, customers, politicians, and employees themselves to dispense only good news. Try not to find yourself in the position of the old pol whose opponent complained, "Half the falsehoods he's telling about me aren't even true!"

In the recent strategic combination with Loral, we sent out some 250,000 letters and packages to employees, customers, retirees, political leaders, the media, and others, all issued on Day One. Among the most rewarding things we did following our mergers, acquisitions, or other major restructurings was to get all the key managers who would be responsible for implementation away from the workplace for a two- or three-day goal-setting and team-building meeting. Such "quality time," away from day-to-day pressures, is priceless. This is, incidentally, a topic about which I have markedly changed my views over the years: from extravagant to invaluable. Although Warren Buffett has named his corporate aircraft "The Indefensible," in reality it is probably *inexpendable.*

6. Reengineering Is Not a Profit Center

There is still a business to run: Reengineering is merely a means to an end. When moving one major half-full plant some 1,000 miles to be combined with another half-full plant producing substantially the same kind of product—in this case, space launch rockets, a highly unforgiving product—we made plans in excruciating detail. Even then a few subtleties escaped our list makers; for example, when some of the factory workers from the old plant arrived at the new plant, it was discovered that they did not have available the more common machine settings they had been using. The reason: Over the years the workers had penciled these numbers on the building's structural posts . . . and we neglected to move the posts! The First Law of Wing Walking applies: "Never let go of something until you have hold of something else."

Over the course of my career, I have seen too large a number of failures of very advanced, complex—and expensive—pieces of equipment. Remember my mentioning the spacecraft that went far off-course on a useless trajectory into outer space because a single hyphen was omitted from the software code? Or the major spacecraft that proved to be badly nearsighted because of a minute error in grinding the primary mirror in its optical train? Or the spacecraft that blew up upon arriving in orbit around Mars after a one-year transit—all due to a tiny piece of blockage in a fuel line?

While all the upheavals of reengineering are taking place, it is necessary to keep reminding employees, managers, suppliers, and one's self of the critical importance of staying focused on everyday responsibilities no matter how many distracting things are happening in the surroundings. After all, no one can simply recall a spacecraft from near Mars or Jupiter or Neptune to fix a loose connector, replace a leaky seal, or repair a sticky valve. Similarly, there are no asterisks in the stock listings on the financial pages to indicate "excused due to restructuring."

When we had to close one plant that built space launch vehicles, we were particularly concerned over possible quality problems. In addition to providing special financial incentives to the employees, we appealed to their pride. Just before each rocket was shipped to the launch pad, everyone who had worked on it lined up and signed their name on it to certify that they had done everything they knew how to do to make it work. We never had a failure among those rockets. People can be great if you'll let them.

7. One Company, One Culture

In the business world, the culture of a dynamic company encourages the incubation of ideas from which those best suited to the prosperity of the company are chosen. All too often, however, the concept is used to thwart, not nurture, change. Sam Walton's suggestion to his hardware store employer that they open warehouse-size stores was rejected as "not the way we do things around here." So Mr. Walton took his idea and started an entirely new culture, one based on meritocracy.

In addition, "culture" can never be an excuse for failure. Culture is an asset, not an excuse. Instructive regarding this point is the apocryphal story (I know it's apocryphal because *I* made it up!) of the professional football player who was traded to a new team. In the first game with his new teammates, he repeatedly missed key blocks. When the coach, flushed with frustration, finally called him to the sideline, the unrepentant player explained, "Coach, I'm having a big cultural problem out there." Okay, that's obviously a ridiculous scenario, but using culture as an excuse for not getting the job done in business should be viewed as every bit as ridiculous.

I know from personal experience that building a new culture can be an enormously positive and rewarding undertaking. This means accepting the notion that everything one did in the past *wasn't* perfect and that everything everyone else did *wasn't* flawed. It means embracing, with an open mind, *the best of the best*. Let the cream rise. It will.

The idea is, first, to convince people they are all in the same boat; second, that the choice is between alternative realistic (imperfect) future worlds, and NOT between some imperfect future world and the status quo. Borrowing from Voltaire in *Candide*, we are not talking about the best of all worlds but rather about the best of all *possible* worlds.

Reengineering Is Dreadful?
Consider the Alternative

Reengineering requires absolute commitment at the top and enormous understanding and patience everywhere else, especially in middle management. It may as well be recognized: Reengineering is painful medicine, so anyone trying to keep the status quo will end up opposing the effort. In today's highly competitive global economy, there is no cavalry to ride in and rescue you. If you're too busy to make reengineering a personal priority, just admit that you're not committed and forget it.

In fact, reengineering is altogether unappealing until you consider the alternative—an alternative emblazoned in the names of once-proud companies that are no longer in business. But even at that, reengineering is not for the faint of heart.

As a result of a decade of reengineering, America is today

in the best competitive position in the world economy in a generation. The Swiss-based World Competitiveness Report recently ranked the U.S. business environment number one in corporate competitiveness for the second year in a row. (And, I'm proud to say, *Aviation Week* just ranked Lockheed Martin as the world's most competitive aerospace company.) Japan, top ranked as recently as 1993, has fallen to fourth position and Germany to sixth. Supporting observations have been offered by Richard Cavanagh of Harvard University, who has noted, "American industry has changed its structure, gone on a diet [and learned] to be more quick-witted." Michael Boskin, former chairman of President Bush's Council of Economic Advisers, similarly observed, "A combination of a major reengineering in corporate America, combined with the depreciation of the dollar, has most of corporate America remarkably competitive to the rest of the world." Another Harvard scholar, William Sahlman, went even further, stating, "[We] will look back on this period as a golden age of entrepreneurial management in the United States."

⊕   ⊕   ⊕   ⊕   ⊕

In today's highly competitive marketplace, business must be brilliant every single day if it is to survive, and this is especially true in the high-tech world. Science and engineering simply won't stand still and wait for our institutions to catch up. We have to reinvent ourselves continually; no one is interested in last year's technology or last year's products. The bad news is that reengineering requires hard decisions. The good news is that success awaits organizations that are willing to make those hard decisions. There are battle ribbons to be worn along with those battle scars.

8

Corporate Governance

On December 31, 1600, history was made in London when 218 merchants were granted a royal charter to engage in a Far East trading enterprise, which became known as the English East India Company. This early version of a multinational corporation was different from other chartered institutions of the era in that it was essentially self-regulating. To guide the fledgling enterprise, the shareholders elected a Court of Committees composed of the Governor, the Deputy Governor, and twenty-four "committees"—or what we now call directors. Perhaps the term is derived from the concept of "commit-ees" . . . at least one hopes so.

The ultimate impact of the enterprise begun on New Year's Eve some four centuries ago is evident today in the extraordinary development of the publicly owned, director-guided corporation. Along with colonists, this concept crossed the Atlantic and took root in the nascent United States of America. The corporation played a major role in the great economic leaps of the burgeoning nation in the 1800s and 1900s, providing the financial framework for prominent industrialists who, as they aggregated immense personal fortunes, built great industries ranging from oil and banking to railroads and telegraphs—and in the process made shareholders rich. In those days, of course, directors tended to be either the owners themselves or fellow executives from interlocking companies—the latter of which, in today's America, would be deemed potentially illegal conflicts of interest.

The Rise and Fall of the Golden Era of Profitable Growth

After World War II, with much of European and Japanese industry in ruins, America's corporations by contrast entered a golden era of profitable growth. Through the 1950s and 1960s, after-tax profits averaged about 10 percent annually, and American products set the standard for world markets. Ownership had passed from the powerful families of an earlier era to a highly diffuse set of shareholders. In the boardroom, directors enjoyed a "sea of tranquility," perhaps best epitomized by the "3-6-3" maxim attributed to some who sat on the boards of financial institutions: "Pay 3 percent interest on deposits, charge 6 percent for loans, and be on the golf course by 3:00 P.M."

The golden era of the boardroom began to tarnish in the 1970s, as resurrected Japanese and German industries challenged American leadership in steel, automobiles, electronics, and a variety of other markets. As a result, directors of American corporations suddenly found themselves contemplating previously inconceivable actions, including widespread employee layoffs.

Then in the 1980s, a number of trends converged on the boardroom, taking directors out of their largely unseen roles and thrusting them front and center in the forum of public opinion. A series of highly publicized attempts to engineer hostile takeovers and leveraged buyouts forced directors to choose between larger short-term returns for the shareholders, often resulting in significant human costs in terms of jobs eliminated and even the possibility of eventual bankruptcy, and the company's long-term prospects.

At the same time, institutional ownership of stocks grew explosively from about 5 percent of all corporate equity in 1950 to more than 30 percent in 1980 and nearly 50 percent today—

concentrating ownership once again in the hands of a few powerful investors or coalitions of investors. The time-tested means
of expressing dissatisfaction with a company's performance ("If
you don't like the way the company is run, sell your stock") was
superseded by a new phenomenon, shareholder activism, which
was the effort by institutional investors to have a more assertive
voice with the board regarding corporate governance and performance. This movement took many forms, but none more
prominent than the Council of Institutional Investors Focus List
of Underperforming Companies. Both boards and management
got the message. "This CII list is a list we don't want to be on,
and we're doing everything we can to get off it," one CEO was
quoted as saying.

Rough Water on the Sea of Tranquility

As if directors did not have enough on their plates, the liability
explosion simultaneously rocked the boardroom. In the 1991–
1994 period alone, according to the National Economic Research
Associates, class-action lawsuits resulted in more than 300 out-
of-court settlements being reached, with some $2.5 billion being
awarded to plaintiffs.

During this period, I once received some very sagacious,
if tongue-in-cheek, advice from the head of a large insurance
company on how directors can avoid such lawsuits. "Always
vote last and always vote with the minority," he counseled.

Reflecting this convergence of explosive issues, heretofore
unthinkable skirmishes between boards and chief executives became much more common—and public. Boardroom revolts in
such blue-chip companies as General Motors, American Express,
IBM, Sears, and Kmart virtually eliminated the prevailing notion
of the chief executive's being all-powerful and unaccountable.
And these skirmishes seemed to yield results, at least as indicated by one admittedly small sampling of five particularly publicized boardroom decisions to replace the CEO.

In these instances, the companies averaged a 7 percent *negative* rate of return for the two years prior to the change and an
83 percent *positive* rate of return for the three years following. Of

course, one could say that starting from the bottom, there is only one way to go, and that is up.

Whatever else might be said, as we close out the twentieth century, the sea of tranquility that once characterized the boardroom had become a roiling ocean of uncertainty.

From the tentative beginnings of cross-border corporate activity 400 years ago, we are now being propelled more and more deeply into the instantaneous, global marketplace—a development that will profoundly affect the boards of companies engaging in that marketplace.

"Déjà Vu All Over Again": Some Leftover Twentieth-Century Board Issues

With all the critical challenges of recent years, it is disheartening that there are probably more thorny, unresolved issues confronting boards as they enter the twenty-first century than at any other time in the past. In a sense, we seem to have run out of century before we ran out of problems. As such, there are lingering issues that boards will have to confront squarely as they enter an increasingly Darwinian twenty-first century.

In years past, being elected to a board seemingly conferred a kind of renewable immortality on directors and an immunity from accountability. Some issues likely to be addressed in the next century to correct these circumstances further include the following:

Having a Lead Director

Choosing a lead director is becoming a popular option with some boards even today. A recent survey by Korn/Ferry International states that 36 percent of the nation's largest industrial corporations now have lead directors, up from 21 percent since last year. Whatever the mechanism, it is becoming increasingly necessary for boards to have in place some means of readily addressing issues that may arise in conjunction with management performance.

My personal view is that every director must have a full membership role on the board, with all the rights and responsibilities attendant to that role, and that designating one director as the "lead" director tends to diminish the influence of the other directors. On the other hand, the establishment of a "coordinating" director whose role would merely be to serve as a "communications central" or facilitator in addressing the concerns of other directors would seem to be very constructive.

The CEO's Role With Committees

To delineate the influence of the chief executive officer responsibly and reduce potential conflicts of interest, it seems appropriate that in the era ahead, the CEO no longer serve as a member of most board committees (with the exception of the executive committee), such as nominating, finance, and public policy, but rather be limited to observer status, as is generally the case today for such committees as audit and compensation. New board candidates will best be selected by a nominating committee composed solely of independent directors, with the CEO having the informal right to reject potential candidates—a right that in a healthy environment should rarely be exercised. The extent of the evolution that such a practice would represent is suggested by the fact that just a few decades ago, most boards did not even *have* nominating, audit, or compensation committees.

Having a Separate CEO and Chairman

The American governmental tradition of checks and balances naturally gives rise in the corporate world to the concept of separating the roles of chairman of the board and CEO. The notion is that an "enforced partnership" will strengthen the oversight function of the board, as well as management's responsiveness to the board. This is a concept that has important benefits under certain transitional conditions, for example, companies in trouble, companies following mergers, and companies undergoing a CEO transition.

But in the ordinary course of governance, I believe there is potential for considerable mischief from having a separate chairman and CEO, unless the arrangement is extraordinarily well handled (which it usually won't be), because such a duality of authority almost inevitably undermines the role of the CEO. Ultimately, as in any other organization, someone has to be in charge. Realistically, either the chairman or the CEO could be the final decision maker, but it had better be clear to everyone which one it is.

Separating these two key positions raises the question of who ultimately speaks for the corporation—to the media, to shareholders, to customers. If an unhappy customer wants to go to the top, who *is* the top? If the customer appeals to the chairman, the chairman is inevitably thrust into operating matters . . . and thus becomes the *de facto* CEO.

Shareholder Representation

The first obligation of a board in the twenty-first century, as has been the case for its twentieth-century predecessor, will be to represent the interests of shareholders and communicate how those interests are being addressed. If current trends continue, twenty-first-century boards will increasingly be confronted with stockholder concerns over board responsiveness. These concerns revolve around several issues:

⊕ *Mandatory term limits for board members?* Having seen constitutional constraints imposed on how long a President of the United States may serve, and reflecting on the current drive for imposing similar limits on the service of members of Congress, shareholders of the future may increasingly seek the forced turnover of board membership after some specified number of years. While agreeing that periodically bringing new blood onto a board is a constructive practice, I hesitate at the notion that a director has only a certain number of "good years" with which to serve the corporation.

It is commonly accepted that there is a learning curve associated with any complex undertaking. Would anyone get rid of a doctor or dentist or stockbroker or auto mechanic simply because a certain arbitrary time limit had been reached? As corporations move into the twenty-first century, an era when wisdom and experience will be at a premium, mandatory term limits for board membership will simply be a bad idea whose time has passed.

⊕ *Board evaluation?* In a global environment in which every member of management will be compelled to "prove" himself or herself continually, it seems appropriate for board members to undergo some form of evaluation as well. The first step in such a direction—annual *terms* for board members instead of multiyear staggering of the board—has already been adopted by many corporations. A likely next step is for the twenty-first-century board to commit itself to a self-evaluation process wherein the nominating committee becomes an ongoing corporate governance committee. As part of this effort, each director up for election might be asked to submit for inclusion in the proxy a brief statement regarding his or her past performance and view of future goals for the company.

⊕ *Reform the annual meeting?* Having participated in my share of annual meetings, I am truly perplexed that what began years ago as an instrument of good corporate governance has in many cases become a sort of theater of the absurd (per end of Chapter Five!). That annual meetings need reform as we approach the next century is becoming increasingly and painfully self-evident. Such meetings hardly ever generate real news, and the media seemingly cover these events primarily to report the oddities that occur. According to one sample, at least 85 percent of the votes cast are typically proffered before the meeting ever takes place. This democratic practice has thus become anything but democratic, with 99 percent of the time being consumed by owners of less than 1 percent of the corporation's shares, and many, or sometimes even most, of the issues raised having little to do with the corporation or even with management's ability to redress the concerns cited.

This is perhaps why, as discussed above, major shareholders rarely expend their time attending annual meetings. And then there is the question of why a globally owned corporation should meet in Fargo, North Dakota, simply because that is where the founder lived in 1907 (or because the lack of transportation offers welcome discouragement to gadfly shareholders).

What is the answer to this conundrum? One option, of course, would be to extend the reach of such meetings and make them "virtual events" via international, closed-circuit television. But this very likely would simply convert the domestic pursuit of fifteen minutes of fame into a global sport. A more productive approach might be, in lieu of annual meetings, for the board to request shareholders once a year to submit comments, questions, and propositions to an independent entity, such as an outside audit firm, to be boiled down and then submitted to management to be answered in the proxy. Shareholders could then vote electronically. Face-to-face meetings would be reserved for those occasions where, say, at least 25 percent of shareholders requested such a meeting. Annual reports would be placed on the Internet, with (costly) hard copies distributed only upon request.

Conflicts of Interest

In contrast with the satisfaction that appears to exist with insider-dominated boards in many other countries, concerns over possible conflicts of interest are likely to lead U.S. companies to compose boards entirely of independent directors, with the exception of the chief executive officer and possibly the chief operating officer. Further, it will likely become standard practice for former CEOs to remain on the board for only a brief transition period after their term of service in that capacity and then step down from the board altogether. There are also likely to be increasingly stringent prohibitions against serving on a board while representing banks, suppliers, law firms, or consultants who conduct business with the company.

Board Compensation

Directors' remuneration has never been quite the hot button that the issue of senior management compensation has been. Nevertheless, the desire for good governance has spurred efforts to bring board pay in line with shareholders' wishes. It would appear that we are moving away from fees for each meeting as well as the more exotic director endowments.

In particular, director pension plans are likely to continue to lose popularity, with one recent survey showing that more than sixty Fortune 500 companies have already either eliminated or frozen this form of compensation, and more are in line.

A common model for the next century will be a simple two-element package composed of an annual retainer for serving on a board supplemented by a performance-based stock ownership formula—possibly stock options.

A related issue stems from the fact that many potential director-candidates have enjoyed financially successful careers in their own right, and as board service becomes more onerous, due to greater time demands, liability exposure, and business pressures, corporations will very likely encounter increasing difficulty finding satisfactory board members. This, in fact, could turn out to be the preeminent problem facing the twenty-first-century board.

Special Issues

Employee pension funds now own approximately one-fifth of the shares of major corporations, a portion that is likely to grow in the years ahead. This trend will inevitably increase pressure for a special *employee voice* in governing the corporation. In this regard, it must be noted that for the good of the entire enterprise, management must sometimes take actions that are not welcomed by employees, particularly with respect to short-term outcomes. Such representation might then become a hindrance to effective action, not a facilitator. Ultimately, boards must choose members who represent the interests of the body of shareholders as a whole, even though each director will inevitably contribute based on his or her own special set of experiences and talents.

A clear trend in the next century will be a marked *increase in women and minorities* as members of boards. As more and more such individuals gain wider professional and managerial experience, they will find boards eager to benefit from their contributions. By the year 2000, fully 85 percent of the individuals entering the American workforce will *not* be native-born white males. Any company that elects not to avail itself of this larger body of talent will find itself trying to mine only 15 percent of the resources enjoyed by its competitors.

As emphasis on performance continues to intensify, *board size* is likely to become smaller rather than larger, simply from the standpoint of workability. The need will be for fewer, more decisive board members who can act on issues promptly and move on. This downsizing of the boardroom will be facilitated by a dramatic decline in the number of insiders on boards.

But the most fundamental responsibility of the board will remain unchanged: that of *CEO selection*. Statistics show that the median term of office for a CEO is now about seven years. One-third of CEOs remain five years *or less*, with some evidence surfacing that even this brief term is diminishing. Such a trend will obviously increase demands on the board (and the CEO) to ensure that a sound succession plan is in place and that able successors are constantly emerging.

Governing in an Age of Rampaging Technology and Globalism

Although many of the challenges faced by the twenty-first-century board will have their roots set solidly in the twentieth century, several challenges are emerging that are unique to the evolving environment:

Technical Competency

In a world where technology plays an increasingly greater role in commerce, boards will need to have a far better understanding of the implications of technical issues than is generally the case today. This does not mean that all directors must be rocket scientists, but the twenty-first-century board will need a greater representation of people who are at least technologically literate.

International Participation

An even greater priority in a global economy will be to have an international board, or at least a board comprising individuals with international background and experience. Today, corporations in most nations have less than 5 percent of their directors from abroad, with the figure for the United States being about 2 percent and for Japan being eclipsed by even that number. The principal challenge in achieving greater international representation will be the mundane matter of enticing directors to fly halfway around the world, even at supersonic speeds, for monthly half-day board meetings. Consequently, despite increasing demands on agendas, *meeting frequency* will probably actually *decrease* in the next century.

A recent survey by the National Association of Corporate Directors (NACD) shows that major companies are now meeting an average of nine times a year, a number that might well be reduced to four. To compensate for fewer meetings and increased workloads, regular board meetings will likely become considerably longer, perhaps lasting two days. Intermediate "meetings" will likely increasingly employ videoconferencing. And it can be expected that there will be a growing propensity toward relying on board committees or even *ad hoc* task forces of the board, backed by the board's own outside consultants, to deal with specific issues. Needless to say, this will pose its own set of legal and fiduciary issues for the board as a whole . . . as well as for management.

Director Commitment

Because of increasing workloads, directors will no longer be able to serve on long lists of boards, a trend that is desirable under any circumstance. One or at most two outside boards will become the norm for a sitting executive, perhaps three or four for a retired executive. There will, in fact, very likely be more retirees on boards as the trend of people retiring earlier continues and as people live longer, more productive lives. Most boards will probably maintain mandatory retirement ages, an arguable practice, at least in principle, but will likely raise those limits to reflect the changing demographics of society and to ameliorate the shortage of qualified director candidates.

Regulatory Requirements

As corporations operate more globally, there will be the increasing challenge of complying with an array of regulatory requirements across the spectrum of countries in which the company has shareholders, customers, employees, investments, or other interests. On occasion, these regulations will inevitably conflict with one another, such as in the case of a company's meeting stringent U.S. disclosure requirements by releasing material information about its operations in another country, while at the same time that country has a policy of not allowing companies to reveal such information for fear that it will be harmful to the country's attractiveness as a place to do business.

The Shape of the New Board

As the modern corporate board is propelled ever closer to the new millennium, it seems likely that the basic responsibilities that have characterized board service for four centuries will continue unabated, but with ever-increasing challenges. It also seems likely that the forces of the marketplace will push the global corporation to build a board more aligned with the U.S. model of independence and accountability than with, say, the Asian model and its less visible, less ecumenical, and less publicly responsive character.

What began 400 years ago as an instrument for building individual and family affluence has evolved into a mechanism that today generates huge amounts of wealth for huge segments of society. While the board of directors continues to evolve, it must still keep in sight two fundamental realities:

1. *There is an important distinction between governance and management.* If this distinction becomes blurred—in either direction—conflict and reduced effectiveness will inevitably be the result. We must never confuse *independence from management* with *adversariness toward management.*

2. *The board's role is to serve the owners.* This is a legal and fiduciary responsibility. Corporations do much good and have much positive influence on the communities where they operate, and the board must be mindful of the corporation's impact on all of its various constituencies. But in the final analysis, the role of the board is to work with management to serve those who own the company—not to serve management, not to serve some subset of shareholders, and certainly not to serve themselves.

What, Then, Is the Right Board for the Twenty-First Century?

I offer the following model of a twenty-first-century board, one that:

- Is highly independent of management but constructive in its relationship with management
- Is understanding of the difference between governance and management
- Is composed of only one or two inside directors
- Has a coordinating outside director
- Includes more members with competence in technology
- Is slightly smaller than today's board
- Contains substantial international participation
- Is compensated largely via stock ownership
- Meets less often face-to-face and more often in cyber-space
- Has much greater participation of women and minorities
- Relies heavily on committees of the board
- Communicates with shareholders by means other than annual meetings

That, then, is a preview of twenty-first-century corporate governance.

SECTION THREE

Quality of Life

AROUND THE WORLD IN EIGHT DAYS, III

My last day in Moscow got off to a bad start with a 5:30 A.M. wake-up call and the realization that, one, it was raining, and, two, the night before, I'd packed all of my shirts in the bag I'd put outside the door to be taken to the airport.

I had two choices. I could wear my pajama top (partly concealed by my cardigan sweater), or I could remain in Moscow forever. I chose the former. Throughout the day, I watched the people I was with for any reaction to my somewhat unusual garb, but no one said a word. If they had, I was prepared. I would say that my "shirt" had been purchased on a previous trip to India, and proclaim, "This is what they wear in India. Didn't you know?"

The L-1011's otherwise routine takeoff from Russia was in fact noteworthy: It was the first time I'd ever taken off from Russia without everyone on board the aircraft breaking out in spontaneous applause. That by itself seemed to suggest that things were at least less stifling than they'd been under the communists.

The trip to Bangalore was considerably longer than might otherwise have been the case since we dared not fly over Iran, Iraq, and a couple of other similarly inclined nations. The time zone change was two and a half hours, thanks to India's being one of the few countries on earth that works on a half-hour basis.

Bangalore, the booming high-tech center of the region, the "Silicon Valley of India," coexists alongside great poverty. In our Time Newstour guidebooks, the per capita income of India was listed at $160 per year, but some say it is much less. We arrived on the heels of the failure of a much-touted business deal involving General Electric, its partner Bechtel, and the local political leadership in Maharashtra (near Bombay) to build a $3 billion much-needed electric power plant. After the deal was put together, the local political leadership in Maharashtra changed following an election, and the new government simply canceled the contract, apparently because it suffered the cardinal sin of having been promulgated by the *previous* government. This was a huge blow to attempts to bring foreign capital into the country, something that is critical if India is ever to overcome its pervasive poverty.

It was dark when we arrived at the airport, so the twenty-five-minute ride into the city offered little opportunity for viewing. We did see an occasional (sacred) cow wandering around the streets, but that was about the extent of anything interesting.

Our hotel was exquisite, as top rate as anything you could find in London, Paris, or Geneva. While the Moscow hotel we'd just left was perhaps the best in that city, it paled in comparison with this one.

When we arrived at the hotel, we were greeted by the manager and several guards dressed in the traditional military uniforms of India, vestiges of the glory days of the British Empire. The women of the hotel staff were all lined up to present us with floral leis, and a violinist played in the background.

We ate a late dinner, and I fell into bed shortly after midnight, having been told that our wake-up time had been changed from 6:30 to 6:00, not a welcome revision.

Apparently wake-up times are very important in India. At 12:15 A.M., the phone in my room rang, but when I answered, no one was there. At 12:30, it rang again, but still no one was there. At 1:00, a young man bearing a silver tray knocked on my door and handed me a note from the hotel manager. It read, "The wake call for the delegates of the Time Newstour '95 has been amended from 0630 hours to 0600 hours. (Signed) The Lobby Manager." But not to worry about any confusion: That morning I received wake-up calls at 5:30, 5:40, and 5:45, followed by my own two (I believe in redundancy) alarms at 6:00, all of this after I'd had a relatively good night's sleep, but one in which, once again, I didn't sleep nearly fast enough.

Throughout the trip we ate well, and often. On occasion, however, the food was a bit nonconventional (we'd already heard rumors that in Hanoi we'd be served *dog*), which served to heighten our anxieties about unidentifiable substances that from time to time appeared on our plates. For example, that first morning in Bangalore I asked for eggs, and the chef responded, "What kind?"

For a startled moment, my mind raced through the kinds of eggs one might possibly find in India other than the chicken kind, but I was brought back to reality when the chef elaborated, to my great relief, "Fried or scrambled?"

Our morning tour began with a bus trip through the city traffic, always an experience in India, given that traffic consists of three-wheeled motorized taxis that dart in and out between buses, trucks, horse-drawn carts, motorcycles, donkeys, automobiles, hordes of bicycles, pedestrians, and, of course, the ubiquitous sacred cow wandering in and out. *Whatever* you hit, you didn't want to hit a cow. Yet as chaotic as it all is, the traffic in Bangalore doesn't come close to Delhi or Bombay, and Bangkok would give

India a run for its money. In this regard, New York and Rome are clearly in the second division.

Bangalore means "City of Beans," but it is also known as the Garden City of India because of the abundance of tropical greenery. The morning's itinerary offered a spectrum of contrasts. Our first stop was for a walking tour of one of Bangalore's infamous slums. The second stop was at a near-replica of Windsor Castle, in floor space about one-fourth as large as the original.

Our tour through the slum began at 9:00 A.M., and all the residents appeared to have been up and about for hours. The area occupied by the shacks was not overly large, but it was overrun with children, a few dogs whose ribs could be counted from afar, and the occasional uneasy chicken. There was no electricity, no running water, and no sanitation system.

Each family (and in some cases several) lived, or tried to live, in a hut about half the size of a one-car garage. Others even less fortunate lived in homemade tents. The "permanent" structures were built of grass (thatch) supplemented here and there with pieces of plastic, metal, or cloth. The floors were dirt, and there was no sign of any furniture. Few men were to be seen. Amazingly, the women and children seemed relatively clean. People were friendly. They even smiled at us (however, this may have been because Time had previously given a donation to the community on our behalf).

We'd been told that in India today, there are 100 to 200 million people living under these conditions; that approaches half the population of the United States. Some of the inhabitants work, but the average daily pay is only about $1.00. Medical care is almost nonexistent, and we were told that a scandal recently broke out when it was discovered that at one of the hospitals where the indigent go for care, some of the doctors had been telling patients they needed one of their kidneys removed, which kidney would then be *sold* by the doctor to someone needing a transplant. Needless to say, this caused the slum dwellers to be skeptical of even the minimal medical care that was in fact available.

While these particular living conditions were not as bad as some I've seen firsthand in parts of East Africa, Cairo, Istanbul, Mexico, and Delhi, the situation endured by these human beings can only be described as tragic—and this in the "Garden City of India." One wonders how to help but hardly knows where to start. Thank goodness for such organizations as the Red Cross. More about that later.

Our next stop was at "Windsor Castle," a remarkable edifice built some years earlier by one of the wealthier families of India. As we enjoyed fruit drinks and coffee in the garden, some men approached leading huge Indian elephants. I had my picture taken standing next to one of the behemoths, gingerly holding on to a tusk. It wasn't as exciting as the time they let me be the honorary ringmaster at the Barnum & Bailey Circus—that time I rode the elephant in the grand parade while the audience cheered. Thank goodness I didn't fall off.

In one of the castle's large rooms, we took part in a panel discussion with various government officials and representatives of local businesses. We were told that software engineers in India are paid a starting salary of $4,000 to $5,000 per year, which actually reflects a substantial increase in the past few years. One local businessperson told us that at his company, "We serve vegetarian sandwiches to our software engineers around 7:00 P.M., and the kids will stay and write software all night long."

The high-tech explosion in Bangalore had begun about eight years earlier, and there was evidence that the growth it had produced was already beginning to saturate the city's infrastructure. Bangalore's population has roughly doubled in the last decade (to 4.5 million people). There is about half the water supply needed for a city of that size, and the electricity is said to be interrupted an average of five times a day.

We asked the representative of the Bangalore Chamber of Commerce which were the best and worst cities in India in which to do business. He answered, "The best is Bangalore, and we can't tell you the worst because whenever we do Bombay gets upset!"

Nonetheless, it is evident that India was betting on technology, especially electronics, to move its people out of poverty and into the twenty-first century. In fact, the Minister of Commerce, who spoke to us at a luncheon, told us, "Technology and capital are equals today." He went on to say that in India there was only one phone for every 100 people, that there were 20 million "street children," and 9 million blind citizens. Yet he said he was convinced it was possible to bring an end to poverty during his lifetime. I fervently hoped he was correct.

Despite the fact that local officials went out of their way to make our visit pleasant and that the people we met were unfailingly cordial, the Indian newspapers criticized our visit, citing the fact that "multinational corporations" were buying up India's assets. For security reasons, Time's management had refused to give the local media our schedule, a decision that appeared to be justified when, on the way to the airport, someone threw a rock through the windshield of our bus. (No one was hurt.) And this happened despite the fact (or maybe because of the fact) that we had a police escort! The windshield was totally shattered, but the driver didn't even slow down.

As we flew out of India in midafternoon, we looked down on still another country that is abandoning a form of centralized economic control in favor of greater market freedom. Two questions lingered in my mind. The first was how in the world Great Britain ever managed to hold its enormous and far-flung empire together for so many years. And the other was whether the United States would export its technological advantage to countries such as India with low labor costs, just as we'd exported our manufacturing advantage to the Pacific Rim—and if we did, how would we provide the quality of life Americans hoped to enjoy in the century ahead?

Everyone seemed pleased to be back on board our flying home (which is exactly what it was beginning to feel like). Each of us had staked out a pair of seats and had begun collecting knick-knacks in our personal overhead compartment. The flight attendants moved about serving Russian caviar, tea, sandwiches, and cocktails. Goodness knows what the people five miles below us were eating.

9

The Gift of Time:
Volunteer Leadership

Why do people volunteer? I'm sure there are as many reasons
as there are volunteers. In my own case, there are not one but
two reasons. First, I have been very fortunate in my life, and I
believe I have an obligation to those who may have been less
fortunate. Second, I enjoy it.

I like being around the kind of people who volunteer. Once
when I was serving as Under Secretary of the Army and was
visiting the 82d Airborne Division, we were introduced to a griz-
zled old sergeant who had over 1,000 parachute jumps on his
record. We remarked, "You sure must like to jump." To our surprise, he responded, "No. I hate to jump."

When we asked why he was in an all-volunteer Army in an
all-volunteer parachute unit if he hated to jump, he answered,
"Because I like to be around the kind of people who do."

I guess that's sort of the way I am. Not only do I like the
kind of people who volunteer, but I also like what volunteers
do. In corporate America, our employees get paid for the work
they perform. In contrast, volunteers get their reward purely
from the satisfaction of helping others and must somehow
squeeze the time they devote to this pursuit in with all the other
demands in their life, including providing a living for them-

selves and their families. (The current movement in the Congress to have companies provide their employees paid time away from work so they can "volunteer" is a concept I find exceedingly difficult to grasp.)

Robert Frost once observed, "The world is full of *willing* people. Some willing to work, and the rest willing to let them." The same is true of volunteerism.

I view the work that volunteers, and especially leaders of volunteers, do with considerable awe. I also think that all successful business executives owe it to society (and to themselves) to give a bit of their lives and fortunes to society in the form of charitable pursuits. That is why, incidentally, this chapter appears in what is otherwise a more (or less) business-oriented book. There is, after all, more to life than balance sheets.

Leading by Example: The American Red Cross

Some things about volunteers will, of course, never change: dedication to helping others, commitment to humanity, selflessness, and camaraderie. On the other hand, some things must change if volunteers are to remain relevant in this ever-revising world, just as we have noted about business. Society itself refuses to stand still. Changes in society mean that today's volunteer has different needs and different priorities, and different problems to solve. As a result, we face the challenge of changing even time-honored traditions and practices within large volunteer organizations—all without undermining their essence.

Take, as examples, the two volunteer organizations with which I am most familiar, the Red Cross and the Boy Scouts of America. (I have served the Boy Scouts as president in the not-too-distant past and currently am in my sixth year as chairman of the American Red Cross. Jere Ratcliffe provides the day-to-day leadership of the Boy Scouts, and Elizabeth Dole does the same for the Red Cross.)

In the opinion of many, the American Red Cross (ARC) is the premier public service organization in the world. Day in and day out, its volunteers lead the way into situations that are rife with challenge and hazard. As one volunteer noted, "The Red Cross goes places that everyone else is trying to leave."

When the American Red Cross was founded, there was little awareness of tragedies in such places as Bosnia, Iraq, Ethiopia, Somalia, and Zaire. Today, sitting in our living room, we see the suffering of people in such distant places as it occurs—and feel obliged to help. In fact, one of the most difficult challenges America will face in the next century is how to satisfy our admirable desire to help alleviate everyone's suffering and yet not become "911-America."

A few years ago, there was no such thing as a tissue bank; today the ARC provides organs and other human tissue to some 60,000 people each year. A few years ago, the Red Cross had no access to records held in the Soviet Union relating to the Holocaust and its possible survivors; today it has the Holocaust and War Victims Tracing and Information Center searching the records and helping to answer questions that often are a half-century old. Witnessing brothers and sisters reunited who last saw one another in Nazi death camps a half-century ago raises indescribable emotions.

Not long ago, most Americans lived on farms and in villages, and natural disasters affected limited numbers of people. Today, we face widespread disasters such as the earthquakes that hit major West Coast cities, the floods that have ravaged the Midwest, and the hurricanes that devastated the highly urbanized areas of Florida. And only a few years ago, we knew nothing of AIDS.

Today concern over HIV/AIDS motivates a significant part of the effort the Red Cross devotes to its educational programs, as well as to its task of providing over half of America's blood supply.

Swift Response: A Red Cross Trademark

Scientists tell us that we might face a nuclear disaster; that diseases heretofore contained in remote parts of the globe can be expected to spread quickly throughout the world, transported by travelers moving at jet speed; that we should expect significantly changing weather patterns, at least over the long term . . . and that with regard to earthquakes, the Big One may be just around the corner.

In recent years, the Red Cross has proved it can respond creatively and energetically to significant challenges:

⊕ The organization committed itself to transforming its Blood Services Program fundamentally, partly to respond to stringent new federal regulations, to be sure—but more importantly, because exciting advances in medicine and technology made these changes possible.

⊕ Similarly, larger and increasingly devastating disasters, coupled with the more intensive needs of today's disaster victims, led the ARC to revitalize its Disaster Services organization, including the establishment of modern telecommunications command centers and mobile units.

⊕ The end of the Cold War and the downsizing of the U.S. armed forces forced the Red Cross to change the delivery of services it provides to the military, which include the transmission of some 4,000 emergency messages each day, or one every twenty-two seconds, to members of the armed forces.

⊕ The ARC responded to changes in how the public provides financial support to charitable organizations by relaunching the Community Campaign, a nationwide effort to invite Americans to donate not only their time and their blood to the American Red Cross, but also their money. (We don't ask for much!)

In the business world, where I, of course, have my day job, there are constant reminders of the need to change. But the challenges the Red Cross faces are, if anything, even more daunting.

A Revolution in the Making

Today we are witnessing nothing less than a revolution in volunteerism in America. This revolution should not come as a surprise to anyone familiar with the volunteer world. Several years ago, in its Volunteer 2000 study, the Red Cross forecast:

- ⊕ A steady increase in the number of women in the work-force, which will erode time available to those making up much of the traditional volunteer pool
- ⊕ Significant growth in minority populations in the United States, which means that one of every three Americans will belong to a racial or ethnic minority by the year 2000, a group from which volunteers must increasingly be drawn
- ⊕ Less long-term volunteer participation, with more emphasis of volunteers on *ad hoc*, project-oriented volunteering
- ⊕ Rapid growth in the number of nonprofit organizations, which will create stiff competition for the time and attention of volunteers

Any one of these circumstances would be cause for reflection. Taken together, they represent a fundamental change in the way an organization that relies on volunteers must carry out the scope of its activities.

Unfortunately, human-created organizations are no more immune to Darwinism than are biological organizations. If the environment changes, but the organization does not adapt to that change, then it will become irrelevant and die. Granted, this is a fairly stark picture of the challenges facing volunteer organizations, but we should not forget that institutions such as the Red Cross have substantial assets in their favor.

First, the Red Cross has a profoundly worthy cause: helping people in times of great need and duress. Second, it has a host of dedicated, able workers who have proved time after time their commitment to alleviate people's suffering. (During 1996 twenty-four of them around the world gave their lives while seeking to help others.) And, third, it has a continuing stellar reputation. A 1994 Yankelovich study showed the ARC to be the "most respected of major charities" in the view of the American public. Incidentally *Money* magazine has named it America's best-managed charity. And it is a good thing, too, since, as the Red Cross is fond of reminding us, "Help can't wait."

Perhaps it is all best summed up by Will Rogers's tribute of some years ago: "I would rather have founded the Red Cross than have written the Constitution of the United States."

BSA: Still Relevant After All These Years

My second personal example of a premier volunteer organization is the Boy Scouts of America (BSA). For many years, I've been a volunteer in the scouting movement, which at this writing is itself in its eighty-eighth year.

Recently, the chief scout executive told me a story about a delegation from Russia that was interested in re-establishing its own Boy Scout movement. (Scouting in Russia died in 1917, along with most everything else at the time.) When they learned that there are over 4 million American youths in scouting, the Russians were impressed. But they seemed confused by the fact that the scout organization had fewer than 3,500 paid professionals. "How do you keep track of 4 million youths with 3,500 adults?" they asked. On hearing the explanation that the professionals were partners with a *million and a half* volunteers, the Russian listeners were all the more puzzled.

"Volunteers? Are these people assigned by the government?"

Volunteerism is, as de Tocqueville has told us, a uniquely American experience.

Scouts Make You Feel at Home

In any gathering of scouts, I always feel at home. There's something about scouting that, no matter where you are in the country, or even the world, when you're with scouts, you're home. The values we share, the traditions we cherish, the institutions we revere—they're what make us feel at home.

Three years ago I traveled 1,000 miles up the Amazon River, and at one point we came upon a good-sized village on the riverbank. To my amazement, when we approached we were greeted by a group of young men wearing Boy Scout uniforms! They had dressed up for the occasion!

A family reunion of all those in America who have ever been scouts would be a gathering equal in population to Mexico.

One reason I feel such a kinship with scouting is that I have been in scouting for fifty years—over half the time that scouting has been around and over 80 percent of the time that *I've* been around. I have been a Cub Scout, a Boy Scout, an Explorer Scout, an Eagle Scout, a camp counselor, a patrol leader, a junior assistant scoutmaster, a member of a national jamboree staff, and an adult volunteer who has served on more councils, committees, and boards and eaten more charred hot dogs and burned beans than any human should have to endure.

Scouts = Volunteers

Without volunteers and people who donate funds, there would be no scouting. Period. Scouting is an extended family for our youths only if we have people who are willing to work to make it available to them. It has been that way from the very beginning of the scouting movement, and it will be that way for as long as the movement continues. You can't have a den without a den leader, a troop without a scoutmaster. Scouting doesn't just happen.

Among scouting's hardest-working family members are its full-time professionals. They are among the finest, most dedicated people I have ever known. But they would be the first to tell you that the scouting movement depends in the end on the volunteers who contribute their evenings and weekends for the sake of young people, and also the contributors who provide the money that is essential for making it all possible.

The More Things Change . . .

Some things in the family of scouting have not changed at all from the early days to the present. The scout oath and law are exactly the same as when I first recited them fifty-some years ago. So, too, is scouting's emphasis on character—because, as scouting says, "Character counts."

But like business, some things about scouting have changed. They've kept pace with the times. The Explorer program is now coed. (That's an innovation I wish they had made about forty years earlier!) Scouts no longer hold scrap-metal drives or grow Victory Gardens as they did when I was a Cub, but last year scouts collected 72 million food items for distribution to needy people. Seventy-two million in one year alone!

Another change is the current edition of the *Boy Scout Handbook*—the tenth edition since 1910, a book that holds the record for the second highest number of copies of any book ever published in the United States. I looked through the new handbook when it came out, and I think it just may be the best yet. The old, familiar instructions on how to pack a knapsack, pitch a tent, orient a map, build a fire with flint and steel, and tie a bowline are still there, but much more has been added.

The handbook now provides a detachable parents' guide on the problems of child abuse and drug abuse. The point here is that a caring family confronts problems and resolves them, and, as we all know, that eventually makes for an even stronger family.

After I finished leafing through the parents' guide of the handbook, I turned to the section on merit badges. There are now 125 badges, compared with 111 when I was getting started in scouting. I earned 42 of them.

Many of the badges I knew from my own scout days are still there: Archery, Bugling, Cooking, First Aid, Swimming, and Lifesaving, among others. But there are also more recent badges reflecting the pursuits of today, such as American Cultures, Cinematography, Computers, Environmental Science, and Handicap Awareness.

Because of my background in the aerospace industry, I am of course acutely aware of the link between scouting and America's space program. Of the 214 pilots and scientists selected as astronauts since 1959, over 125 have been active in scouting. The first man on the moon was an Eagle Scout. I wouldn't be surprised if the first astronaut to land on Mars were a Cub Scout (or a Brownie) today! Some 1.2 million Americans have attained Eagle rank since 1912.

Scouting can lead to careers that have unlimited upside potential. Some scouts seem out to prove from the very beginning that they have no limit, as I found out some years ago when I was asked to serve on a panel of long-time scouters. The purpose of this panel was to select from a group of six finalists one outstanding scout to spend a season at an American scientific outpost in Antarctica.

I knew that we would be presented with a crop of outstanding candidates—they'd been selected from an initial field of something like 15,000—and that the selection process would be difficult. But I didn't realize *how* difficult it was going to be until we interviewed the first youth on the list.

I figured our candidate might be a little nervous, so I thought I'd put him at ease by starting off with a very simple question. I asked what was the longest distance he'd ever backpacked alone.

"Two thousand miles," came the reply.

It seems that this extraordinary young man had hiked the entire length of the Appalachian Trail—from *Maine to Georgia*—by himself. When I asked how he was able to hike the whole trail by himself without any assistance whatsoever, he gave me a detailed description of how he had planned the trek, which lasted several months. He described how he had located U.S. post offices near the trail and had mailed packages of dehydrated food to himself that he could pick up at appropriate intervals along the way! Suddenly all my hikes in the Rocky Mountains in my native Colorado seemed to pale a bit.

A Family Affair (Sort of)

The pleasures and adventures I experienced in scouting have influenced my whole family, and in fact still do. My son, the other Eagle in the Augustine clan, eagerly accompanied me on a dogsled trip within 1,000 miles of the North Pole, on a hot-air balloon trip in East Africa, on a raft through the Grand Canyon, on a camel to the Pyramids, in a covered wagon across the Oregon Trail, on a jaunt to photograph polar bears at the Hudson Bay, and a dozen other such adventures. On my own, I've expanded the list with snorkeling on the Great Barrier Reef, watching whales on the Inside Passage, camping in the Empty Quarter of Saudi Arabia, boating the Amazon, traveling to the South Pole, visiting the outback of Australia, snowmobiling on the (frozen) Bering Strait, and the like. When my son graduated from college, we gave him (and me!) a trip to Antarctica. (His friends wanted to know what we would have given him if he had *not* graduated!)

This has all been tough for my wife, Meg, who is a wonderfully good sport, but I must confess that her idea of "roughing it" is a slow bellhop. (Sorry about that, dear.)

The success of scouting rests on the people who love scouting so much that they are willing to make the extra effort, go the extra mile, take on the extra project, and motivate someone else to do the same. (The qualities of leadership I mentioned in Chapter Two apply to volunteer organizations just as well as to businesses.)

Once again, it was Will Rogers who said it best: "The only problem with the Boy Scouts . . . is that there aren't enough of 'em."

Pick Your Passion, and Pitch In

Obviously, there are any number of other outlets for volunteer efforts than the Red Cross and the Boy Scouts. Pick your own passions. Maybe you'd rather volunteer to help someone learn how to read—or to read better. Or, like former President Jimmy Carter, you might like to join Habitat for Humanity. And then there is Christmas in April, or Reading for the Blind, or the Salvation Army, or the Girl Scouts. Or you could volunteer to drive the elderly to their doctor's appointments, or take meals to people consigned to their beds.

There are just *so many* organizations out there that could use your help. And it doesn't have to be one that deals with sickness or poverty. All sorts of organizations in the arts need help, as do countless numbers of clubs and groups that run activities for kids, from sports to science projects. Just pick your passion.

All it takes to make a difference in someone else's life is a few hours a week from yours. Not only don't you have to be the president of something for your time and effort to count, but you don't even have to measure your contribution by a monetary standard.

Find out where you are needed, and—to borrow an expression from the 1980s—go for it!

I have been surprised by the number of my major corporation CEO friends who are active in volunteer organizations. Quite a few of them have told me that they learned a lot more in their early lives about leadership from the Boy Scouts than they ever learned in school or anywhere else.

I happen to believe that volunteer efforts make you happier in every phase of your life, *and* they make you better at working with and managing other people. I must confess that when I learn that a prospective employee—or one up for a bigger job—has a serious history of volunteerism, I pay a little bit closer attention.

Be Careful; It May Be Contagious

Not long ago, I received a letter from a man who had been a vice president at Lockheed Martin. In his letter, he reminded me that when he had retired, I had encouraged him to become a Red Cross volunteer. He wrote to say that he had just spent his entire day standing knee-deep in floodwaters, passing out rolls of toilet paper. He said that for some reason he thought of me!

And then he went on to say that it had been the finest day of his life.

10

Preparing for the Education Olympics

A recent book addressing the international currency markets by the Dutch economist Geert Almekinders carries this intriguing dedication: "I am grateful to the numerous tennis players who defeated me over the years and the soccer players who outplayed me. Unknowingly, they helped to convince me that my advantage is in economics, rather than sports." (In my own case, it was a course in accounting that reintroduced me to engineering at a time when I'd been flirting with the idea of a master's degree in business.)

I dare say that many of us could make a statement similar to that of Dr. Almekinders. We fell short on the athletic field but were able to overcome that temporary setback and go on to contribute in other fields of endeavor. Instead of our legs, we were forced to use our minds, and that has made all the difference. Which is not to suggest that I am other than a great believer that many lessons from the sports world carry over into the business world (and into life). But more on that toward the end of this chapter.

Embracing the Future

As compared with almost any other nation, we live in a meritoc- racy, one wherein education is the most powerful escalator to a good life and the opportunity to contribute in society. In the words of Thomas Jefferson, "If a nation expects to be ignorant and free, in a state of civilization, it expects what never was and never will be." Education is the very foundation of a free and prosperous society.

In my ancestors' case, my mother was the only one to attend high school (as I was the first to go to college). But they all knew the value of an education. In fact, they probably understood that value better than many so-called educated people today.

A half-dozen years ago, I joined a group of other business- people to form the Maryland Business Roundtable for Educa- tion. I said at the first meeting, "Because those of us in business have a great stake in the quality of education in this country, we are going to focus very much on bringing accountability into the schoolroom." In fact, we would be bringing a lot of things from business—things such as competition, training, planning, and accountability. We recognized then that we were at a turning point, and the time had come for a change.

Accepting the Challenge

At the meeting, the governor challenged us, saying, "We need something new from the business community, something spec- tacular." Well, I'm thrilled to be able to report that we have al- ready begun to see spectacular changes in the public schools in Maryland and elsewhere, changes brought about because five years ago we entertained previously unthinkable notions, such as admitting failure with individual schools. The Maryland De- partment of Education has taken such heretofore unheard-of ac- tions as stepping in and taking over schools that cannot or will not compete in today's demanding educational environment. Everyone pulled together—the governor, the teachers, the unions, the parents, business—and an incredibly able leader of the state's educational system.

Looking back, I would say that the best thing we did was to establish educational *standards*, and not just any kind of standards, but *tough* ones. In recognition of the wide range in individual children's rates of development during their early years, performance in standards in kindergarten through eighth grade is measured by schools; if individual schools do not perform, they are penalized. Conversely, those that improve are rewarded. Rigorous individual examinations that reflect our tough standards are being developed for high school. Our plan is that students will not get out of high school with a diploma without passing difficult statewide tests.

We decided that these examinations shouldn't be retroactive, but would start in the lower grades so that students would have some years to adapt to this new reality. The standards were determined by committees of teachers put together and approved by the state department of education and were implemented at three specific compass points on the educational journey. If students did not pass the tests, they stayed where they were until they did.

Five years later, we had real progress to show for our efforts. In 1996, the Maryland Department of Education released the "state school report card," which showed, among other things:

- Student performance improved in twenty-one of thirty performance evaluation areas.
- Four out of ten students met the *very challenging* School Performance Assessment standards (we still have a lot to do).
- More schools are making gains, with 72 percent of schools at grade 5 and 70 percent at grade 8 now meeting or approaching standards.
- Fewer schools are below the Performance Assessments' satisfactory standards (in grade 5, the number of schools below the standards fell from 122 in 1993 to 68 in 1995).
- Entire school systems are making gains, with eighteen of twenty-four systems improving in all grade 5 Assessment Content areas.

These are significant, even remarkable, achievements in such a short period of time. But they also show just how far we still have to go. They reflect how far down we were, as far as educational performance is concerned, when we started our quest for educational reform.

As part of the program, all of the CEOs involved agreed to teach a class or two to get a "feel" for what teachers are up against. In my case, I taught an eighth-grade math class and helped out in a fourth-grade science class. In the evening of the day I taught the math class, I had agreed to speak to a group of graduate students and faculty members at the Kennedy School of Government at Harvard University. I was far more scared by the prospect of teaching eighth-grade math.

As a result of our innovative program in Maryland, the Business Roundtable, a group of CEOs of the nation's largest corporations, cited the state as a leader in educational reform. And when U.S. Secretary of Education Richard Riley announced the results of the Maryland State Performance Assessment Program, he said, "What Maryland is doing is exactly what we would like to see the rest of the nation do."

I take a great deal of pride in a statement like that. In a similar vein, I get excited when Maryland plays UCLA in a game of basketball, as do the local newspapers and television stations and citizens. But the importance of a basketball game pales in comparison to the largely unnoticed intellectual competition that is going on day in and day out between Maryland and California and a host of other locales throughout the world, which ultimately determines where the jobs go.

What was it that brought about the improvements in Maryland? The answer, in a word, was standards. As the results of various schools in meeting these standards became public, the pressure to improve became irresistible. It was surprising that it took so long to discover the power of standards. Just as in business, one must set goals, measure against those goals, and have consequences for meeting or not meeting those goals.

Educating the American Dream

Maryland, however, is but a single state. The Business Roundtable believes we need to see to it that every state has a similar program. As a nation and as a society, we will be no better than our educational system. We can, of course, be less, but not more. As Benjamin Disraeli, the legendary British prime minister, once stated in Parliament, "Upon the education of the people of this country the fate of this country depends." What was true for the Industrial Revolution is true with a vengeance for the Information Revolution.

Another push by the Business Roundtable is to get businesses to ask to see high school transcripts before they hire people. That may seem like a fairly obvious thing to do, yet most businesses don't do it.

One of the reasons they don't is that in many large corporations, when the CEO suggests asking for transcripts, he or she is opposed by the company's lawyers on the grounds that it might *appear* that the company is biased and that there might be lawsuits alleging discriminatory hiring practices. As it turns out, it's perfectly legal to use transcripts if you consider only the parts of the transcripts that are relevant to the job the person is being hired to perform. If nothing else, you can ask to look at prospective employees' attendance records to see if they even showed up for school; if that isn't a good indicator of potential job performance, I don't know what is. Isn't there a saying about showing up being half the battle?

Eastman Chemicals, which took the lead in this effort about five or six years ago, got some intriguing results. Not only did it enjoy lower training costs, but it produced a "feedback" in the high schools. The word got out among the students that if you want a job at Eastman after you graduate, you'd better take math and science, and forget about the gut courses. This is yet another example of the marketplace's working.

Another innovative approach to incentives was introduced by Peter O'Donnell, Jr., a very successful retired businessman in Texas, who used his own money to set up an academic reward program. If a student achieved a set score on the Advanced Placement test of the Educational Testing Service, that student would receive $1,000, his or her teacher got $500, and the school $1,000! It was another example of bringing the marketplace to the schoolroom.

The idea worked so well that not only did more students

start taking the test than ever before, but more of them did well. (The test results are graded 1 through 5, with college credit given for scores of 4 or 5.) You could plot a beautiful rising curve that showed how the students in his program were doing better than those who weren't in it—and then how the scores dropped back down after the prototype program ended. It's about as convincing a set of experimental data as you can imagine.

Being a technologist myself, it's hard for me *not* to believe that technology in the classroom enhances the educational experience. However, I've come to see that the overall results concerning the introduction of technology are somewhat mixed. The schools that have strongly embraced technology have in fact tended to do better (setting aside for the moment the fact that in most schools the prevailing technology is at about a 1940s level) *but* those have almost inevitably also been the schools with the most imaginative teachers and the most involved parents. And the more I've observed, the more I've become convinced that, at least thus far, the determining factor in producing scholastic improvement and achievement has been the strong interest of the parents and teachers rather than having a computer at every desk. The enthusiasm and excitement of these teachers whom I met from schools all across the economic and social spectrum are absolutely contagious.

Most of us have forgotten 90 percent of our former teachers, but we all remember the best ones. One of the reasons I am a reasonably good speller today is that back in the sixth grade, Mrs. Gleasner motivated me to become one. I had been transferred into her class at midyear, and when I looked up at the blackboard (they *were* black in those days) and saw the scores for the weekly spelling tests—one wrong, two wrong, sometimes none wrong—I thought it would be a struggle to meet that standard. On the day Mrs. Gleasner gave back my first spelling test, I saw that my not-exactly-backbreaking study effort had paid off; I had only one wrong—far better than my past performances in other classes. But Mrs. Gleasner stunned me when she said, "I'm very disappointed in you. I thought you were going to be a good student." I suddenly realized that the one or two wrong marked on the board had not been, as I'd thought, the average number of mistakes per student, but the *total* number of errors made by the *entire class!* I'm proud to say that for the rest of that year, I never missed another spelling word. It wasn't that I couldn't do it previously; it was that nobody had expected me to.

Now for a Little History

For over two centuries, America's schools have been educating and inculcating values in *two* broad categories of immigrants. One category, obviously, is that of the many people who come to this country every year to seek a new life. My wife was one of those. In her case, she arrived alone on America's shores on a ship from Sweden at the age of nineteen with $50 in her pocket and a job obtained by answering an ad in the *New York Times*. She can tell you the "American Dream" is no dream. (During a visit by her father, someone complimented Meg on "adjusting" so well to America, and her father, a very wise man, reminded her, with a wry smile, "It's not so hard when you adjust *up*.")

The second category, however, we often overlook: the children born into our families who "immigrate" into a highly competitive, globalized, fast-forward economy.

Infusing educational and character-building traits into young people has never been more challenging, or more important, than it is today.

Aiming High, Falling Short

America's business world tends to get the first real-world view of the young people who emerge from the educational pipeline. The young people whom executives encounter in business today are cause for both celebration and concern.

The best rank with the very best on earth, with world-class abilities in subjects ranging from the classics to calculus and from macroeconomics to microbiology. Such is the pace of advancement of knowledge that it is not unusual to walk through a high school science fair today and find a project that demonstrates a scientific principle that Nobel prize winners were struggling with only a few years earlier.

It is a sobering experience to try to explain to a high school student, born in the 1980s, the sense of excitement and wonder we all felt when the first moon landing occurred in 1969. They take all that for granted. And when you say that you got to see it *on TV* (in grainy black and white) straight from the surface of the moon, they wonder if you've still got rabbit ears on your set (or maybe on your head) and whether your favorite entertainment is watching the *Ed Sullivan Show* or *Leave It to Beaver*.

That's the good news. The bad news is that many of the graduates we see fall *far* short of this level of world-class accomplishment. More and more are simply ill prepared, not just for jobs and careers but also for the basics of survival in an advanced democracy and technocracy. We see less consistency and more polarization across the spectrum of educational preparedness, with ominous implications for the future of our country and its citizenry. In short, America's public education system is becoming increasingly bimodal. To paraphrase the Longfellow rhyme, "When it is good, it is very, very good. But when it is bad, it's terrible!"

Actual examples from the classroom front lines are dismaying, such as the comment by a student at Grover Cleveland High School in Los Angeles, who said, "You mean Cleveland High was named after a former president? I thought it was named after that city in Canada."

Lest we think that disoriented underachievers somehow magically become Einsteins by the time they reach college, a telling anecdote comes from a journalism professor who asked a group of undergraduates to identify certain terms and names every aspiring journalist should know. Among the responses received were that Alzheimer's is "an imported beer," Sandra Day O'Connor is "an actress on *L.A. Law*," and OSHA is "a killer whale at Sea World."

Is it any wonder that in a recent survey, a large fraction of adult Americans queried could not locate the United States on an unlabeled world map? Or that another survey revealed that a majority of Americans do not know that the sun and the earth are both in the Milky Way galaxy? Or that the dinosaurs were extinct for some 60 million years before the first humans trod the earth?

In 1992, the Educational Testing Service reported that nine of every ten U.S. students receive test scores below international *averages* in math and science. In a 1983–1986 survey of twelfth-graders in thirteen industrialized nations, the average score of U.S. students was lower than the average scores of students in all other systems in biology, nine other systems in chemistry, and seven other systems in physics. Results of the most recent tests, released in 1996, suggest progress: Our fourth-graders scored above the international average in both math and science, while our eighth-graders improved in science but remained slightly below average in math. But another survey, this one by the National Science Foundation, found that only one in ten Americans could define a molecule, and even fewer, about 8 percent, could describe in even rudimentary fashion how a telephone works.

Marketplace "Disconnect"

Perhaps these examples would be less disconcerting if the economy of the United States were still based on an early industrial model, where hard work, a strong back, and common sense could secure a decent job. But today's economy is unforgiving. As Peter Lynch, the prominent Wall Street money manager, recently observed, "Twenty years ago, you could get a job if you were a dropout. You could work a lathe, you could work a press. Those jobs are gone now."

Unfortunately, many of those who do graduate from high school arrive at the doors of industry unable to write a succinct business letter, fill out simple forms, read instruction manuals, do essential mathematical calculations, or understand basic scientific concepts. Just a few examples illustrate the enormity of the problem.

A major New York bank interviews forty applicants to find one who can successfully be trained as a teller; a major high-tech company, which previously accepted about eight of every ten applicants for entry-level jobs, today screens as many as fifteen to hire just one, and the company now requires only seventh-grade English skills and ninth-grade math skills; and, in a recent year, New York Telephone gave 23,000 applicants an entry-level exam—and 84 percent flunked.

Let me hasten to add, before I give the wrong impression,

that it's not solely math and science skills that are needed. There's every bit as great a need for communications, decision-making, and problem-solving skills, all of which are also taught on the liberal arts side of the aisle. Chapter 3, "Giving Value," recounts how incredibly well rounded was the great artist and scientist Leonardo da Vinci. Obviously, that's a near-impossible standard; nonetheless, more effort in the direction of that magnificent mix could greatly benefit today's students.

Surveys of our workforce at Lockheed Martin (as well as at other corporations) show that our liberal arts graduates bemoan their lack of even a rudimentary technical and scientific background, while our engineers fault themselves for what they consistently term their poor communciations skills, both verbal and written.

Given that today's economy is defined by constantly evolving technology, how can we expect high school graduates entering the workplace to understand the use of personal computers or numerically controlled machines? Instantaneous communications, advanced manufacturing techniques, worldwide marketing practices, a much more sophisticated capital formation system, and a much less forgiving legal system continue to increase the velocity of change to an extent unprecedented in human history and create a "disconnect" between much of our emerging labor force and the demands of a global marketplace.

A survey conducted as part of the 1992 National Education Goals Report suggests that many American graduates are not only unprepared for the twenty-first-century economy, but they are also blind to its implications. The survey showed that only 13 percent of Japanese workers believed their existing job skills would be "very useful" in five years. West German workers were a little more sanguine, with 35 percent feeling confident their job skills would hold up over five years. But 57 *percent* of American workers contentedly predicted continued relevance of their job skills.

This survey reminds me of the epitaph on the century-old tombstone I saw in Arizona's Boot Hill graveyard: "I was expecting this, but not so soon." Worse yet, in our case we seem not even to be expecting "it."

In a world of fiber-optics, robotics, bioengineering, space

telecommunications, microelectronics, and artificial intelligence, falling behind is a recipe for disaster.

How has our society been responding to this extraordinary challenge of preparing young people for an ever-more demanding economy? Generally, our response has been to give our kids more free time—to watch television! Surveys show that the average youth in America today watches 1,200 hours of television annually. The average high school *graduate* will have spent about 20 percent more time in front of a television screen than in front of a teacher. For better or for worse, and it could prove to be either, using the Internet is beginning to crowd in on those couch-potato hours.

Business Must Do More Than Just Apply Band-Aids

Now, given the state of public education today and the simultaneous market demand for higher-quality goods and services, one might ask what business has been doing in recent years to help take up the slack. The stop-gap answer is that both business and our institutions of higher learning have discovered the mixed blessings of "remedial education." A former University of Chicago chancellor summed up the situation this way: "We [don't] have the three R's in America, we have the six R's: remedial readin', remedial 'ritin', and remedial 'rithmetic."

According to the New American Schools Development Corporation, American businesses spend some $30 billion annually on the education of the current workforce. Most of this is remedial education, including basic literacy.

A recent article in the *Wall Street Journal* highlighted the McDonald's Corporation's training course for its new hires. In images reminiscent of an Army boot camp of fifty years ago, the program takes tens of thousands of teenagers each year—many from impoverished inner-city areas—and instills in them the rudiments of adulthood, including simple courtesy, proper clothing, hygiene, personal responsibility, enthusiasm, and discipline. Discipline—or the lack thereof—turns out to have been a major factor in the failure of many experiments in hiring the hard-core unemployed; once again, merely showing up *is* half the battle. As one McDonald's executive summed up the teaching program, "Whether we like it or not, it's a role we're thrust into." And I might add that it's a great national contribution by McDonald's.

If there were any doubts about the extent of the remedial education challenge, the recent news that the Harvard Business School would begin requiring incoming students to prove their mastery of basic writing and math skills before taking courses reemphasized the seriousness of the issue.

Waiting for the Cavalry

The blame for education's current problems is abundant enough for everyone to assume some share. One key factor in understanding today's difficulties is the appalling lack of consistency over the years as to what we want our educational system to accomplish. A professor of education at UCLA recently observed, "Education, like so many other social and human services, is beset by fads and quick-fix solutions. . . . But if we blame education . . . we need also to indict the culture at large, which is always looking for quick solutions to complicated issues."

But when it comes to repairing America's educational process, there is, once again, no cavalry that will come riding over the hill to save us. And the need to find solutions cannot wait. We should never forget, as we climb aboard an elevator or airplane, that the person whose design, manufacturing, or maintenance skills we are betting our lives on was very likely the product of our public school system.

The Business Roundtable has been running a series of public service messages on television that follow a theme illustrated by one showing an eight-year-old fastening an engine onto a model airplane. The announcer drones in the background, "This is Johnny. One day when Johnny grows up he wants to work on airplanes." Then, suddenly, the engine breaks loose and falls to the floor, just as the announcer says, "Maybe one day Johnny will work on an airplane *you* fly on." Other ads in the series show Freddy, who wants to build bridges, and Susie, who wants to be a surgeon—you get the idea.

Mixed Messages

As a society, we send highly mixed signals as to what we expect from our schools. As a recent editorial in the *Washington Post* pointed out, American students ranked nineteenth among industrialized nations in the number of class days attended. The typical U.S. school year is 180 days long, while "students in South Korea, Taiwan and Japan spend 220, 240 and 243 days of the year, respectively, in the classroom."

The editorial went on to note that parents "balk at the idea of putting off summer vacations for a couple of weeks. When the Polk County, North Carolina, school board tacked an extra month onto its school year in 1983, parents sued in court, lost, then launched an electoral campaign that ousted the board. The new board's first order of business was to return to the old school year."

Voters seem to be of two minds: wanting better school performance and being unwilling to shoulder the responsibilities inherent in meeting that goal. A school board in Half Moon Bay, California, actually voted on a proposal that would have abolished homework.

Part of the dichotomy with respect to the way we seem to view our public education system stems from the differing perspectives various constituencies hold with regard to the quality of education being provided in America's schools today. For example, a 1991 Lou Harris poll revealed that 78 percent of the students surveyed believe they read well. In contrast, only 67 percent of the parents believe that to be the case. Less than 30 percent of employers agree with this assessment.

Unlike most other countries, whose educational systems are highly centralized, ours is, of course, highly decentralized. In many other countries, curricula, textbooks, course content, standard teacher training, and salaries are all determined by a central governmental organization. In the United States, such decisions are made by state legislatures, state education departments, and more than 15,000 local school boards. We have a tradition of local control of schools, and most Americans, myself included, want to keep it that way. But this system can, if not carefully nurtured, lead to great disparity in quality among the schools that constitute America's public education system.

A Commonsense Prescription

Everyone concerned about American education, which *should* include everyone who is concerned about America, needs to continue to press forward on the initiatives already underway and to entertain further steps to improve education, most of which I believe would apply to any state or municipality seeking to improve its school system.

I am, of course, a businessperson, but I possess a citizen's concern about the future because, as the saying goes, that's where I plan to spend the rest of my life. I have seen the product of our nation's public educational system as a student, as a parent, as an employer in the private sector, as a government employee, and as a trustee of two universities.

I don't pretend to offer an expert opinion, but, personally, I have often fallen back on the time-tested axiom, "When all else fails, go back and read the directions." And in that sense, I would venture to offer some basic observations and recommendations:

1. Money is neither the problem nor the solution for our nation's K–12 educational problems. (We spend more per student than most other nations, and more than we ourselves were spending in the past.)
2. More studies of our educational system will not solve education's problems. Analysis *is* paralysis.
3. Business can, if it must, train skills, but it is too late to teach character.
4. Technology offers a partial, but only a partial, solution to the learning shortfall.
5. The primary solution to our current problems is to raise

academic standards substantially, verify achievement through rigorous testing, and have consequences.

You Can't Have Achievements Without Standards

The central point I would like to make is that if we want our public education system to be world-class, there is no substitute for rigorous, uncompromising, world-class standards of performance. Such standards must, above all, be measurable.

Standards are the *sine qua non* of virtually every human endeavor. Lou Gerstner, chairman and CEO of IBM, recently made the following impassioned plea on behalf of educational standards and accountability: "I have to confess I find the whole [issue of K–12 standards] baffling. In virtually everything else we do in the U.S., we set high standards and strive to be number one. Why not in education? In basketball, you score when the ball goes in the hoop, not when it hits the rim. In football, you score when you cross the goal line, not when you show up in uniform. In track and field, you must jump over the bar, not go under it and around it. And who would practice baseball with the fences 150 feet from home plate?"

To Lou's list of questions, I would add: Would anyone settle for a surgeon whose primary accomplishment was the person had tried hard? Would anyone step onto an airplane knowing it was designed by engineers who had a B average—A's in physical education and the study of religious cults but an F in physics? Every time I watch an astronaut climb into the space shuttle prior to launch, I think of the thousands of people at Lockheed Martin and other companies whose expertise and abilities are about to be put to the ultimate test.

In my opinion, national standards are badly needed; the laws of physics are the same in California as they are in New York. But at least for the time being, it seems that we can best concentrate on public education in those states where we are fortunate enough to have an aware and highly supportive constituency.

There are, of course, many other changes that would improve America's schools, including longer school days, longer school years, greater discipline, additional required courses, greater social recognition for teachers, greater parental choice, prekindergarten care, safe classrooms, increased focus on core subjects, incentives to reward teaching achievement, more emphasis on character education, day-to-day decision making at the operating level (including authority to hire, fire, promote, reward, and transfer), the elimination of assured lifelong employment, and the expectation that when customer goals are not met, you go out of business. Pretty imaginative stuff for a country built on the idea of the free enterprise system!

Remember the inspiring movie *Stand and Deliver?* It portrayed the story of math teacher Jaime Escalante and the barrio kids in Los Angeles whom he helped pass Advanced Placement tests in calculus. I see no reason why we could not have a Jaime Escalante story in every public school in America, and in fact in many we already do.

Reading the Signs

I said at the beginning of this chapter that I firmly believe one can learn valuable lessons for business and for life in general from participating in sports. The lessons I learned from playing sports have helped me a great deal in both life and business—with things like how to win, how to lose and bounce back, and how to get that last ounce of effort out of yourself when you think you have no effort left to give. This, too, is part of the educational process. You could call it character education. You could also call it leadership training—a subject that is rarely taught in the classroom but which permeates athletic fields.

I'm speaking here of *participating* in sports . . . not just watching them on TV. It's less important that one be a world champion—although that is probably nice—than that one step into the arena and try. And I don't mean to hold all aspects of today's athletes as positive examples. In fact, were I commissioner of sports, things would be a lot different. For example, clear cheating—like *corking* a bat—wouldn't just get you a four-day suspension. It would get you a start on your new career.

During World War II, President Roosevelt (whose magnificent new monument is being dedicated in Washington, D.C., as I write this) was asked by the major leagues if they should suspend baseball games for the duration of the war. No, insisted the President, the games should continue. Never mind that some of the best players were fighting their way across Europe or storming the beaches of previously little-known islands in the South Pacific. President Roosevelt said baseball was a fundamental part of American life and that it was critical for the nation's morale that major league play continue uninterrupted. And, of course, it did.

I believe that what was true in regard to the value of sports in this society fifty years ago is every bit as true today. Maybe even more so. Whether it's an amazing effort that results in a win, such as Tiger Woods's thrilling victory in the 1997 Masters golf tournament or a similarly amazing effort that ends in a loss—such as that put forth by "my" Washington Bullets, when they tried valiantly to resist the superior firepower of Michael Jordan and Co. in the first round of the 1997 NBA playoffs—we all come away with a renewed determination to improve the quality of our own efforts, and not just in sports themselves.

The following examples illustrate my belief that we can learn a great deal from athletics, especially if we know how to read the signs. (As Jim Bouton, the great pitcher, once said, "You spend a good piece of your life gripping a baseball, and it turns out it was the other way around.")

The importance of *teamwork*—one of the most critical ingredients of success in business—can be learned from participating in any number of sports. As I once observed, "Trying to defy gravity on a daily basis is very good for one's humility." Watching people you've come to know and care about ride aloft on a space shuttle launched by thousands of your employees is a little like coming out of the bull pen as a relief pitcher with the score tied in the bottom of the ninth in the seventh game of the World Series with the bases loaded and a count on the batter of 3-and-0. There is not a lot of margin for error.

Bob Uecker seems to have caught the essence of teamwork

when he said of his roommate Eddie Mathews, "Between me and my roommate, we've hit 400 home runs." Eddie Mathews, of course, had 399.

The next lesson we can learn through sports is *the value of quality people*. It's as important for a business to have extraordinary people as it seeks to challenge world-class competitors or place a spacecraft on Mars as it is for a baseball team to have talented performers as it tries to make up three games in September.

This point is perhaps best demonstrated by my favorite trivia question: "During his record-breaking home-run quest in 1961, how many times was Roger Maris walked intentionally?" The answer is "None." And the reason was that following Maris in the batting order was a fellow by the name of Mantle. No matter how good we are, we all look a little better when we have a legendary home-run hitter behind us.

Whether you are in the executive office, your cubicle, or the third-base coaching box, *motivating* your team to perform at peak levels is the most surefire way to win. As Vince Lombardi put it, "Those not fired with enthusiasm will be fired with enthusiasm."

The ability to *dig deeper*, to demand more and more of yourself and by doing so setting an example for those around you, is a priceless attribute. In the movie *Bull Durham*, Crash Davis, the crafty old veteran, advises that the difference between the minor leagues and the big time can be a dribbler through the infield or a Texas Leaguer once a week.

This business of toughing it out becomes particularly important when everything is going wrong, when you are dog-tired and then you get bad news. Every business manager can empathize with the hockey goaltender who said, "How would you like it in your job if every time you made a small mistake, a red light went on over your desk, and fifteen thousand people stood up and yelled at you?"

The history of sports is replete with instances where a team was being blown out but leapt out of the grave to produce an inspiring win. The same is true of business. And these are far and away the most rewarding wins one can ever have. When it seems that all is lost, think of the Houston Oilers in the 1993

National Football League sudden death playoff game, down 32 points at half time, who went on to beat Buffalo in overtime. As Churchill said, "Never, never give up."

Risk taking is also a clear requirement for success in both business and sports. Both astronauts and ballplayers can appreciate Tug McGraw's comment about being a relief pitcher: "Some days you tame the tiger, and some days the tiger has you for lunch." Or, as a stock-car racer—another sport that involves a lot of risk taking—put it, "You win some, lose some, and wreck some."

A *winning attitude* is critical in competing for business against all-star competition. It's also very much a part of sports. One baseball manager with an interesting slant on winning said, "You only have to bat 1,000 in two things, flying and heart transplants. Everything else you can go four for five."

Unfortunately, some teams, like some businesses, have attitudes that inevitably guarantee failure. A Pittsburgh Pirates coach once said, "I managed a team that was so bad, we considered a 2-and-0 count a rally." And a former Pirates manager knew he was in for a rough season when on opening day as the team lined up for the playing of the national anthem, he heard one of his players say, "Every time we hear that song we have a bad game."

Frank Robinson had a similar problem with one of the Indians teams he coached. "In Cleveland," he said, "pennant fever usually ends up being just a forty-eight-hour virus." But one of my favorite comments in this same vein was made by a hurler with a miserable won-loss record: "I'm working on a new pitch. It's called a strike."

Preparation and *discipline* are as essential in business as they are in sports. This is true whether you are firing a fastball 100 miles an hour past a batter or firing astronauts into space at 17,000 miles an hour to fly around the earth as human satellites (which is what Lockheed Martin did a few years ago with its Manned Maneuvering Unit, a rocket backpack for astronauts).

Any lack of discipline is a sure-fire formula for a short career in baseball, rocketry, or business. Witness the *former* NFL linebacker who said, "I'm a light eater. As soon as it gets light, I start eating." That's not the kind of hunger you need to make it to the top in business or in sports. Nor is the kind displayed by the very overweight Orlando Magic player who was described by his coach as thinking "a balanced meal is a cheeseburger in each hand."

Despite all the planning and preparation, sometimes fate—some call it luck—intervenes. It depends on how you look at it. After years of enormous success, our company once had two spacecraft fail within an hour and a half of each other, one in orbit around earth and the other approaching Mars some 212 million miles away. Consider the feelings of baseball player Cesar Geronimo. He had the dubious distinction of being Nolan Ryan's 3,000th strikeout victim only six years after becoming Bob Gibson's 3,000th victim. Cesar observed philosophically, "I was in the right place at the right time." But Tim McCarver's slant on luck strikes a responsive chord with me. Of the same Bob Gibson, he once said, "Gibson is the luckiest pitcher I've ever seen. He always picks the night to pitch when the other team doesn't score any runs." In business or sports, we make a lot of our own luck.

Two more characteristics shared by both business and sports are *competitiveness* and *performance under pressure*. There are times in business, as in baseball, when you have to slide head-first. To illustrate the need for day-in-and-day-out competitiveness, the legendary Lefty Gomez once said of the equally legendary Charlie Gehringer, "Gehringer is in a rut. He bats .350 on opening day and stays there all season." And Reggie Jackson, a somewhat more contemporary legend who's been accused of being *too* competitive on occasion, once said of his own performance during a game in Boston, "We needed an insurance run, so I hit it to the Prudential Building."

Competing in the *Real* Olympics

The title of this chapter refers to the Olympic Games. The reason for this is to draw a parallel with how hard Olympic athletes train. Does any athlete train to come in *twelfth* or *twenty-first*? Of course not. They all work toward the goal of being the best. The best in the entire world. Unfortunately, almost all of them will not reach that goal. Only one person in the world can be the best at any given individual endeavor. But in the pursuit of being the best, running faster or vaulting higher or jumping farther than anyone before, each one of those thousands of athletes will attain personal bests that they may at one time have considered impossible. And in the aggregate, the rising tide *will* raise all ships.

Let us not forget that long after any Olympiad is consigned to the history books, we will still be competing in the Real Olympics: sending our young people into the global marketplace to meet the best of Europe and East Asia and India and China and Mexico. What took place in Atlanta in the summer of 1996 was for pride and medals. What takes place at the Grover Cleveland School is for *survival*.

11

"Sociotechnology"

or The Challenge of the Machine in the Garden

This chapter deals with two topics that I think are terribly important in this high-tech age: the ability of the liberal arts–educated individual to cope in an era where everything except one's toothbrush is electronic (come to think of it, some toothbrushes do have motors), and the need to teach our engineers at least one language not including the software languages Ada or C++.

Today we take for granted that telephones work, skyscrapers don't fall down, airline travel is boringly safe, automobiles start, electric lights go on when you flip the switch, computers do not make errors in tracking your bank account, and televisions not only bring you more than 100 channels of programming but do so in virtually perfect color and at an enormous data rate (but too often with near-zero *information* rate).

But despite the many positive contributions of my original, and in a sense only, profession, and despite all the amazing technological innovations that are constantly being produced, many of the greatest challenges for engineers today come from nonengineering sources. And, increasingly, the challenges one meets in life, whether trained in the liberal arts or in engineering, are technology related. That's why I call today's age the "Socioengineering Age." To explain why, it'll be necessary to do a little time travel.

The View From 1897

I have a recurring dream in which two engineering graduates meet at the dedication of their alma mater's new engineering lab. One is from the class of 1897, the other from the class of 1997. In my dream, they're having a heated discussion about their respective experiences as engineering students. The old fellow from the class of '97 (*1897*, that is), who is by nature rather acerbic, apparently has not kept up with the times, professionally speaking. In my dream, I overhear parts of their conversation. Clearly there's a communications gap. In fact, there's a chasm.

The young engineer is complaining that although she likes her Macintosh, she has a problem with her mouse, and she goes on to say that her favorite academic pursuit is virtual reality, but that fuzzy logic was proving troublesome, as was artificial intelligence. She mentions that she is on her way to the electrical engineering lab to pick up some chips to take to her next class.

The old graduate is dismayed. In a rather emotional outburst, he asserts that if she would stay out of the campus pub, she wouldn't have problems with fuzzy logic and virtual reality. And, yes, he says, they *did* have artificial intelligence in his day. It was what they used to answer true-false questions on exams. Regarding the chips, he suggests that it was *her* logic that was fuzzy if she didn't know that neither the buffalo type nor the potato type is to be found in the engineering lab . . . and, as for the mouse, she should get a cat.

At this point in the dream, I begin to hope that the alarm will go off.

The View From 1957

I suppose you could say that my own engineering career traces its roots to the public schools of Denver, where my first action was to get myself expelled from kindergarten for misbehavior. I now gloss over the incident by saying I skipped a grade—in my case, directly into first grade a year later.

I recovered, at least partially (though my mother never did), from that inauspicious beginning and eventually decided, as I recounted at the beginning of this trip, to pursue a career in engineering. I still remember the day during summer break when my father and I scoured the pawnshops on Denver's Larimer Street in search of a slide rule that I could afford to take with me to Princeton (as with all scholarships at Princeton, mine was "need based," not "achievement/ability based"). When we failed in our search, I dejectedly concluded this must be a bad omen. My father, however, was obviously enthused. "Good news," he explained, "not many engineers have to hock their slide rules."

In those days engineers proudly displayed their status symbol: a holster clipped to their belt festooned with a K & E log-log duplex decitrig slide rule ready to engage any numerical challenge at a moment's notice—sort of a battle flag that separated us members of the clan from the unwashed, i.e., liberal arts students. The liberal arts students simply thought we were weird.

But in the coming millennium, liberal arts–trained persons *and* engineers had better understand each other if they plan to survive in the world (and business) they *both* inhabit.

Anyway, equipped with our slide rules at our sides, we could *calculate* things (unlike today's students, we were immune to power failures)—although, in retrospect, to have had a calculator that doesn't add or subtract or keep track of where the decimal point goes does seem a bit weird. At least that's what my son, another engineer, tells me. I tell him that at least all our mistakes were *big* ones! In any event, even that marvel seemed far superior to those thick books of logarithms that preceded it, and it was much more portable than the revolutionary new electromechanical desktop calculators of my early working days.

A few short years later, in my first job, I worked in a huge room seated in formation with several acres of other young engineers, all wearing short-sleeved white shirts and ties (but no jackets!). The building was actually the upper half of an aircraft hangar where a floor had been added, and it was so large that birds flew around inside it. (Our bosses weren't the only thing we had to look out for.) Each Friday afternoon, we would all ceremoniously greet the beginning of another weekend by simultaneously dividing by zero on our electromechanical calculators (at least those of us important enough to *have* calculators) and marching smugly out the door. Our hopes for a breakthrough in perpetual motion were dashed when, each Monday morning, we would discover that our bosses had unplugged all the machines, as they good-naturedly did each Friday evening to begin the celebration of *their* weekend!

In those days, a budding engineer was presumed to be *adorned* in a short-sleeved white shirt equipped with a plastic pocket protector holding six pens, all of different colors, plus, of course, the trusty hip-mounted slide rule. Often, safely tucked into another pocket would be a linen handkerchief, representing the remains of an engineering drawing that was to have been produced on a piece of expensive starched linen, that is, until it had met a premature demise late the night before with a splotch of ink (or, as I mentioned, there were the birds . . .). After a rinsing out, it became a quite adequate handkerchief.

Actually, these items were not *mandatory*, but if you did not display such symbols, the danger was ever present that you might be mistaken for one of those aforementioned pre–business school types who marched to such a strange oscilloscope—and who seemed to have so little to do with their afternoons.

In the fall of 1957, just as I was about to begin graduate school, the Russians launched *Sputnik,* and a whole new world was born. We were dismayed and shaken at the thought that the Russians had beaten us into space. Today, with the illuminating perspective of time, I realize that they did us a favor. They shook us out of a complacency that had engulfed us: the unquestioning belief that since we had the greatest country on earth, the world's most advanced engineering must be an entitlement. In short, they woke us up.

Along with that grudging sense of admiration for the Russian engineers, I soon became appreciative of the incredible good fortune I had to pursue an aerospace engineering career in that narrow sliver of time when humans first began to climb above our planet and explore what lay beyond.

Today that horizon is obscured by an accumulation of storm clouds. Since 1986, the number of engineers graduating each year in the United States has actually dropped—by some 19 percent, or almost 15,000 fewer engineering graduates. And while the United States has twice the population of Japan, we graduate 25 percent fewer engineers than Japan. In this country, starting salaries of engineers with a master's degree are substantially lower than what novice business school graduates receive. Comparisons with running backs and rock stars do not warrant the effort.

This brings me to the subject of where technology and the education of those who pursue new technology might be headed. In this regard, it seems to me that we have lived through four distinct technological ages and are now entering a fifth. Actually, each of these ages has had a beginning but no end. Each new one simply ran in parallel with the ones that preceded it, ebbing and flowing over the course of time. But for a true understanding of this new and quite different age into which we are now being propelled, we again need to look backward in time.

The Technological Ages

The Structural Age of Technology—From 2900 B.C.

For most of the history of the human race, building shelters and other physical structures that did not fall down was the primary engineering challenge. It was an age in which the principal enemy was straightforward; it was gravity.

During most of the Structural Age, education consisted simply of passing knowledge from one practitioner to another through apprenticeships, leading to a gradual improvement in technological skills through trial and error over a period of many centuries. But despite the lack of formal institutionalized education, the builders of several millennia ago achieved some remarkable feats, for which they were widely acclaimed. The fellow who designed and built the pyramid complex was an Egyptian named Imhotep. Like modern tourists, the Egyptians marveled at Imhotep's work, so much so that when he died, they put him in their pantheon of deities and worshiped him as a god. My son tells me *that's* the way engineers *should* be treated.

The Egyptians and others of their time were also quite adept at such things as building walls, aqueducts, and tunnels. Some historians believe that the walls of Jericho came tumbling down due to Joshua's army's digging caverns and vents beneath them and then lighting a fire that destroyed the excavation's wooden supports. And, of course, there were the Seven Wonders of the Ancient World, which, even ignoring the hyperbole of the day, were still remarkable engineering achievements.

One of the important lessons to be drawn from this period is that builders have to bear responsibility for their work. The Code of Hammurabi proclaimed that "if a builder builds a house and the house collapses and causes the death of the owner, that builder shall be put to death." No such thing as liability insurance in those days.

Perhaps the ultimate example of accepting responsibility for one's work, at least one's *construction* work, was embodied in the visionary Crystal Palace, built in London in 1851 by Sir Joseph Paxton. The design was said to have been inspired by Paxton's observations of the strength characteristics of the Amazon water lily. The building was iron-framed and consisted of 300,000 panes of glass, which gave the complex an airy openness that revolutionized architecture and building construction. But that very airiness also contributed to the fear that the structure was unsafe.

In fact, Prince Albert wrote a letter to a concerned dignitary, saying only half in jest, "Mathematicians have calculated that the Crystal Palace will blow down in the first strong gale; engineers [have suggested] that the galleries would crash in and destroy the visitors." Contributing to the general unease was the fact that iron railway bridges were in fact failing at the rate of about one in four during the period, and suspension bridges were periodically collapsing under the dynamic loads generated by marching soldiers.

To demonstrate that the "ferro-vitreous" structure, as it was called, would support the thousands of people who would visit it, Paxton undertook a series of extremely rigorous "practical tests," as he called them, which were recounted in a newspaper article of the time in the following fashion: "The first experiment," the article explained, "was that of placing a dead load of about 42,000 lb., consisting of 300 of the *workmen of the contractors,* on the floor and the adjoining approaches. . . .

"The fourth experiment—and that which may be considered the most severe test . . . was that of packing closely that same load of men, and causing them to jump up and down together for some time."

The Crystal Palace not only withstood the tests; it withstood the test of time, lasting until a great fire destroyed it in 1936.

A further lesson from the Structural Age was that a sound theoretical underpinning accompanied by experimental verification are the key ingredients of all sound engineering.

The Mechanical Age—From the Mid-1800s

The Industrial Revolution changed the world in the mid-1800s, marking a whole new era in the application of technology. It was during this period that engineering principles were formally applied to mechanical (moving) devices. The earlier waterwheel and the steam engine were among the first in a long series of powered machines that transformed the work that people performed, extending their reach and amplifying their muscles.

But with movement came complexity. The mechanical devices that characterized the period—the steam engine, the mechanical thresher, the cotton gin, the internal combustion engine, and eventually the gas turbine, the airplane, and so on— all required the interaction of moving parts and increasingly sophisticated materials. The goal of the Mechanical Age was to produce working devices that did not fail under repeated use; the principal enemy of the period was friction, and the major challenge was to convert various forms of energy into motion safely.

It was during this era, at about the turn of the present century, that one contemporary textbook insightfully began its chapter on mechanical systems with the simple pronouncement, "The horse is dead."

It was also during this era that there emerged a new school of thought that would have a major impact on a technological era still well into the future. Specifically, it was discovered that technological progress is possible only if the force applied is greater than the friction of occasional public opposition and the inertia of business as usual. The former aspect of this opposition was epitomized by the Luddites, who opposed advanced technology as a matter of principle and demonstrated their convictions by *smashing* new machinery—they believed machines would eliminate jobs.

It was during this era that Robert Fulton in 1807 attracted a large crowd to witness the first full-scale demonstration of the steamboat on the Hudson River. It is reported that as he tried to get the engine started, the crowd shouted, "It will never start!" When the engine finally did start and the ship took off with a flurry of sparks and heavy smoke, the crowd was silent for a moment, but only a moment. It then screamed in unison, and fear, "It will never stop!"

But among the most important legacies of the Mechanical Age was the recognition of the need to disseminate the accumulating body of technical knowledge better. Thus, the concept of a formal engineering education was born. The first institution offering such a curriculum was the French School of Bridges and Highways, founded in 1749 under that nation's military. By 1775, the standard engineering curriculum consisted of three years of study. America's first engineering school was at West Point, which, although founded as a military academy, devoted considerable effort to ensure that graduates were trained in so-called civilian technologies.

Other schools followed, offering formal engineering degrees in the 1830s time frame. Curricula generally followed the French model, that is, three years of study, still less than the traditional four-year course now required for a bachelor of arts degree. Unfortunately, in those days college was still a rich man's endeavor, and the engineering degree suffered the stigma of being a "practical art," which was often afforded less respect than was devoted to the loftier liberal arts. Even dining facilities used by engineers were segregated from those frequented by liberal arts students at some of the older institutions in the eastern United States, much as facilities for athletes are segregated today.

But as the quality of engineering education advanced, so too did the roots of skepticism over the value and viability of technology, roots that a century later would begin to have a profound impact on virtually all scientific as well as technological endeavors. George Washington Ferris was to discover this firsthand at the World Exposition of 1893. The promoters wanted an attraction that would surpass what the French had achieved with the Eiffel Tower four years earlier at their exposition. The fair director challenged local engineers to create something huge and magnificent to bring in the people. Various proposals were considered, including one grand scheme to buy the Roman Colosseum, tear it down, and rebuild it in Chicago. No doubt they even considered such preposterous ideas as moving London Bridge to, oh, say, Arizona.

In any event, Ferris, a local architect and bridge builder, like Eiffel hit upon the idea of building an enormous metal structure, but in this case one that would *move*. Some 265 feet high, more than four times as big as most Ferris wheels today, and capable of holding more than 2,000 people, Ferris's wheel opened on schedule and was an immediate best-(ticket)seller. More than one and a half million people flocked to ride it just in the interval of that one summer.

Critics, of course, staged a circus of their own, saying the giant wheel would keel over in the first of Chicago's gusty winds. Seemingly defying my theory of the nonbelligerency of nature, a storm packing 110-mile-per-hour winds soon approached the fair. Ferris decided to ride out the storm at the top of the wheel. He was joined by his loyal wife and a thoroughly frightened newspaper reporter, who later wrote, "The inventor had faith in his wheel. Mrs. Ferris had faith in her husband. But the reporter at the moment believed neither in God nor man."

The wheel performed flawlessly not only through the storm but also throughout the entire fair.

To teach students how to design and build such complicated structures, academic curricula from the era show that in addition to mathematics and physics, courses in metallurgy, chemistry, and applied mechanics made their way into a prospective engineer's studies. These were, of course, in addition to such established liberal arts courses as French, German, and English composition (pursuits that in a later era would largely disappear from the standard engineering education).

The ultimate examples of the Mechanical Age were the steamship, the railroad engine, the automobile, and the airplane. When you look back at the hundreds of years of experimentation, setbacks, and refinements that went into the mechanical processes that culminated in the first successful machines, you can't help but conclude that perseverance is another attribute that serves well those who would innovate and create, no matter what the century.

The Electrical Age of Engineering—From 1879

The one exhibit that overshadowed even the mighty Ferris wheel at the World Exposition in 1893 was the Electricity Building, which demonstrated this new phenomenon and its ability to power devices that produced mechanical force, heat, light, and even communications. Here was a source of energy that was truly convertible, transportable, and able to satisfy a wide variety of needs.

Today we tend to forget how controversial electricity once was. People were fearful that unused electricity would "leak out" of sockets and onto the floor, electrocuting anyone in the area.

The first flashlights were regarded by some as a sort of "witchcraft." Even Thomas Edison, the Father of Modern Electricity, had limited faith, calling alternating current "just a waste of time. Nobody will use it, ever. It's too dangerous . . . it could kill a man as quick as a bolt of lightning."

In spite of all these concerns, electricity was soon to be found everywhere. Great dams were built to generate it, complex power grids to distribute it, and sophisticated devices to use it. In the case of the airplane, about one-tenth of 1 percent of an aircraft's weight in the 1920s was devoted to electrical devices. By the 1940s, this had increased tenfold to 1 full percent. In the 1980s, in the case of military fighter airplanes, it had become 10 percent of the airplane's weight (and one-third of its cost).

Engineers learned that public reluctance to embrace revolutionary new technologies could be overcome if the applications of that technology could be made safe, reliable, affordable, useful, and, above all, user friendly (as opposed to user vicious). This latter point would be largely forgotten in another, not yet imaginable, period, which would follow.

The Information Age—From 1906

When Lee De Forest invented the vacuum tube in 1906, he unleashed a whole new realm of technological achievement, and the Information Age was upon us—albeit in its infancy. Advancing quickly from the vacuum tube to the transistor to the integrated circuit, these devices enhanced the human mind in much the same way that the Mechanical Age had magnified humankind's muscles. Interestingly, the two discoveries that laid the foundation for today's global village had their origin only three years apart: the airplane (which would rapidly move people) and the vacuum tube (which in another embodiment, the semiconductor, would process information rapidly). But as is so often the case, few people (if indeed any) realized the implications of the discoveries that had been made.

Technology, which had already rendered obsolete many of the tedious yet strenuous physical activities that had bedeviled humans for ages, was now moving into the realm of what might be called "cerebral engineering," freeing people of routine mental pursuits and vastly extending their thought capacity. In short, unlike earlier periods, the challenge of engineering was to process and move not *things* but *knowledge*.

The real breakthrough came when the transistor and, later,

the semiconductor integrated circuit were invented. The latter has profoundly changed the entire world—and has yet only begun to reveal its full impact. I have often thought that Bob Noyce and Jack Kilby, two friends of mine who invented the integrated circuit, though nameless to most people, may one day be judged by history as among the most important people to have lived in this century.

There is a certain irony that sand, the substance that made the modern electronic revolution possible, is the same material that humans had trod upon for some 2 million years, not realizing the potential beneath their feet. In much the same fashion, Theodore von Kármán, the great aerodynamicist, once compared the profile of a highly sophisticated airfoil that had been derived by the theoreticians at the National Advisory Committee for Aeronautics (the predecessor to today's NASA) supported by a bevy of wind tunnels, with the cross-section of a trout that Sir George Cayley had caught, dissected, and documented some 150 years earlier. The two profiles were virtually indistinguishable.

The lesson is that there are discoveries in science and technology all around us, just waiting to be unlocked, and that with each new discovery, we are left not with less to know but rather with more to access, almost as a nuclear reaction propagates itself.

Perhaps sooner than most people realize, it will be possible to carry a pen-sized device in your pocket that will enable voice conversation anywhere on earth. Individuals will also carry the equivalent of a huge library in their pocket or purse. But the greatest breakthroughs of the next couple of decades will very likely be the ability (1) to talk with our machines just like we talk to each other, and (2) to engineer new living things.

But when we realize that we are in only the first century of the Information Age and then extrapolate forward, say 500 years, about the time since Columbus visited America on his sailing ship, we can barely imagine the possibilities that lie ahead, assuming, of course, that we elect to pursue them. And this brings us to the Socioengineering Age.

The Socioengineering Age—From 1979

To a not inconsiderable segment of the public, the word *technology* conjures up images of Chernobyl, Bhopal, and thalidomide, *Exxon Valdez, Challenger,* and atomic bombs. Too often technology is perceived as the problem rather than the solution, as something to be broadly avoided and feared rather than something to be selectively embraced and controlled. But people cannot be expected, even when viewing the wonderful freedom the automobile gives them, to overlook the quarter-million automobile-related deaths these devices cause worldwide each year or the carbon monoxide pollution they produce. Even when recognizing the enormous enjoyment people derive from their television sets, they cannot simply disregard the impact television has on a generation of youth, who on average spend more time in a living room watching a cathode-ray tube than in a classroom watching a teacher.

And that is the challenge of managing technology—so that it doesn't manage you. Much of technology can be used for good or for evil . . . that choice is, of course, up to us, not to technology itself. Examples, in addition to those already noted, range from nuclear energy to pesticides and from rockets to petroleum. And another big genie may have just jumped out of the bottle in the form of bioengineering of humans.

If we were to search for a specific date as the beginning of today's increase in societal uneasiness over technology, we might choose March 28, 1979. On that day we witnessed the breakdown of the sophisticated controls that had been installed at the Three Mile Island nuclear power plant in Pennsylvania. Despite the fact that not a single person was killed and no one seriously injured in the Three Mile Island "incident" (engineers use words like that) and that, indeed, there were no external signs that anything unusual had happened within the confines of the plant, this event has had a profound, and in many respects constructive, impact on the American public's willingness to accept on faith every new innovation that scientists and engineers unleash.

The lesson from this new age is increasingly evident: In this modern era, scientists and engineers must become as adept in dealing with societal forces as with gravitational forces, and, candidly, up to this point I would not give us a passing grade.

Tomorrow's engineers must recognize that they are no longer constrained simply by the laws of nature, as was generally the case in the past, but also by the laws of the land. And they owe it to society to become far more adept at explaining the consequences—both good and bad—of their creations.

Questions for a Cautious Age

⊕ Could we send men and women to Mars? Technologically speaking, I believe we could. But politically there is at present no will to do so.

⊕ Could we build a supersonic jet transport superior to the Concorde? The answer is unquestionably yes, but the mood of the country has not significantly changed from the late 1960s when we opted out of the supersonic transport development race, probably wisely for the time, but for all the wrong reasons.

⊕ Could we vastly increase the amount of electricity generated by nuclear power plants in America, creating safe, nonpolluting power throughout the country? Almost certainly (as is in fact being done in Europe and, ironically, in Japan even today), but communities in America are still repelled by the notion of nuclear power, especially after the horrendous example of Chernobyl.

⊕ Could we build automated highways that would increase convenience and reduce automobile accidents? Absolutely. But who is to pay for them, and who is to insure their builders in today's litigious society?

⊕ Could we build a superconducting supercollider? Open the Alaskan oil fields? A ballistic missile defense against numerically small attacks? Almost certainly—if anyone wants us to.

⊕ Could we build a railroad through the Grand Canyon? Or perhaps a dam across it? Amazingly, both of these projects were once seriously considered and, fortunately, relegated to that file of very bad ideas whose time had not come.

The Tacoma Narrows Bridge did collapse. So did the walkways in the Kansas City Hyatt Hotel. The *Challenger* explosion still reminds us that technical skills, although extraordinary, are in the end still subject to human error.

Herbert Hoover wrote eloquently, some forty years ago, "The great liability of the engineer compared to men of other professions is that his works are out in the open where all can see them. His acts, step by step, are in hard substance. He cannot bury his mistakes in the grave like the doctors. He cannot argue them into thin air or blame the judge like the lawyers. He cannot, like the architects, cover his failures with trees and vines. He cannot, like the politicians, screen his shortcomings by blaming his opponents and hope the people will forget. The engineer simply cannot deny he did it. If his works do not work, he is damned."

In a sense, engineers were fortunate in the past, for they became accustomed to being measured by nature itself, an unwaveringly fair and consistent, yet unforgiving, judge. Today, in contrast, they are also judged by humans, with all the vagaries, special agendas, and inconsistencies that entails. But they still have a responsibility to society.

This leads to Augustine's Second Law of Socioengineering, with due apologies to Sir Isaac Newton: "For every engineering action, there is an equal and opposite social reaction." But this, like technology itself, is not inherently bad.

The time has arrived for the technologically literate to come down from the ivory tower and enter the arena of real-world debate and controversy and to help society understand *all* the consequences of what they can produce.

The practice of socioengineering (despite the fact that the very word makes many people uncomfortable) combines the elements of a traditional technical education with the far broader skills needed to survive and indeed prosper in the twenty-first century, skills ranging from such basics as written and oral communications to political science, economics, international relations, and, yes, even ethics.

It should be noted that this broadened concept of a technical education is necessary but not sufficient, as the mathematicians say, if humankind is to deal with the broad family of issues already confronting it. Many of these issues are steeped in techno-logical content, ranging from such challenges as energy production to transportation, from health care to environmental protection, from national security to economic competitiveness.

Importantly, there is a companion action that must be un-dertaken, and that concerns eliminating widespread technologi-cal illiteracy among many, even most, of those who were educated in the liberal arts and who hold high-level decision-making positions. Some even take pride in this form of illiteracy: the syndrome evidencing itself with statements beginning, "I don't begin to understand this technical stuff, but I hire . . ."

More than thirty years ago, C. P. Snow, the British scientist *and* novelist, was appalled at the lack of technological understand-ing on the part of much of the public. He would ask someone if he or she could describe the Second Law of Thermodynamics, and almost always got a negative response. "Yet that," said Snow, "is about the scientific equivalent of 'Have you read a work of Shake-speare's?' "

Only 5 of the 435 members of the U.S. House of Representa-tives hold engineering degrees. When last seen, there were none in the Senate and an equal number in the cabinet. Of the 50 governors, only 3 hold engineering degrees.

The danger to all when those to whom we entrust our well-being do not understand even the rudimentary technological as-pects of critical issues was noted by the late Isaac Asimov, who wrote, "Increasingly, our leaders must deal with dangers that threaten the entire world, where an understanding of those dan-gers and the possible solutions depends on a good grasp of sci-ence. The ozone layer, the greenhouse effect, acid rain, questions of diet and heredity—all require scientific literacy. Can Ameri-cans choose the proper leaders and support the proper pro-grams if they [themselves] are scientifically illiterate?"

In order to survive in the technologically driven twenty-first century, it will not suffice merely for engineers to be exposed to the liberal arts, although that will be very important. There will in fact be an equally compelling need for our universities to offer physics for poets.

It is one thing to be unable to program one's VCR; it is quite another to sit in the U.S. Senate and have not an inkling of what causes the greenhouse effect, what are the implications of genetic engineering, or what might have been the consequence of nearly losing a leadership position in the manufacture of dynamic random access memory devices.

A Missed Opportunity

If we are to have our leaders equipped with at least a nominal understanding of technology, and if we are to have numbers of engineers capable of leading in fields beyond technology, we must rectify one other failing of our technical education system. That failing is its apparent unattractiveness to women and minority students.

Women and minorities are grossly underrepresented in the ranks of engineering schools. To solve this problem, one cannot just look to the incoming freshman class; rather, one must look to eighth-grade math classes and even before. Engineering involves a highly hierarchical educational process—you can't take calculus until you have had algebra, etc.—such that, unlike law, medicine, and accounting, a student has to make a decision in the eighth grade whether or not to preserve the *option* of becoming an engineer. Too many decide not to (or, more often, default). And this is particularly true of women and minorities.

But it doesn't have to be that way. The legal profession, for example, has made significant strides in attracting women and, to a lesser extent, minorities. So too has medicine. One of my favorite stories in this regard concerns a business acquaintance of mine who practices law with the large New York firm of Skadden Arps. She has a son about five years old who has become quite accustomed to being surrounded by his mother's friends, most of whom happen to be women lawyers. On one occasion one of these friends asked the boy what he wanted to be when he grew up, and he promptly replied, "a garbage man." It seems that he had always been impressed with the giant trucks they drove and the clanging of the huge barrels they threw around. Continuing the conversation, the friend asked the boy if he might not like to be a lawyer. With a note of genuine surprise in his voice, he asked, "Can *boys* be lawyers, too?"

Well, that's progress. More or less.

Educating the Technologists of the Future

Drawing on the lessons learned from each of the five ages into which the evolution of technology seems to fit, what then should be the key ingredients of an engineering education for the twenty-first century? I believe there are eleven important elements worthy of attention:

1. *Emphasize the basics.* Despite the rapid evolution of technology, the primary emphasis of an engineering education should still be on the fundamentals—mathematics, physics, chemistry, thermodynamics, and the like.

2. *Expose engineers to the liberal arts*—especially history, government, geography, literature, economics, and ethics.

3. *Develop team skills.* The day of the brilliant loner is largely over insofar as engineering is concerned, if indeed it ever broadly existed.

4. *Teach the political process.* We must equip engineers of the future to understand public policy formulation and to present their cases in a balanced fashion in almost every forum imaginable—from town meeting to state legislature, from the *New York Times* to *Sixty Minutes,* from the Congress to the Oval Office.

5. *Develop communications skills.* Living in a "sound bite" world (the average network evening news sound bite is 17 seconds) engineers must learn to communicate effectively (and efficiently). If we put our trust solely in the primacy of logic and technical skills, we will lose the contest for the public's attention, and in the end, both the public and the technologist will be the loser.

6. *Place greater emphasis on systems engineering.* The modern field devoted to the integration of a variety of elements representing a combination of diverse disciplines has become known as "systems engineering," and has taken on steadily increasing importance ever since the 1950s. The implications for an engineering education in the twenty-first century would seem to be that all engineers should be exposed to at least some courses that teach systems engineering practices, particularly the practical, real-world aspects of the field.

7. *Understand the internationalization of human activity.* Marshall McLuhan's global village has arrived. (In fact, as I have noted from my unbiased perspective, it has largely been brought to us by engineers.) Technological innovation and commerce no longer recognize geopolitical boundaries, a circumstance that has profound implications for our economy and our society.

8. *Open the doors wide to women and minorities.* We must fully benefit from the technical talent represented by this larger body of individuals if we are to have any hope of remaining competitive on a world scale.

9. *Commit to continuing education.* College diplomas in technical fields should have an expiration date on them. Whether through refresher courses at a university or *in situ* continuing education courses at one's place of work, lifelong learning is an indispensable ingredient of a modern engineering education. It is also a personal responsibility of anyone who deems herself or himself a professional.

10. *Ensure that an engineering education is affordable.* A quality education is almost certainly one of the finest investments available today. Additional means of ensuring that qualified individuals have an opportunity to receive an education, should they want one, are essential.

11. *Adopt a five- to six-year course of study for the basic degree of the engineering profession.* The *de facto* recognition of the need for such a change is that the average undergraduate engineering education even today takes some 4.7 years. We should continue the current bachelor's degree program, but that should be equated to the education of a "paraengineer," much like a paralegal or a paramedic. The basic engineering professional degree should become the master's degree, and the entire curriculum should be revamped to center around that longer and more extensive program. There is simply too much material that needs to be added to the engineering curriculum to cling to the mindset of another long-gone era.

The Twenty-First Century

An engineering education that embodies these elements can, I believe, ensure that we will continue to generate into the next century technological progress capable of enhancing the lives of all humankind. To do so, we must learn to understand and work with the Second Law of Socioengineering, for our limits are no longer simply the laws of nature. They now include the nature of the law. The socioengineering education has already begun for many engineers—but it is largely being acquired the hard and costly way: through OJT (on-the-job training).

In the opening words of *Winnie-the-Pooh*, A. A. Milne wrote: "Here is Edward Bear, coming downstairs now, bump, bump, bump, on the back of his head, behind Christopher Robin. It is, as far as he knows, the only way of coming downstairs, but sometimes he feels that there really is another way, if only he could stop bumping for a moment and think of it."

The time has come for *us* to stop bumping heads and prepare to bring the profession of engineering into the twenty-first century.

12

After the Fall

If I were to write an entire book and not discuss the changes in the aerospace and defense industries—the industries I've been around for four decades—that have come about as a result of the fall of communism, my friends would wonder if I'd developed amnesia. As those folks know, it's a topic much on my mind. More important, it's a volatile and controversial topic, for in the defense and aerospace industries, the winds of change are still blowing mightily, and they will affect the future of our nation as well as the one and a half million people still involved in those industries. The question is: Will the winds be destructive, or will they propel us forward?

And it *is* a confusing world. I recall a rather distraught politician whom I once met in what was then Leningrad in what was then the Soviet Union. His curiosity over democratic political processes soon became apparent: He had just run for reelection unopposed . . . and lost! Like the Red Queen in *Alice in Wonderland*, we are asked to believe three impossible things before breakfast each morning.

Astride the Fault Lines of a Tectonic Shift

Turning first to the aerospace industry, let's examine the extent of this change. Consider for a moment the enormity of all that has transpired in just under 100 years. In less than a century, we have progressed from the Wright brothers' first tenuous flight at Kitty Hawk to the point where each day in the United States alone, the equivalent of the entire population of San Diego climbs on board commercial airliners and travels safely to their destinations. In fact, commercial aviation has become downright boring. Some say it now competes with Greyhound, but without the class.

The success of the Wright brothers helped spur other seemingly outlandish theories into reality, theories such as those of college professor Robert Goddard, whose early experiments with rockets in a Massachusetts cabbage patch gave way, almost a half century later, to the landing of Neil Armstrong and Buzz Aldrin on the moon.

Just how fast and how high the progress of the aerospace industry has been can be appreciated by looking at it this way: The entire first flight of the Wright brothers could have taken place *inside* the external fuel tank which I mentioned serves as the structural backbone of the space shuttle; and Goddard's famous rocket launch reached about half as high as the Apollo booster—while the Apollo was still sitting on the pad.

As a tribute to the amazing accomplishments of this field, some terms have entered the language as standards for purposes of comparison, as in, "You don't have to be a rocket scientist." And, conversely, one no longer hears people say, "You could no sooner do that than fly to the moon."

Why Should Anyone Care?

In a sense, the aerospace industry of today is paying the price for its past successes. There are people who wonder why we should build new airplanes when the ones we already have can carry passengers to many of their destinations in less time than it takes to go to and from the airport (*and* find their bags). During the era of the Cold War, many people argued that the government shouldn't buy the equipment the industry was making because it wouldn't work. Today, having experienced the Persian Gulf War, many of these same people now argue that the country shouldn't buy the equipment the industry produces because it works so well that we don't need any more of it! And there are people who look back at the Apollo flights to the moon and the planets and dismiss further investment in space, simply saying, "Been there. Done that."

Here's another ironic touch. The life expectancy of the unmanned spacecraft this industry builds for space exploration and for telecommunications is now so long that soon most of them will ultimately fail from technological obsolescence, not malfunction. Spacecraft built by Lockheed Martin have an average life span that is nearly *double* the life specified in their contracts, which in turn means that each time we sell a satellite, we are in essence giving one away free (the Little Caesar's Pizza of the space business). The two Viking spacecraft we built to land on Mars were designed to operate for sixty days. One lasted over six years (and finally failed owing to a human error in sending an incorrect command to the spacecraft). But the question remains, "Why should anyone *care* that America's aerospace industry has fallen on hard times?"

Not One, But *Four* Good Reasons

Here are four reasons why I believe every citizen should care about America's having a healthy aerospace industry:

First, the aerospace industry still provides employment, quality employment, to some 700,000 of our fellow citizens (only a decade ago it was more than 1.3 million). And the services and materials required by the industry create jobs for nearly another million people. (The *defense* industry, with which much of the aerospace industry is often lumped, today employs about 1.5 million people, as I've already noted.)

Second, when it comes to the balance of trade, within the manufactured goods sector, aerospace is America's largest positive contributor, with a net annual positive balance of $21 billion.

Third, new technology generated by the aerospace industry has improved the lives of people throughout the world. It was aerospace that made the world air transportation system a reality, created near instantaneous space-relayed communications around the world, and developed satellites, which permit accurate weather forecasting—to name but a few achievements.

Fourth, the aerospace industry is a cornerstone of national defense. In today's world, with technology so important and U.S. military forces so reduced in size (not many people realize that the United States now has the world's eighth largest army), it is no exaggeration to say that a healthy aerospace/defense industry is every bit as important to the nation as a healthy Army, Navy, Air Force, or Marine Corps.

Yet despite this extraordinary record, relatively few people outside the industry itself understand the extent of the crisis it has been facing.

I would never argue for spending money on national defense to preserve jobs. That is bad logic and bad economics. But I believe there are other important reasons to maintain a reasonable national defense capability.

And What About the Defense Industry?

In general, Americans have been reluctant warriors. The desire to avoid even preparing for the possibility of war has been prevalent throughout our history. Despite George Washington's warning in his first address to Congress that "to be prepared for war is one of the most effectual means of preserving peace," the size of America's army was reduced from about 11,000 in 1778 to a grand total, some six years later, of 80 soldiers.

Even our cultural icons reflect this basic aversion. Like the townspeople in the movie *High Noon*, we strenuously avoid conflict, are slow to react to obvious danger, and rise to defend ourselves and our allies only when it becomes unavoidable. But unlike the movie, we don't have Gary Cooper to call on to bail us out.

What's the Problem?

Why are we so reluctant to defend our interests in a sometimes brutal world? Perhaps it's because we are a nation whose heritage is one of immigrants fleeing persecution and violence, or perhaps it's because we have considered ourselves protected from the troubles of Europe and Asia by two vast oceans. Harry Truman characterized America as "not a warlike nation. We do not go to war for gain, or for territory; we go to war for principles."

Yet time after time, and despite our best efforts, we have found ourselves at war. Here's the all-too-predictable pattern:

Step One: The United States wins a conflict, having finally fielded a superior force, usually with the most numerous and, only recently, most capable equipment. Thus our country stands as a leader of the world's democracies, setting terms for the peace to follow.

Step Two: The prospect of enduring peace causes us to disarm to a point where our military capabilities become incompatible with our ambition to influence international events or to deter certain of those events . . . particularly without significant loss of life.

Step Three: Growing tensions among other peoples, leading to conflict, create frustration as we try, through moral suasion or economic pressure, to mediate disputes and change deep-seated attitudes.

Step Four: Belatedly, we respond to the increased international danger, only to be shocked by unexpected violence, such as the surprise attack at Pearl Harbor or the invasion of an ally, as in Kuwait or Korea.

Step Five: Finally roused to action, the country mobilizes to meet the now-unavoidable threat and, after the loss of precious lives, emerges victorious—only to begin the pattern one more time.

D-Day, by this analysis, was preordained. Our historic reluctance to recognize the need for a sustained, viable military has severely handicapped our fighting forces. Consider this century. In World War I, the majority of American troops reached Europe in British transports, fought with French and British artillery pieces, fired French ammunition, flew Allied planes, and manned French tanks. Of the 23,000 U.S. tanks on order, only 76 had been completed by the time of the armistice, *after* we had slogged our way from trench to trench across Europe and lost 117,000 lives in the process.

Following World War I, with the Weimar Republic crushed, the horizon looked remarkably cloudless. We reduced our military capability drastically, believing that we had fought "the war to end all wars." The fledgling aircraft industry saw 90 percent of its capacity disappear almost overnight. The country was eventually assured that through political maneuvering and diplomacy, we would enjoy "peace in our time." This, of course, proved tragically ephemeral as World War II unfolded against a backdrop of broken promises and repudiated treaties.

After losing more than 400,000 lives in World War II, we slashed our forces yet again. Barely five years later, we were nearly chased off the Korean peninsula by a third-rate military force. Historians have noted that our obsolescent projectiles simply bounced off the advancing enemy tanks. We had a new generation of tanks on the drawing boards, but very few of *any* generation in inventory. Scrambling to find *something* to repel the North Korean invaders, decommissioned M-26 Pershing tanks sitting on concrete pedestals around Fort Knox as displays were actually taken down from their mounts and shipped into combat. By the end of that war, the cost was 54,000 lives.

Oh, Oh, Here We Go Again

Today the familiar pattern appears to be happening once again. Step One was the demise of communism in central and Eastern Europe and the Soviet Union and the victory over Saddam Hussein and his forces in the Persian Gulf. Step Two was the precipitous cutting of the defense budget, which has caused procurement dollars to plummet by over two-thirds in real purchasing power since the mid-1980s—almost 80 percent in the case of the Army—and brought defense spending, as a percentage of gross domestic product, to its lowest level since just before Pearl Harbor. In business terms, our armed forces are now on a fifty-four-year equipment replacement cycle—in a world with a two-to ten-year technology cycle. Step Three was recently suggested by the respected British publication *Jane's Defence Weekly*, which counted twenty-seven military conflicts in the world, twelve "flash points," and thirty-one "areas of tension."

Step Four—the halfhearted buildup to overcome earlier excessive reductions in order to deal with an emerging threat—is not yet here, but we would be unwise not to heed the lessons of the past. In the words of General Norm Schwarzkopf, "If someone had asked me on the day I graduated from West Point where I would fight for my country during my years of service, I'm not sure what I would have said. But I'm damn sure I would *not* have said Vietnam, Grenada, and Iraq."

A haunting reminder of the nature of the world we are entering was suggested by the Indian minister of defense, in his comment that the real lesson learned from Desert Storm is: "Never fight the Americans without nuclear weapons." And the really tough part is that the military equipment we are developing today will largely fill its role in carrying out whatever might be the U.S. global objectives in the 2010–2030 time frame; objectives, if history is any guide, are very difficult to foresee. In my own observations of the world political scene, I have noted a certain "rationality" at work: Nations that are strong set the agenda; nations that are weak get swept along in someone else's agenda.

A Word to the Wise

Some people dismiss these and other hypothetical events as being so remote that they should be disregarded—and they may even be right. But who among the world's leaders could have predicted the assassination of Archduke Ferdinand; the attack on Pearl Harbor; the invasions of Korea, Kuwait, Afghanistan, and the Falklands; or a host of other unexpected eruptions over the past century? Speaking of the post–Cold War world, Margaret Thatcher observed, "The ice is most dangerous when it's breaking up."

Today many people seem to believe that military conflict has become passé. Not long before World War I, a young Winston

Churchill confronted a similar sentiment that was prevalent in his day. He wrote, "War is too foolish, too fantastic, to be thought of in the twentieth century. . . . Civilization has climbed above such perils. The interdependence of nations in trade and traffic, the sense of public law, the Hague Convention, liberal principles . . . have rendered such nightmares impossible."

After stating this popular view, Churchill then mockingly—and, unfortunately, presciently—added, "Are you quite sure? It would be a pity to be wrong."

Here's some fairly recent editorial wisdom from the *New York Times:* "[After the success of Desert Storm, it's obvious] U.S. weapons systems are unrivaled, so production of new tanks, planes, and ships can be put off for a decade or more." Sound familiar?

What is so often overlooked is that in this era of the "come-as-you-are" war, where outcomes can be determined in days, the only equipment our forces will have will be that which was planned for and acquired years earlier. The systems that performed so well in the Persian Gulf War represented the technology of the 1960s, the development of the 1970s, and the production of the 1980s—all utilized by the people of the 1990s. To a considerable extent, the decisions of the 1970s determined the casualties suffered in the Persian Gulf in the 1990s. The decisions made in the 1990s will very likely determine the extent of any casualties we might suffer in the 2020s. As historian Donald Kagan wrote, "Peace does not preserve itself."

Some Swords Don't Seem to Want to Be Plowshares

Five years ago, Ken Adelman (former director of the U.S. Arms Control and Disarmament Agency, a professor of Shakespeare, and a syndicated columnist) and I wrote an article for *Foreign Affairs* that began: "The record of massive defense conversion is one unblemished by success." For the most part, that remains true today . . . but there are some notable exceptions based on new approaches to so-called defense conversion.

In our article, we mentioned two major exceptions from the past, "the defense-dominated economies and mammoth military facilities of Japan and Germany, which were converted into civilian production after World War II. Then, the two defeated powers were militarily occupied, their defense industries were immediately destroyed and new industries built with extensive foreign aid; now, decades later, both countries enjoy economic prosperity."

The situation could hardly be more different in the former Soviet Union and Eastern Europe following the fall of communism. In the case of these nations, there is no benevolent conqueror standing by to level the landscape of defense-oriented industries, to help them follow the biblical admonition to turn their swords into plowshares.

Ken Adelman and I did original research for our article in *Foreign Affairs*. As we wrote, "In our travels throughout the one-time communist countries—talking to plant managers, workers, academics and government officials alike—we came to sense the staggering obstacles they confront." The greater these obstacles appeared relative to anything known in the West, where defense conversion has until now largely failed, the darker their prospects seemed.

Even before communism fell, the occasional Soviet attempt to convert a plant from weapons of destruction to something, anything, "benign" did not go well. For example, when Mikhail Gorbachev ordered the plants that had been producing nuclear weapons to start manufacturing cheese-making equipment, they made a mighty attempt. The orders, for ten units, they handled with relative ease, but when, within weeks, they received orders for 2,300 units, the plant manager threw up his hands, "Of course we are now somewhat bewildered." Similar (mis)-matches produced rumors, within the international defense industry, of childrens' sleds with titanium runners and of gasoline refineries turning out somewhat suspect champagne.

Back in Khrushchev's day, he bragged the Soviets could make rockets like sausages. Recently the Iuzhmash factory tried to convert to doing that, literally. Its chief engineer reported,

"Our first 30 sausage machines fell apart." A much better result was obtained by the Znamya Truda Plant 30 in Moscow, which went from making MiGs and transport planes to making the Il-114 civilian airliner. One snafu: Along the way they tried to ease the transition by building industrial-strength juice processors, but all they produced were lemons (pun intended).

The study that Ken and I made came up with one main message regarding defense conversion: Bulldoze the corporate culture.

Home Remedies

In Re Aerospace

So after we have provided for whatever level of military-industrial base our national leaders decide is needed here in the United States, what do we do with the part that is left over? Better to ask, what are we already doing?

Some people said the answer is to do nothing, hunker down, and wait for things to get better. I say, forget that. The "let's-wait-and-hope-things-get-better" strategy always reminds me of baseball player John Lowenstein who, when asked what changes might improve the game, answered, "Move first base back a step to cut out all the close plays."

As for quickly diversifying into consumer products, we've tried that. Here's the opinion of several people who know what they're talking about, mainly because they've done what they are talking about.

"We've learned our lesson," says John McDonnell, then the CEO of McDonnell Douglas. "In the late 1980s, I was the prime advocate of diversification in the company; now I'm the prime advocate for aerospace."

Renso Caporali, the CEO of what was then the Grumman Corporation, agreed. Asked why his company didn't invest more in converting to other product lines, he replied, "We've already watched that movie twice." (If he'd run it backward, it might have had a happier ending.)

And Wolfgang Demisch of BT Securities, in my opinion one

of the most perceptive aerospace analysts on Wall Street, says, "The idea of defense conversion is a fraud. It's basically been hype from the beginning." (That may be a *little* overstated, but not by much.)

Some people argue that the practice of defense companies' buying companies not in the defense business is diversification. For example, until recently when it sold the business, Lockheed Martin was the nation's second-largest producer of crushed rock. Owning this business had increased our range of products from rockets to rocks, so it was truly a diversification, and a very profitable one at that. (My favorite part of the business was that we never had a rock blow up.) But, to be candid, our being in the aerospace/electronics business brings very little value-added to the rock business. Nor does the rock business add much to the arsenal of democracy.

But diversification *is* important, and it *can* be accomplished successfully, but it has to be pursued very deliberately and over a number of years. There are no quick victories to be had here.

The leaders of the defense industry were thus faced with a dilemma: There was not enough work left in defense to keep most companies alive, and the record at diversifying outside of defense was at best dismal. To quote Woody Allen: "More than at any time in history [we] face a crossroads. One path leads to despair and utter hopelessness. The other, to total extinction. Let us pray we have the wisdom to choose correctly."

Okay, Then What *Is* the Solution?

Here's my bare-bones prescription: *First, the defense industry needs to do those things it does well. This requires becoming efficient in its core business by building market share through consolidation and then downsizing. Second, the industry should move into adjacent, that is, closely related commercial markets.*

In Re Defense

Obviously the world is not yet a peaceful place, and I suppose that some people would expect me, as a defense industry executive, to call for more spending on defense. But I would be the first to argue that the end of the Cold War has fundamentally changed the nature of the threat and that America should never spend money on defense simply to preserve jobs. It's clear that in the post–Cold War world, America can afford to shrink, safely, its defense posture. And we are doing that, having laid off the one-millionth defense worker some three years ago. And there *was* in fact a substantial peace dividend. The problem is that the growth in the rest of federal spending ate it up. (We now spend more on interest on the debt than on defense.)

What America should spend on defense depends entirely on the national objectives we wish to embrace (and, importantly, forgo) and what risks we are willing to take.

I would note with some concern that we seem to be in the process of inventing a new type of hollow military force, one whose funds for modernization are so out of balance with the size of the force that it will ultimately find itself ill equipped, just as in the past we have built forces that were ill trained or ill supported. But choices regarding national objectives and risks are the province of government policymakers acting on behalf of the American public, not of industrialists.

In Re Diversification

Defense diversification of a type different from that pursued in the past can in fact be successfully implemented by following four straightforward rules:

1. Engage in high-tech products matching one's core competencies.
2. Focus on large customers, such as corporations and governments.
3. Concentrate on markets where new demand is being created as opposed to markets saturated by established competition.
4. Move deliberately over a period of time.

Most importantly, stay away from consumer products, a market that entails everything the industry doesn't understand.

Take Ike's D–Day Advice

I can think of no better advice than General Eisenhower's order that launched the D-Day invasion, the most massive military action in history: "Okay, let's go."

AROUND THE WORLD IN EIGHT DAYS, IV

The Time Newstour flight to Vietnam took us across the southern part of India and the Bay of Bengal, across Burma, Laos, and up the Tonkin Gulf to Hanoi. The last time I had flown along the Tonkin Gulf off North Vietnam was in the fall of 1967 when I worked in the Johnson administration for Secretary of Defense Robert McNamara. I never in my wildest imagination expected that I would be landing in Hanoi one day, or that if I were to do so I would be anticipating a reasonably cordial greeting.

Today, U.S. relations with Vietnam hinge on a number of counterbalancing factors, including the POW/MIA issue, human rights, business opportunities in a booming region, and the need to maintain a balance in Asia among China, Japan, and such other countries as Korea, Malaysia, Vietnam, Taiwan, Singapore, and Thailand.

Communism is still, of course, the government "of choice" in Vietnam, and the party controls the political system tightly. In contrast, the economy is being opened to a degree not seen in years. This cutback in central control has led to burgeoning economic growth. Change is evident everywhere. Ho Chi Minh City, formerly Saigon, is far surpassing the more rigidly controlled Hanoi—much to the chagrin, I am sure, of Vietnam's victorious leadership in the North.

Shortly after landing—in heavy darkness and slightly overcast weather—we were reminded of what it was like to be back in a communist country. Until our arrival in Vietnam, our encounters with customs had been totally uneventful. We had simply walked on and off our aircraft and gone about our business. No so in Hanoi.

Actually, we did okay with customs and immigration. Our problem was that the gentleman in charge of the "opening-the-gate department" of the airport wouldn't let us out! It developed that the Gate Opening Bureau had not properly coordinated with the airport authority, so they were a bit out of joint. I later learned that a few boxes of the Cuban cigars we'd been given by Castro played some part in our eventual release, but I decided it was best not to pursue the matter.

I was up before the alarm—set for 5:30—and went to the lobby in search of breakfast. I wandered across the street where a small park was located in front of the government compound. It was crowded with people doing their morning exercises, which are quite different from what we (or at least *some* people, like my wife, for example) do in America. Where we Americans tend to do a lot of jumping and flailing about, the Vietnamese exercises are more like the Chinese, with slow, contortion-like movements.

Our day in Hanoi officially began with a (second) breakfast, this one with a number of businesspeople from the Vietnamese and the expatriate communities. We were told that there was little residual adverse feeling toward Americans in spite of the long war (an assertion we later confirmed). In contrast, there was said to be outright hatred of the Japanese because of the cruelty they dispensed when they occupied Vietnam during World War II. Also, there was still evidence of a residual dislike of the French because of their occupation following that war, and the Russians were disliked because they were, as it was explained to us, Russian. The Chinese were *feared,* largely because of their overbearing presence as a next-door neighbor. We were told that the Americans were the only ones who ever went to bat for *any* Vietnamese, even if we had done so for, in their view, the *wrong* ones. Apparently our good intentions, albeit again in their view improperly directed, were enough to make us acceptable to these northerners.

Next on our schedule was something listed as a "cyclo" ride. The cyclo, which is the basic taxi in Hanoi, turned out to be a three-wheeled contraption with two wheels in front plus a bench seat big enough for just one person, and the rest being the back half of a bicycle where the "engine" is located—that is, the peddler, who does all the work. Soon we were hurtling down the street in a caravan of thirty "CEO-clos," and were immediately engulfed in chaos.

It was as if we'd been dropped precipitously into the middle of an anthill. Along with the hordes of cyclos, there were a few small trucks, thousands of bicycles, and a number of motorbikes, the last a recent addition to the chaos that signaled the owner's affluence. Right-of-way belonged to the least intimidated.

Each street was lined on both sides with tiny stores that doubled at night as homes. One street would be filled with sheet metal shops, another with food stores, another with paper goods, and still another with carpentry shops. Bordering the street was a ten-foot-wide sidewalk upon which most of the community's daily life took place, including such activities as cooking, bathing, barbering, socializing, and bartering. At night, straw mats placed on the shop floors served as beds. I could have stood for hours in total fascination watching the activity—all of it punctuated by the bleat of motorcycle horns and the jingle of bicycle bells. I felt much as I did standing on top of the Berlin Wall during the Cold War or on a street corner in China during my first visit in 1978—I just wanted to drink it all in.

After lunch, we boarded our buses for a forty-five-minute drive to visit a small farming village. In the center of the village was a pagoda, where a ceremony had been arranged so that we could take part in the presentation of gifts to the appropriate gods. Although the structure looked like the Buddhist temples in Japan, China, and Thailand, we were told it was actually Taoist. The women were all dressed in long yellow dresses, and the men wore uniforms that dated back to the eleventh century.

In the background was the same extraordinary flute and drum music I'd first heard at the opera in Beijing nearly twenty years earlier, and had found so fascinating with its strange whines and drumbeats. On that former trip, I'd been somewhat disconcerted to learn that the Chinese characters on the large red banners that flanked the stage at the theater we were visiting in fact read, "Kill the capitalist running dogs."

When we finally got back to our hotel, we had all of twenty minutes to shower and change clothes, yet that proved to be one of the highlights of the trip, given the heat of the day and the length of our travels. It was almost as good as when I had visited the U.S. Antarctic Station on the way to the South Pole, where each person is allotted two minutes of shower water a week.

Late that afternoon we went to what is, in effect, Vietnam's White House for a "discussion" with Do Muoi, the General Secretary of the communist party of Vietnam. I put the word in quotes because it was a most unusual interchange (and, as you will see, that isn't the right word either).

The seventy-four-year-old Do, the most powerful person in Vietnam, entered the room and slowly circled it, shaking everyone's hand but saying absolutely nothing. Not just no small talk, but *no talk*. He was wearing a Mao suit, the first one I'd seen since the trip to China in the 1970s.

Do took his seat at one end of the long, narrow, and elegantly appointed (mostly in red) room and stared at us in silence. After an awkward period of time, an aide said Do would take questions, so someone asked a question. The communist leader sat expressionless. When the question was repeated, it was followed by another awkward silence. Eventually the interpreter said we should proceed with *all* our questions and that Do would answer them at the end! (Hmm, I thought. Could I try this on Evelyn Davis at the next Lockheed Martin stockholders' meeting?)

When Do finally did begin to speak, of course through an interpreter, which complicated things even further, he spoke slowly and in a monotone for an hour and a half. Instead of answering our questions, he basically gave us a lecture on the condition of Vietnam, and soon I could see that many in our group were struggling not only to hear but simply to stay awake.

I managed to figure out that Do believed Vietnam suffered from three major problems: social inequality, the economic gap between the rich and the poor, and declining moral standards. He wasn't kidding about the economic gap. One of our group told us later that his company had explored the possibility of building a factory in Vietnam and found that the hourly wage was thirteen cents plus transportation, breakfast, and lunch. (He decided to build the factory in China, where the cost at the time was eight cents an hour.)

Mercifully, the meeting came to a close just short of two hours after it had begun, and we left the building puzzling over the apparent contradiction that was involved: Communist ideology still seemed to pervade Vietnam's leadership while capitalism flourished in its streets.

That evening was our first unscheduled moment, so a group of us walked the five blocks to the Metropole Hotel (having determined ahead of time that its dining room did not serve dog) and had a thoroughly enjoyable meal.

I had trouble sleeping (the night before I'd found mouse droppings under my pillow) and was up an hour before the 6:00 A.M. departure time, but it turned out my night had been downright restful compared to that of those on the tour who'd gone nightclubbing. They'd ended the evening drag-racing down the streets of Hanoi—in cyclos! It was rumored that the drivers were "adjusting" the outcome of the races to factor in the monetary incentives being slipped to competing cyclo drivers to slow down. The entrepreneurial drivers made enough money to make them eligible for early retirement. (Apparently there are limits to ethics!)

And some people say CEOs aren't generous!

⊕   ⊕   ⊕   ⊕   ⊕

Friday the thirteenth, in Hanoi! Lucky I wasn't superstitious—and that I had my rabbit's foot with me. This time our passage through the airport was uneventful, although a few more boxes of cigars disappeared. There was no sign whatsoever of customs or immigration, and our old nemesis, the gatekeeper, was nowhere to be seen.

All the people we had met in Hanoi, with the exception of Do and the gatekeeper, were both cordial and seemingly devoted to dragging the nation's economy into a new era. If their political system doesn't do them in, it seemed that the energetic people of Vietnam have a good chance of making it. This was in sharp contrast with the impact that communism has had in Cuba, where the people appeared to be utterly defeated.

The flight to Hong Kong was only one hour and twenty minutes long, and we were told that there would be "some weather" upon our arrival. This could make for an exciting landing given the approach to that city, which even in good weather is an experience. Planes descend virtually alongside the skyscrapers.

Like all of the other places we visited, Hong Kong was undergoing its own transition. Specifically, the British lease of the island that had been granted for a period of ninety-nine years would expire in July 1997. At that point, ownership of the island would revert to China, a prospect that was causing a good deal of consternation among the Hong Kong citizenry. Some 300,000 Hong Kong citizens had already emigrated, and another 1.5 million had made the necessary legal arrangements to flee should the need appear. Hong Kong thus had the distinction of being the only country we visited on our tour that was proceeding in a direction *away* from capitalism and democracy to some unknown system overseen by communist rulers.

Our approach into Hong Kong, although in a moderate fog, was uneventful (the *only* kind of landing; I know—I once had the other kind in a small jet that ended up in a snowbank!), and we promptly cleared customs and headed to Kowloon to attend a luncheon at which the speaker was to be Tsang Yok-sing, the head of the provocatively named "pro-Beijing party."

His presentation after lunch was absolutely unfathomable, an oriental mystery wrapped in an enigma. He argued in favor of communism and for support of the Beijing government; however, he said that China needed to move toward democracy. He admitted that the thing that had made Hong Kong successful was capitalism and then professed that capitalism was not inconsistent with Marxist beliefs. We ferreted out during lunch that, despite the fact he'd said he was "more communist than the communists in China," he

drove a Mercedes 300E. Dismissing our protestations, he explained, "Marx never said you could not drive a Mercedes!" It had
recently become public that his wife and children had applied for
emigration visas to Canada—"Hongcouver," as he put it—just to
hedge their bets when the Chinese government took over.

On Saturday, October 14, we attended an early breakfast
meeting at which the British Governor of Hong Kong, Christopher
Patten, was our speaker, and he was absolutely outstanding. Patten
is the last British governor of Hong Kong, a distinction he did not
particularly seem to relish. He began his remarks by pointing out
that Hong Kong is where the British Empire ends, and he con-
trasted other decolonizations with that occurring in Hong Kong by
pointing out that in all the other instances, the British had handed
the countries their own independence. Hong Kong was to be the
unfortunate exception.

He went on to describe Hong Kong as a city of 6 million people
with no natural resources and made up entirely of refugees, yet
which had produced a GDP that was 26 percent of mainland China's and had become the eighth largest trading community in the
world. He said that in contrast with earlier eras, technology was
now making totalitarianism impossible. The key question would
be whether rulers could open a country economically but maintain
a grip politically.

We lifted off from Hong Kong at 11:00 A.M., and our route
home took us over Taipei, Taiwan, and into Sapporo, Japan, for a
refueling stop. About an hour out of Sapporo, we flew over a vol-
cano that had erupted a few days earlier and was still spewing
smoke, ashes, and molten lava.

When flying eastward at just under the speed of sound, there
is, of course, a considerable "time compression" due to the continual crossing of time zones. Anyone who tries to squeeze in three
meals between each period of darkness, as we had been trying to
do, is eating continuously. (That evening I overheard someone ask
a flight attendant, "What does hunger feel like?" We finally prevailed on the attendants to show mercy and eliminate a couple of
meals so that we could sleep.) It seemed as if we had been flying
forever. At one point, after eight hours of flying, I remarked to the
person across the aisle from me, "Just think, we'll be home by this
time tomorrow," and everyone groaned. Tomorrow seemed an
awfully long time away.

Paradoxically, we were in the ninth day of our eight-day trip
around the world. This, of course, was the very problem—or,

rather, solution—that the travelers in *Around the World in 80 Days* had encountered. We had, of course, crossed the international dateline and thus regained a day, having celebrated Saturday, October 14, for the second time.

As it happened, that day was the birthday of one of our journeying journalists, an event we had celebrated in-flight the day before with champagne, cake, and the flight attendants' leading us all in singing "Happy Birthday." As we crossed the international date line, the birthday boy demanded that we do it all over again. But he gave up on the idea once we explained that if we did so it would make him not one but *two* years older. (It's part of Einstein's theory.)

Having flown through yet another night, the second night in a row on this leg of the flight, we finally landed at Anchorage, Alaska, at 6:00 A.M. in darkness and with the temperature hovering slightly below freezing. U.S. customs required us to take everything off the airplane, pass through inspection, and then reload everything, including all the baggage in the hold. Over two hours were consumed. Finally, we reboarded the aircraft and continued on to Chicago, where I separated from the group, most of whom went on to New York and then scattered from there. I finally returned to Washington, D.C., around 8:00 P.M. Saturday night.

⊕   ⊕   ⊕   ⊕   ⊕

Our trip had covered 30,000 miles in just eight days, and we had touched down in nine countries, having flown over a dozen others. We spent forty-eight hours onboard the L-1011 aircraft, which performed flawlessly, I might add, and another twelve hours in transit to and from airports, although these were often educational hours in their own right. Each of us felt that we must have eaten several hundred meals and talked with dozens and dozens of people, ranging from people on the street to the senior political leaders of the countries we visited.

At the outset of our trip, we'd been told that we were all "journalists" and that we had to "think and act like journalists." Trying to do that turned out to be a once-in-a-lifetime experience. Without any doubt, I'd learned more in this week than in any other single week of my life.

The beauty of the trip was that there was no schedule on which business had to be transacted, almost no interruptions from telephone calls, and no one to persuade of anything. We merely asked a lot of questions to gather the news.

Most of the honorary correspondents felt that the "lead" (as we *journalists* call it) would clearly have to be that communism is in retreat almost everywhere, and even the most ardent of the remaining communists are embracing capitalistic principles, albeit not always in entirely recognizable forms. Many of these hard-liners are simply declaring victory and calling whatever it is they are now promoting "communism." The only problem with our overall conclusion was, as we were told by our more legitimate news brethren, "That's not news."

To me, the bottom line (correction, "wrap") to our trip was that although there has been a plethora of writing during the twentieth century about how to convert from capitalism to communism, no one had thought to write the book on converting communism to capitalism, which has to be the ultimate irony.

And that, as we say in the journalism business, is

—30—

Epilogue: The Next Journey in Augustine's Travels

On April 18, 1997—two days ahead of when we had planned to do so—we rushed out a three-and-a-half page corporate press release headed: VANCE D. COFFMAN TO SUCCEED NORMAN R. AUGUSTINE AS CEO OF LOCKHEED MARTIN CORPORATION.

Here are a few sentences from that release.

"The Chairman and Chief Executive Officer of Lockheed Martin Corporation, Norman R. Augustine, announced today his decision to retire August 1, 1997, and step down as CEO. He will continue to serve as Chairman of the Board of Directors. . . . In accepting Augustine's retirement, the Lockheed Martin Board of Directors affirmed the Corporation's established succession plan. . . .

"About his announcement, Augustine noted that he has discussed with the Lockheed Martin Board of Directors, for several years, his interest in pursuing additional outside interests and had delayed retirement until Lockheed Martin was fully integrated. 'This is the right time to move on to the next generation of leadership now in place at Lockheed Martin,' he said.

"Augustine, who will turn 62 in July, 1997, plans to focus on education and public service. Beginning this fall, he will join the faculty of the School of Engineering and Applied Science at

Princeton University, his alma mater, as lecturer with the rank of Professor. He will also continue serving on several corporate boards, as well as continue as Chairman of the American Red Cross."

✤   ✤   ✤   ✤   ✤

So begins the next journey of my travels through life. I took this step for a number of reasons. For one, having worked in both government and the private sector, I've always wanted to try academia. I have had chances to do so in the past, but these opportunities never seemed to occur at a time when it was possible to leave my then-current responsibilities. I have been a CEO since 1987, well beyond the average tour of CEO duty, and this seemed like the right time. There is an outstanding team in place to take over the company, because we have followed our basic succession planning strategy to ensure that would be the case.

So, I decided to follow my own advice, as specified in an earlier chapter, and "Be opportunistic; go for it!"

A lot of people seemed to be stunned by the announcement. They shouldn't have been. I had been talking about teaching for quite some time, and planning this move with our board for over two years. Maybe no one on the outside thought I was serious; it *is* a heck of a great job to just walk away from, especially three years ahead of the Lockheed Martin retirement deadline.

Once again the story leaked to the newspapers on the Friday before the planned Monday morning announcement, which meant we had to "crash" the release forward by two whole days—but then we have gotten to be pretty good at that!

My son, the young electrical engineer, had his own spin on the story. A decade earlier, when he graduated from college, he had wanted to work for Martin Marietta (he'd been properly brainwashed)—a proposition I discouraged as I was then CEO of Martin Marietta. Accepting my view, he went to work for IBM in its Federal Systems Division . . . which was later bought by Loral . . . which was later bought by, you guessed it, Lockheed Martin. After my impending departure was announced, he simply told reporters and anyone else who asked, "The company just wasn't big enough for both of us."

At Princeton, I'm going to teach courses for engineers *and* liberal arts majors, all together in one classroom. It's the same idea I've mentioned several times in this book. I hope to share with students some of the lessons learned in my travels, much as I've tried to do with you, the reader, so they can make their own mistakes rather than repeat mine.

There was one bit of bad news—in the hours following the announcement of my retirement, Lockheed Martin stock *rose* $^7/_8$ of a point.

And within hours of the press releasing the story, someone in a group of my closest colleagues at LM, seeing me in the hall, stage-whispered, "There goes old what's-his-name!"

⊕   ⊕   ⊕   ⊕   ⊕

Oh, oh. I thought I was finished, but I'm not. I'm afraid I *have* to tell you about just one more event. I guess I can't even get the timing of my retirement right!

In mid-afternoon on Thursday, July 3, 1997, John Greenya, the writer who's been working with me on this book, called my office to talk about the possibility of including a picture from that morning's *Washington Post,* which showed me on the pitcher's mound at Camden Yards with Baltimore Orioles' owner Peter Angelos, baseball superstar Cal Ripkin, and First Fan William Jefferson Clinton. When John asked for me, my secretary Laura Cooper (who knew it was now safe to say what she did), replied, "He's not here. He's in New York buying another company."

What we had bought—for $11.6 billion—was Northrop Grumman, the missing piece in the puzzle we'd been working to assemble ever since the collapse of communism and the reductions in the U.S. Defense budget. In addition to the purchase itself, what had made me particularly happy was that for once we'd managed to pull off a major acquisition in *complete* secrecy. (It didn't hurt that a certain reporter at the *Wall Street Journal* was on vacation in the wilds of Montana when it happened.)

I'd already had a few preliminary talks with Kent Kresa, Northrop Grumman's top man, but we didn't sit down seriously until about a month before the deal went through. (To enhance secrecy, our meeting was in a "neutral" hotel in Paris, one where neither of us was staying. When I got there, I discovered I didn't know his code name! There was a man waiting in a room off the lobby, said the concierge, but he was French. I looked in, and it was Kent. I never did learn how he'd managed to pass for French, but he *is* an amazing person.) Right after that meeting, our respective teams of lawyers, bankers, and businesspeople went to work, and by the time a month had passed, one hundred people knew about the deal, yet no one leaked news of it to the media, or, apparently, to the market.

The last question at the press conference announcing the deal was from a reporter who wanted to know how we'd managed to keep it such a secret. I replied, in a reference to the fighters and bombers produced by our two companies, "Lockheed Martin and Northrop Grumman are famous around the world for *Stealth*."

There were a number of fascinating aspects to the deal, not all of which were financial. The purchase brought the industry back together again, so to speak, because Jack Northrop, the company's founder, had been chief engineer for the Loughead ("Lockheed") brothers in the infancy of their company. Another point was that our buying Northrop Grumman revivified several deals we'd attempted to make in the past.

For example, as I mentioned before, Northrop had beat us out when we tried to buy Grumman several years earlier (though we had to pay more for it this time). Also, when Lockheed and Martin Marietta (before they combined) had tried to buy Vought, Loral got one half and Northrop got the other; so when we bought Loral, we got the first half of Vought, and with this purchase (as long as the federal government approves it, which we anticipate it will), we will get the second. Finally, I had spent at least a year in (ultimately unsuccessful) talks with Westinghouse's CEO about our buying their defense electronics business, but Westinghouse later sold it to Northrop. By buying Northrop, we will soon own that, too. Because of this deal, we finally pulled together all the pieces that, over the years, we had made serious attempts to buy. I guess it *is* true that "all things [including defense companies] come to those who wait." (But this form of "waiting" can be like the advice given by the jungle guide to the tourist: "Carrying a flashlight will protect you from the alligators, but, of course, it depends on how fast you carry it.")

Earlier in this book, I said that Lockheed Martin is made up of seventeen companies; you can now make that twenty-two. And the number of employees jumps to 230,000. And our rank among the Fortune 500 companies climbs to number 17.

This purchase will undoubtedly be the last major deal in the U.S. aerospace industry. Except, of course, for our very secret "Project Big Bang." Just kidding . . . we like to keep our friends at Boeing on their toes.

Speaking of friends, as this deal (which some in the media dubbed "Norm's Last Hurrah") fell into place, it occurred to me once again that business successes are the result of large numbers of people working together, each contributing in his or her own way. I've long felt that CEOs get too much credit—though there are also times when they get too much blame—for it has always been my good fortune to find myself surrounded by extraordinarily talented people, all of whom deserved a lot more credit than the media gave them. So, I used the opportunity of my final letter to Lockheed Martin employees to cite, one last time, the story of the baseball pitcher who, when asked the secret of his success, answered, "fast outfielders."

⊕   ⊕   ⊕   ⊕   ⊕

It has been quite a trip. The travels continue, and I can't wait to get fitted for my academic gown. However, this doesn't mean the travels are *over*. There are still places to go and things to see while I still have, as we say in the aerospace business, some runway left.

Index